FACING DEATH IN CAMBODIA

17 APRIL 1975

FACING DEATH IN CAMBODIA

PETER MAGUIRE

COLUMBIA UNIVERSITY PRESS NEW YORK

Columbia University Press

Publishers Since 1893

New York   Chichester, West Sussex

Copyright © 2005 Columbia University Press

All rights reserved

Library of Congress Cataloging-in-Publication Data

Maguire, Peter (Peter H.)

  Facing death in Cambodia / Peter Maguire.

    p. cm.

  Includes bibliographical references and index.

  ISBN 0–231–12052–4 (cloth)

  ISBN 0–231–50939–1 (electronic)

  1. Political atrocities—Cambodia. 2. Cambodia—
History—1975–1979. 3. Trials (Genocide)—Cambodia.

DS554.8.M34   2005

959.604'2—dc22

                                2004050214

Columbia University Press books are printed
on permanent and durable acid-free paper.

Printed in the United States of America

c 10 9 8 7 6 5 4 3 2 1

Frontispiece: Young Khmer Rouge soldier in Phnom
Penh. Al Rockoff

FOR ANNABELLE LEE

Contents

ACKNOWLEDGMENTS

     I began this project in 1994, and many people have helped along the way. A special thanks goes to those who encouraged me to continue my research in Cambodia when I was struggling with my unpublished Nuremberg book: Brian DiSalvatore, Conrad Crane, Jörg Friedrich, Gary Solis, Ron Steel, Ron Olson, Rebecca Mclennon, Anders Stephanson, Mark Norris, and Michael Kloft.

     I owe a debt of gratitude to Chris Riley and Doug Niven for inviting me to Cambodia in 1993. Doug Niven generously shared his research and was a gracious host in both Phnom Penh and Bangkok. A special thanks goes to Michael Hayes and Kathleen O'Keefe, the cofounders of the *Phnom Penh Post*. Not only did the *Post* archive their back issues onto a CD-ROM, they generously allowed me to quote from them. Aun Pheap, the *Post*'s walking encyclopedia, was also a great help in finding obscure citations. Thanks to the *Post* alumni who kept me informed during my long absences from Cambodia: Nate Thayer, Kevin Barrington, Tom Fawthorp, Matthew Grangier, Moeun Chhean Nariddh, Jason Barber, Anette Marcher, Hurley Scroggins, Ker Munthit, Robert Carmichael, Phelim Kyne, Bill Bainbridge, and Pat Falby. Chris Decherd of the Associated Press was a generous host who introduced me to key sources and greatly increased my understanding of Cambodian politics. I also must thank the *Phnom Penh Post*'s crosstown rival, *The Cambodia Daily*. Robin McDowell, Seth Meixner, Matt Reed, and Kevin Doyle were also generous with both time and resources.

     I am especially grateful to scholars Craig Etcheson and David Chandler. Both carefully read and constructively criticized early drafts. Their good-faith efforts restored some of my faith in academics. Youk Chhang and his staff at the Documentation Center of Cambodia taught me a great deal about their country. Sorya Sim, Meng Tre Ea, Dara, Kosal Phat, and Bunsou Sour all helped me in more ways than they will ever know. Tuol Sleng Museum's Sopheara Chey was also extremely generous over the years. Thanks to Al Rockoff for generous permission to use his remarkable photographs.

Thanks to the Foreign Correspondents Club Cambodia. Owners Anthony Alderson, Tom O'Connor, and Michelle Duncan provided good humor, food, loans, and unflinching generosity that I won't soon forget. A special thanks goes to kickboxer/linguist Sylvain Vogel. Not only did the remarkable Alsatian introduce me to another side of Cambodia, he and his wife Nea provided me with a home away from home in Phnom Penh.

At Columbia University Press, thanks to former editor Kate Wittenberg for signing me to a two-book contract. My patient and supportive editors, Leslie Kriesel and Peter Dimock, were all that I could have asked for. My research assistants, William Gouveia, Tim Hogan, Richard St. Onge, Martin Splichal, and Heilwig Nations all helped me a great deal. My former professor Ron Grele of the Columbia University Oral History office and his successor, Mary Marshall Clark, enthusiastically supported my research.

Thanks to my friends for various forms of support: John Danaher, Gen, Renzo Gracie, Rickson Gracie, John Peretti, Kevin Jackson, George Greenough, Bamboo Opperman, KK and Regina Jackson, Mary Kennedy, Sam Garkawe, Terry and Jo Harvey Allen, Leonard Brady, John Milius, Duncan Bock, William Caming, Jon Bush, Michael Cundith, Rusty and Tricia Miller, Steven Niles, Ron and Jane Olson, Pete Bill, Mike Perry, Sara Powers, Ian Warner, William Powers, Mike Ritter, Spencer Rumsey at *New York Newsday*, Russell Bridge, Luke Hunt, and Dan Kraker.

A special thanks to the Maguire clan. First and foremost, my father, Robert F. Maguire III, who encouraged and funded most of my research. My uncle, Gil Maguire, provided sharp criticism and unflinching support. I won't soon forget his efforts at the 1998 Bard College War Crimes Conference. My brother Alec Maguire and sister Robin Maguire were both generous with their sofas and hospitality during numerous visits to Los Angeles. Last but not least, my grandfather, Robert Maguire Jr., encouraged my research and bolstered my spirit.

A special thanks goes to the late Robert Worth Bingham, who was the most significant, reliable, and enthusiastic sponsor for Niven and Riley's Photo Archive Group. Bingham paid for part of my travel to Vietnam and Germany.

To Sok Sin, Im Chan, Karl Deeds, Rob Bingham, and Telford Taylor, James P. Shenton—rest in peace.

My parents, Joan Tewkesbury and Robert F. Maguire III, supported me and my research every step of the way. Finally, thanks to my wife, Annabelle Lee, without whose support I could not have completed this book.

INTRODUCTION

This is a book with few heroes, plenty of villains, and no easy answers to some of the most vexing questions of our time. Those looking for the "glass half full" optimism that characterized much of the human rights scholarship during the 1990s should read no further. This is a sad story with an inconclusive ending. Its only certainty is an insistence on the necessity for humility when trafficking in the pain of others.[1]

I have spent much of the past decade searching for legal, historical, and moral forms of accountability for the three-year, eight-month, and twenty-day rule of Pol Pot's Democratic Kampuchea (1975–1978). Their experiment in Stone Age communism cost Cambodia close to two million lives. Most shocking to me was Tuol Sleng prison (also referred to as S-21)—a former high school in Phnom Penh that was transformed into the regime's primary interrogation and torture center. Approximately 14,000 men, women, and children entered the prison between 1976 and 1978. In 1979, less than a dozen were still alive. Before the prisoners were interrogated, tortured, and executed, they were carefully photographed.

Simple, wordless documents more eye-opening than the mounds of human bones, the instruments of torture, or even the killing fields, the Tuol

Sleng portraits have become a sad distinguishing artifact of Khmer Rouge brutality. The images that are forever seared into my mind are the stoic ones: the boy with the padlock and chain around his neck who stares straight into the camera; the delicate little girl with the pageboy haircut posing as if it were school picture day; the half-dissolved image of a dignified Khmer beauty; the *sangfroid* of the bare-chested young man with the number seventeen pinned through the flesh of his chest; the sadness in the eyes of the boy thrust into the frame by a disembodied fist clutching his tricep. Susan Sontag compared the photographs to Titian's *The Flaying of Marsyas,* "where Apollo's knife is eternally about to descend—forever looking at death, forever about to be murdered, forever wronged. And the viewer is in the same position as the lackey behind the camera; the experience is sickening."[2]

I began the research that would make this book possible in 1993. I was completing my Ph.D. dissertation at Columbia University on the Nuremberg war crimes trials and the laws of war. The dissertation was awarded honors, but it was cold comfort. I felt hollow and fraudulent, like a boxing commentator who had never been in the ring. I was writing about modern conflict as a civilian leading a secure life at an Ivy League university. Twenty-eight and a product of one of the softest generations in American history, what did I know about conflict resolution beyond what I had read? To teach undergraduates about how the world should be without addressing that rapidly changing world on its own terms was to perpetuate a familiar cycle of fraudulence.

My Nuremberg research led me to Cambodia quite naturally because Cambodia had shattered the "never again" promise once and for all. The Khmer Rouge had committed the most brazen atrocities since the Third Reich. There was overwhelming evidence that they had violated the Nuremberg Principles, the United Nations Charter, the laws of war, even the UN Genocide Convention. During the decade after their regime's collapse, the Khmer Rouge had been rescued by China, the United States, and Thailand. Pol Pot and the other leaders lived in freedom and still wielded considerable power. Genocide was carried out and the perpetrators were rewarded. I began to see Cambodia as the modern paradigm for the resolution of a genocidal conflict, and Germany/Nuremberg as the anomaly.

Like post–World War II Germany, Cambodia was the beneficiary of a costly and hugely ambitious reconstruction effort. Between 1992 and 1993, the UN imported 15,000 soldiers and 5,000 civilian advisors in a $3 billion effort to end 20 years of war and build democracy in a country that knew only oligarchy and dictatorship. According to the UN's "expanded peacekeeping" model, neutrality was the highest political virtue; military affairs were viewed as another facet of police work. "Expanded peacekeeping operations had ambitious objectives, which included conflict resolution and Wilsonian goals such as nation building and creating democratic societies," wrote Fredrick Fleitz Jr. Above all, the UN leaders were unwilling to use force. Once that became clear to the Khmer Rouge leaders, the peacekeepers' political leverage was gone.[3]

While the United Nations Transitional Authority Cambodia (UNTAC) successfully repatriated 362,000 Cambodians living in Thai border camps and introduced modern ideas such as party politics and human rights, but failed to address the question of war crimes accountability. The UN was able to hold an election without igniting civil war, but the incumbent prime minister refused to step down and was allowed to rule as co-prime minister. These basic problems raised major questions about "expanded peacekeeping" and the UN's passive approach. Rather than face the fact that the paradigm was flawed, UN leaders sent many UNTAC veterans on to former Yugoslavia to commit similar errors.

Just as the UN was folding up its tents in Cambodia in late 1993, I learned that a friend from high school, Chris Riley, and his colleague, Doug Niven, were in Phnom Penh preserving, printing, and cataloging the negatives of the photographs taken of the inmates at Tuol Sleng prison. Although Cornell University had microfilmed most of the Tuol Sleng documents in the early 1990s, Niven and Riley found the original negatives covered in mold and rotting in steel file cabinets at Tuol Sleng Museum in 1992. The pair created a nonprofit organization called the Photo Archive Group the following year and began to raise funds and recruit volunteers to restore the negatives and reprint them in Phnom Penh. Given the legal immunity enjoyed by the Khmer Rouge leaders and their ongoing claims that the Tuol Sleng photos were fakes manufactured by the Vietnamese, I believed that preserving this historical evidence was particularly important. Niven and Riley were only restoring what was recovered; the majority of the negatives either had been destroyed or were in private hands.[4]

I traveled to Cambodia for the first time in 1994 in the hope of answering a deceptively simple question: How had the Khmer Rouge gotten away with genocide? My inquiry was redefined as a result of early interviews with Tuol Sleng survivor Im Chan and Tuol Sleng Museum director Sopheara Chey. Both men pushed me to the limits of theories of perfect justice that sounded much more convincing in university seminar rooms than in the hot, dusty back streets of Phnom Penh. More than anyone else, Chan forced me to confront the conflicting demands of justice and national reconciliation in an unresolved civil war, in a Buddhist country. While I thought and still believe that the Khmer Rouge leaders should be punished, Cambodians expressed a much more ambivalent attitude; many were reluctant to reopen the old wounds. Fear was and remains the biggest obstacle. Many Cambodians, even today, are reluctant to speak about politically sensitive issues in a country where political views come with a price.

War crimes trials would not be seriously discussed until the Khmer Rouge began to break up in 1996. The question of individual accountability could no longer be ignored as thousands of former Khmer Rouge rank and file began to defect to the new Cambodian government. After 1996 it became much easier to find and interview former Khmer Rouge, including many of the former Tuol Sleng prison staff. Given the lack of information about the Tuol Sleng photographs, I was most interested in interviewing the photographer.

Nhem En appeared in the Phnom Penh office of the Associated Press in 1997, looking for work as a press photographer. When one of the Cambodian employees asked about his background, he explained that he had been one of the photographers at Tuol Sleng prison. When I first interviewed En that year, I found him to be a smooth operator unburdened by regrets of any kind. He had entered the Khmer Rouge as a small boy and had served the revolutionary army with distinction. At the age of fifteen En was sent to China, where he was taught photography. When he returned to Cambodia in 1977 En was sent to Tuol Sleng to photograph prisoners. In 1997 he claimed that he was scheming to overthrow Pol Pot and the remaining Khmer Rouge hard-liners. I did not trust the aggressive En. Within two hours of our first meeting, he was pressing me for cash and an introduction to the U.S. ambassador.

After the Khmer Rouge collapse, the death of Pol Pot, and Hun Sen's 1997 coup, war crimes trial discussions between Cambodia's Prime Minister Hun Sen and the United Nations began in earnest. The back-and-forth negotiations quickly became a battle between national sovereignty and the new demands of international justice. The Cambodian government insisted that the trials take place in Cambodia with a Cambodian majority on every level of the court. But as the talks dragged on into the new millennium, I wondered if the Hun Sen government even wanted a trial. Many of the most important potential defendants had already died of old age. More than that, it was difficult to remain optimistic about a tribunal that was twenty-five years late. A trial would have little impact on the Cambodians who live far from the cities and whose chief concern remains filling the rice pot twice a day. Basic survival is still difficult in a land where tragedy, poverty, corruption, violence, and injustice are regular features of everyday life.

By 2000, the tribunal negotiations had been dramatically overshadowed by more human tragedies that, for me, erased the dividing line between the personal and the professional. Several of my Cambodian associates tested HIV positive in 2000 and 2001, and many other Cambodian acquaintances were dying of AIDS. I tried unsuccessfully to steer them away from the many AIDS "cures" offered by charlatan doctors in Phnom Penh. One Cambodian friend rejected my offer of western AIDS medicine with a laugh and told me confidently that the herbal doctor had "cured" his AIDS: "Asian HIV different." After that discouraging encounter, I arrived at the Foreign Correspondents Club's bar in time to watch jet planes smash into the Twin Towers in New York City. In those moments, the four-year-old discussions over a Khmer Rouge war crimes trial looked supremely irrelevant.

I wondered if the efforts by outsiders like myself to find "justice" in the wake of such atrocities were more to ease our guilty consciences as westerners raised on slogans like "never again" than to compensate the victims of the horrors. By 2001, that slogan had failed both as a promise and as a universal commitment. It was little more than an obscene fiction after unchecked power demonstrated its capacity for atrocity throughout the 1990s in places like Kigali, Dili, and Freetown.

Many western academics and human rights activists became very utopian in the wake of the Cold War. Throughout the 1990s they formed a powerful coalition, best described by Alex De Waal as "the human rights international." By the decade's end, the line between advocacy and scholarship had been completely erased. To me, this renewed interest in war crimes trials and international law was an admission of defeat in the face of overwhelming reality. I remember being baffled and enraged by the evangelical optimism so common in the West during the 1990s. I believed that risk-averse western leaders from Washington to Bonn to London were offering the victims of massive human rights violations a cynical deal. Instead of the satisfaction of immediate and palpable vengeance—the kind victims can see, smell, and feel—they gave only the promise of perfect "justice" in a UN courtroom, far from the scenes of the crimes.[5] Although there was unprecedented interest in trying the perpetrators, there was very little interest in preventing the ongoing atrocities, not to mention a general feeling of condescension for all things military. This struck me as very strange: civilians who had never been in a fistfight were trying to write the rules of war for the soldiers they held in contempt.

My graduate school teacher Telford Taylor taught me that war crimes prosecutions—under any circumstances—signified failure: failure to act, failure to deter, and finally failure to prevent. Nobody in his or her right mind opposed the punishment of war crimes perpetrators, but after the bloodiest century in the history of man, could there be salvation in new codes of international criminal law and world courts? I did not think that expanding international law was the solution. Until global powers can define and enforce simple standards of international conduct, morality will pose no deterrent to strategy and the world will slip deeper into the morass of ethnic and religious war.[6]

From 1999 until 2004, the Cambodian government has haggled over a war crimes court while the potential defendants have been living out their lives in freedom. We are told that trials are set to begin in 2005. I want to warn the reader in advance that my search for legitimate international structures of accountability for what happened in Cambodia has been a failure. The gap between what I studied and what I saw was too great. As a result, this book is written in two voices: that of the academic historian and that of the often stunned observer. I have come to no clear-cut conclusions, only a visceral awareness of the hollowness of my thousands of words when weighed against the survivors' individual historical experiences, as either victims or perpetrators. This is a cautionary tale: good intentions are never enough and war crimes trials cannot be relied upon to teach historical lessons. The decade I spent coming and going to Cambodia has been humbling. It has forced me to perceive and to acknowledge things as they really are, not as I would like them to be. Never again will I ignore the limits of the possible and never again will I confuse what should be with what is.

1

"SO YOU'VE BEEN TO SCHOOL FOR A YEAR OR TWO . . ."

i

In 1993, I ran into a friend from California in the Columbia University library. He told me that two mutual friends from high school, Chris Riley and Mark Norris, were going to Cambodia to restore the original Tuol Sleng prison photographs. I had been curious about Cambodia since I had first heard the name Pol Pot in the Dead Kennedys' 1980 punk rock anthem "Holiday in Cambodia." Their machine-gun lyrics described a hell on earth. While I knew that over one million Cambodians died during the reign of the Khmer Rouge, I had never heard of Tuol Sleng prison.

Riley and I had been friendly in high school, but I had not spoken to him in a decade. I talked to him on the phone, and his project sounded interesting. With Agence France Presse reporter Doug Niven, they planned to build a darkroom at the AFP villa in Phnom Penh, where they would soon begin cleaning, restoring, and reprinting all 6,000 original negatives. I was hooked when a package containing reproductions of the Tuol Sleng photos arrived on my doorstep in late 1993: dozens of portraits of men, women, and children, staring at me as they were literally facing death. It was clear that most knew what was in store for them, and this final, human, visceral record spoke to me in a way that academia never had.[1]

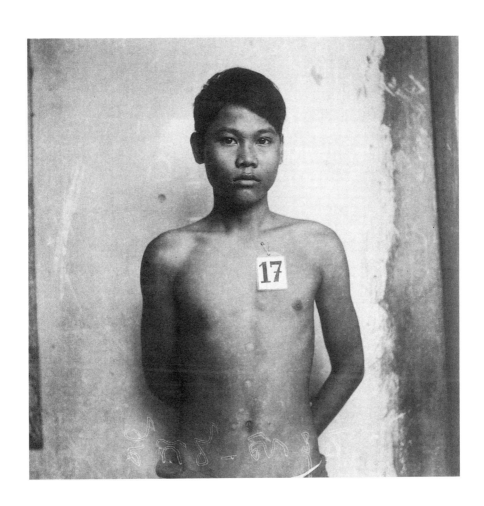

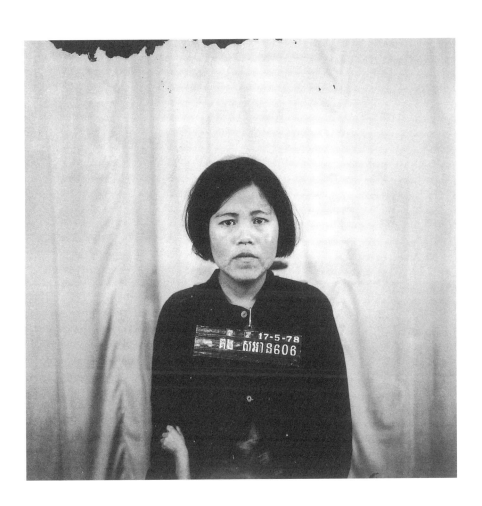

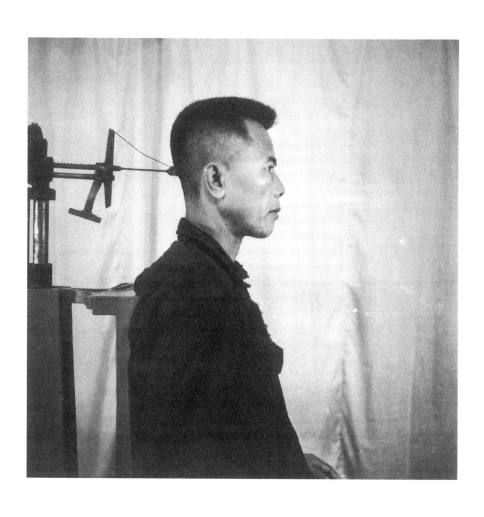

One afternoon in early 1994, I ran into Telford Taylor at Columbia Law School and told him that I was considering a trip to Cambodia. While he knew that the Khmer Rouge had killed at least one million people in four years, he did not know that Pol Pot and most of the regime's leaders were alive and did not fear prosecution. The old lawyer just shook his head and sighed: "Politics." He had taught me not to try to divorce politics from international law and, above all, not to confuse what is with what should be. I opened my briefcase and handed Taylor a notebook containing the Tuol Sleng photographs that Riley had sent me. He took one glance and winced. "This is very bad."

The eighty-five-year-old lawyer studied each image. He pointed to a very young Khmer girl who probably wasn't ten years old. "Why?" he asked with incredulity. I had heard that the photos had been taken to prove to Khmer Rouge leaders that their orders—to interrogate and eventually kill—were being followed. The little girl was probably some accused person's child. Furthermore, the Khmer Rouge leaders would probably never be tried; they even challenged the authenticity of these photographs. I told my professor that I had been invited to Cambodia and wanted to look more closely into the question of Khmer Rouge war crimes. "Cambodia is not like postwar Germany, the levels of literacy and education are much lower," I explained. Compounding this problem, the Khmer Rouge had killed most of the nation's educated people. Taylor agreed that the original Tuol Sleng images were a valuable empirical antidote to revisionism.

Why had the world allowed the Khmer Rouge to get away with genocide? The Third Reich was then, but this was contemporary—the Khmer Rouge leaders were living freely in the countryside. These were my Hitlers, Ribbentrops, and Himmlers, and most were above the law. The Khmer Rouge's leaders were blaming the atrocities on the Vietnamese. Political scientist Craig Etcheson offered the best analogy: "It is as if Himmler, Goebbels and Goering had all retired to Munich after World War II, spending the remainder of their lives publishing tracts asserting that no Jews were ever killed by the Nazis, and that any trouble the Jews might have had, they had deservedly brought upon themselves."[2]

I prepared to go to Cambodia in early 1994, just as the Cambodian army began a dry-season offensive. The Royal Cambodian Armed Forces appeared to have captured Pailin, the Khmer Rouge stronghold on the Thai border. Government soldiers found paved roads, a cinema, even color-photocopied currency that pictured smiling peasants atop water buffalo. There were doubts about the longevity of the government hold on Pailin; some observers suggested that the victory was a trap, because the city and army could be cut off from reinforcements once the wet season began. Had the Khmer Rouge only made a tactical retreat?

In March 1994, Khmer Rouge soldiers kidnapped an American aid worker and announced that they would begin kidnapping westerners as a matter of policy. Shortly thereafter, Cambodia's King Norodom Sihanouk issued a blunt warning: "I cannot continue to assume responsibility for accidents that could happen to travelers in Cambodia because I have repeatedly warned that my country can provide no safety guarantee to travelers without a big escort."[3] My second thoughts mounted: my date of departure corresponded with the UN inspection deadline of North Korean nuclear sites. I hoped that it wasn't some sort of omen, as my discount Korean Airlines ticket would take me to Bangkok via Seoul.

After a decade "back east" in academia, the Dead Kennedys' lyrics had special resonance in 1994, as I prepared to leave:

> So you've been to school
> For a year or two
> And you know you've seen it all
> In Daddy's car
> Thinkin' you'll go far
> Back east your type don't crawl. . . .
> It's time to taste what you most fear
> Right Guard will not help you here
> Brace yourself my dear
> It's a holiday in Cambodia
> It's tough kid but it's life
> It's a holiday in Cambodia
> Don't forget to pack a wife
> Well you'll work harder with a gun in your back
> For a bowl of rice a day
> Slave for soldiers
> 'Til you starve
> Then your head is skewered on a stake
> Now you can go where people are one
> Now you can go where they get things done. . . .
> Pol Pot, Pol Pot, Pol Pot, Pol Pot, etc.[4]

ii

The thirty-six hours of travel time was a blur of cramped, smoke-filled planes and transit lounges. When my flight from Seoul to Bangkok was called, I was nearly trampled as everyone in the boarding area rushed for the gate. There was no boarding by row or class, just a scrum of mostly Chinese and Thai businessmen. On the final flight from Bangkok to Phnom Penh, there were only a handful of passengers, mostly journalists and khaki-clad workers from nongovernmental organizations, or NGOs. By 1994, NGOs represented a vast range of private interest groups in Cambodia promoting everything from human rights to evangelical Christianity to land mine removal. Previous generations of young, educated, and privileged Americans joined the State Department and later the CIA to assume the white man's burden. My generation seemed to have assumed a mutated version: the white guilt burden.

On our final approach to Pochentong Airport, it was clear that Phnom Penh was only a hub of civilization; the paved roads radiating from the center dissolved into parched red dirt spokes just outside the city limits. The bone-jarring, three-point landing required all of the runway. When the stewardess opened the door, heat filled the plane's cabin like a blast furnace. I descended the stairs and there was Chris Riley beyond the customs checkpoint, looking crisp and stylish in khakis and a button-down shirt, despite the blistering heat on the tarmac. After I cleared customs, we walked out the terminal door. A tall white guy in a sweat-stained oxford shirt stood out among the soldiers, beggars, and taxi drivers. It was Mark Norris, whom I had not seen in a decade. Norris was suffering from amoebic dysentery and taking the dreaded nightmare-inducing drug, Flagyl. He looked hot, red, and the worse for wear, and I was touched that he had turned up at the airport.

I was saying hello to Norris when I noticed a surging crowd that could only mean one thing: violence. Cambodians fanned out and formed a ring around two combatants who became only a blur of knees and elbows. Neither Riley nor Norris reacted; they continued walking to the car and put my bags into the trunk. Getting into the car, I looked back. The fight was still in progress and had gone to the ground. Now, even the National Army soldiers manning the airport gate had taken notice. While they watched with great curiosity, they made no effort to try to break it up. We drove away as the two fighters continued to toil under a cloud of rising dust. Riley said with an unsettling grin, "Welcome to Cambodia."

We arrived at the Agence France Presse villa where Doug Niven worked as a photographer and Norris and Riley were staying. Niven had arranged for them to set up a darkroom in a spare room. It was a nice old French colonial villa with a large yard, staffed by a full-time security guard and maintenance man named Sam, his wife, and their lovely daughter, Saban. The AFP office was run by a chain-smoking Khmer named Mr. Song, who told me that because he had a *"septieme sense,"* he had left Cambodia in 1974. Skinny as a reed and constantly in motion, Mr. Song returned to Phnom Penh in 1979 to work as a cyclo (three-wheeled bike taxi) driver. *"Oh! Tres difficile!"* Song exclaimed as he began to pantomime the cycling motion and then clutched his thighs. "Oh! Oh!" Like so many Cambodians who had survived the Khmer Rouge, Mr. Song was full of energy and constantly in motion, as if he was making up for lost time.[5]

The ground floor of the AFP newsroom was dominated by a large map of Cambodia that hung on one wall; spent artillery shells, rocket tails, Khmer Rouge currency, and other trinkets of war littered the room. The Tuol Sleng Photo Archive Project was well under way: Doug Niven, Chris Riley, and their volunteer staff (Mark Norris, Michael Perkins, and Jeff Apostolu) were reprinting the original Tuol Sleng negatives in their homemade darkroom. This day, Apostolu, Perkins, and Riley were hand cleaning each image with isopropyl and Q-tips. The villa's greatest attribute was a shaded veranda on the second floor that overlooked a busy intersection. That afternoon, Riley, Norris, and I sat in the shade and drank iced tea. It was nice to catch up and to relax for the first time since leaving Honolulu more than thirty hours earlier. Our reunion was broken up when a white Toyota Land Cruiser, driven by a young white woman, pulled into the driveway. "She's a UN official who might be able to help us," Riley said.

Although roughly my age, she had a very condescending manner. When I described my current interest in Khmer Rouge war crimes—more specifically, the UN's failure to account for them—she grew defensive and dismissive. "Nobody, well . . ." she paused, obviously trying to decide how to break the news that my questions weren't worth asking. "Well, nobody is really interested in those questions anymore." I politely reminded her that I was a historian, not a journalist, and that the war crimes impunity in Cambodia raised serious questions about war crimes accountability in the late twentieth century. She sharply rebuked me for using the word "genocide," as the official term was now "autogenocide." After fifteen minutes she realized that I would not be easily convinced and urged me to examine my questions from a "psychological and sociological point of view." Her final piece of advice floored me: "Don't bother talking to Cambodians, they will only confuse you," she said curtly before wishing me "good luck." She and Riley drove off in her Land Cruiser to a classified meeting. Apparently, I had failed her litmus test. Most jarring to me was her assumption that the subject of Khmer Rouge atrocities was a dead issue. I would hear that opinion often in coming months, and the idea that she might be right haunted me. Someone who knew much more about Cambodia than I did seemed to have accepted the idea that amnesty for war criminals was the price of peace. Apparently, as far as the UN was concerned, their mission in Cambodia had been a success because they had held an election without sparking a civil war, and now they were off to save Bosnia. Those responsible for the Cambodian atrocities were alive and well. The UN's conspicuous silence on the question of war crimes accountability only deepened the confusion for ordinary Cambodians.

Doug Niven took me for a ride on the back of his 100 cc Honda motorcycle, through Phnom Penh's anarchic and treacherous traffic. Stoplights were nonexistent; turn signals were not used; driving on the right side of the road was optional; and above all, police were extortionists to be avoided at all costs. Niven fetched a block of very sketchy-looking ice from a café across the street and we returned to the villa. My doubts about a mixed drink increased as Michael Perkins doubled over and winced. "Hurry up with my drink, I want to put my amoeba to sleep." He too had dysentery. Soon I would be sick like everyone else; it was the price of admission. For now, I had a beer. Talk turned to Cambodia's newest business/sport: kidnapping westerners. According to Niven, the Khmer Rouge were offering a bounty of $5,000 for the heads of "long-nosed westerners," preferably Americans. Several days earlier the Khmer Rouge had kidnapped Australian Kellie Wilkinson, Englishman Dominic Chappell, and New Zealander Tina Dominy. The trio of tourists was traveling by taxi to Phnom Penh from the coastal town of Sihanoukville when they were stopped at a roadblock and marched into the jungle. At that point we were only speculating about their fate and thought that they were still alive. Both the British and the U.S. embassies had issued warnings to travelers to "exercise extreme caution."[6]

Perkins began to groan and said that he was too ill to eat. Niven and I went to a restaurant around the corner where many of the patrons wore holsters containing big, state-of-the-art sidearms. Shoot-outs and cowboy-style banditry were common in Phnom Penh. I nervously ate vegetables and rice. Several nights later, I walked a few blocks from my guesthouse past the Royal Palace and on along the main street to the Foreign Correspondents Club. It was an assault on the senses that made Times Square during the 1980s seem as serene as Bel Air. If you could cross the street without getting hit by a motorcycle carrying dozens of honking geese or by the cars speeding into oncoming traffic, there was still the gauntlet of the infirm to pass on the sidewalk in front of the palace. One-legged soldiers, people of all ages with battle scars and birth defects unseen in the West for decades, mothers with dying babies—each more horrifying than the last and all in your face, tugging at your sleeve and your conscience.

The Foreign Correspondents Club was a beautiful, four-story, yellow building with an open-air veranda that overlooked the Tonle Sap and Mekong rivers. The street-level entrance was mobbed with moto taxi drivers, more crippled and deformed beggars, out-of-luck mothers, and land mine victims. A man with pincherlike arms, a normal-sized head, and a torso no bigger than a basketball sat at the foot of the stairs at the doorway, upside-down hat in his lap. Two flights of stairs led to a third-floor barroom that was divided by rank. At the top of the natural elite, at least in my eyes, were the Vietnam-era photographers I would meet later, like Al Rockoff and Roland Neveu, who had been working in Cambodia since the early 1970s.

A couple of ranks below them, a new generation of reporters were cutting their teeth in Cambodia. At the head of the pack was the *Phnom Penh Post*'s star reporter, an unlikely Yankee named Nate Thayer. Tall and athletic with a shaved head, Thayer had excellent contacts within the Khmer Rouge and would break most of the major stories during the 1990s. Mark Norris was off the Flagyl and bouncing back. He introduced me to Nate, who was friendly but distracted by his many female admirers. A French photographer named Franck came over and spoke with us briefly. The gaunt European had a shaved head as well, and a 10,000-yard stare. Franck had just returned from a few days in Pailin with the Cambodian army. The tank he'd ridden on had run over an antitank mine, and he was blown into the air. Franck was fine, but two soldiers on the front of the tank were killed. He'd spent the next four days dodging bullets and rockets.[7]

When I called it a night and descended the FCC stairs, as soon as my feet were visible from the street, some of the moto taxi drivers began running toward me, grabbing at my sleeve: "You go with me okay." Others ran for their bikes, kick-started them, noisily revved their engines, and instructed me to hop on. While Phnom Penh's moto drivers appeared to be cowboys, they also served as eyes and ears. Little did I expect that I would get to know all of them in the coming decade: "Smiley," "Pouv," "Big Man," "Ken," "Panda," "Vesna," and others. Their cunning and *sangfroid* would pull me through many checkpoints and close calls. My guesthouse's gate was now locked, and a guard came out carrying an old AK-47. He unlocked it and let me in.

Despite the uncertain security situation, I was struck by Phnom Penh's colonial charm. The old buildings and the natural beauty of the land and people overwhelmed me, particularly in contrast with what I knew about their recent history. Life in the capital was soft for foreigners, if not for the natives. Phnom Penh had long catered to the bacchanalian tastes of western colonials. Green marijuana was $5 per kilo; a dozen Valium tablets were a dollar; opium, heroin—you name it, you got it, ultra cheap. I had met hard-boiled newsmen who were raging opium addicts as well as junkies from all walks of life who'd gotten hooked in Phnom Penh and now could not leave. We seemed to be only the most recent generation of colonials. Irrespective of our efforts to appear down at the heels, most of us could come and go as we pleased, as long as we had credit cards.[8]

The next day, Riley took me to the Tuol Sleng Museum of Genocide for the first time. The former high school seemed small and serene. At the gate stood a pack of one-legged men wearing various remnants of their military uniforms; they were begging for change. Inside the gate, it looked like a typical school; a U-shaped collection of buildings faced a grass courtyard with pull-up bars and lawn bowling pitches. Due to the recent spree of widely publicized kidnappings, there were very few tourists in the country and the museum was virtually empty. In one corner of the courtyard stood an ominous-looking scaffold; at the other end of the compound a handful of men played boules. Three of them had artificial legs; they were living reminders of Cambodia's millions of land mines.

The ground-floor classrooms appeared as they might have in 1978, when the prison was operating at full capacity. Each spartan interrogation room was furnished with a school desk and chair that faced a steel bed frame with shackles at the head and feet, and an ammunition box that served as a water container and toilet. On the far wall of one room was a photo of a bloated, decomposing body chained to a bed frame with a large pool of blood underneath it.[9]

I walked into the second building and saw that the classroom walls were papered with thousands of S-21 portraits. They clearly conveyed the horror. At first glance, the photo of a shirtless young man appeared typical. Yet upon closer inspection I realized that the number tag on his chest had been safety-pinned to his pectoral muscle. A mother with her baby in her arms stared into the camera with a look of dignified resignation. Suddenly, a photo of a

TUOL SLENG SURVIVORS
HEYNOWSKI & SCHEUMANN FILM STUDIOS

young westerner leaped out at me. Before I had left for Cambodia, a friend in California had asked me to look for any records of an American acquaintance he had known in Hawaii during the 1970s who was rumored to have vanished in Cambodia. Besides this man, James Clark, Americans Lance McNamara, Mike Deeds, and Chris Delance were also captured by the Khmer Rouge in 1977 and 1978 while sailing near the Cambodian coast. While I was sadly overwhelmed by the thousands of Cambodians portraits, this Australian looked like me.

I found the Americans' confessions in the prison's records. After weeks of torture and interrogations, both broke down and claimed to be working for the CIA. In his confession, Clark claimed that he was a drug smuggler and CIA agent whose handler thought he "could be useful in South East Asia since at this time America's greatest weakness is there, and the changes there are biggest. My first job was to be very simple. Besides our regular smuggling as cover, he wanted me to sail close by the coast of Cambodia to photograph." I could only imagine what their final months had been like. Even worse, the Delance and Deeds confessions were dated December 26, 1978, one week before the Vietnamese arrived to liberate Phnom Penh.[10]

Down the hall was Tuol Sleng Museum's *pièce de resistance*: a map of Cambodia made entirely of human skulls and bones. It had been constructed under the supervision of a Vietnamese colonel named Mai Lam, who turned the former prison into a museum in 1979. Many Cambodians objected to this map and the Vietnamese efforts to use the evidence of Khmer Rouge atrocities for propaganda purposes. I later asked the museum director, Sopheara Chey, about the map, and he described the gruesome process of construction. The skulls had been taken from the nearby killing fields at Choeung Ek and arrived at the prison with bits of hair and scalp still attached. Museum employees were first given rice wine, then told to clean the skulls. To him, the map and the skull-filled pagoda at Choeung Ek, another Vietnamese/Mai Lam creation, were more than ghoulish overstatements; they were religious transgressions. According to Sopheara's Buddhist beliefs, the souls of the dead could not rest until their bones were either burned or buried. To this day, each year at the time of the Pchum Ben festival and the Khmer new year, the museum director brings in a group of monks to hold a special ceremony to calm the former prison's restless spirits. "All of us have been haunted by ghosts, even myself."[11]

I asked Sopheara Chey if I could walk around the prison's upper floors. He said that they had fallen into a state of disrepair and warned me about the deteriorating staircases, but said I was free to roam. I pushed the bent gate

Declaration of Michael Scott DEEDS

My name is Michael Scott DEEDS. I am American citizen. I was born on november 15th. 1949 at Long Beach, California.

My father's name is Cameron Scott DEEDS and my mother's name Katheen DEEDS. They have 4 son and I am the second son. My father is professor of physical education. He teaches tennis and leads and controls the other sports. My mother is a wifehouse. ~~They~~ Their home address is 5920 Appian Way, Long Beach, California. My father is 58 years old and my mother 57 years old.

My ~~young~~ brother names Robert and is 31 year old. And my two other young brothers are Karl and Timothy.

I was captured on november ~~xxx~~ 1978.

DATED ENTER PRISON TUOL SLENG
November 26th. 1978.

to enter the large stairwell leading to the top floor of the building. The bottom of the staircase was strewn with Khmer Rouge hats, shoes, bowls, ammo boxes, and rotting black uniforms. Suddenly something moved in the rubble: an unsettled soul? My nerves calmed when a scrawny kitten showed its head, revealing a small litter that looked like rats. I climbed the stairs, walked down the outer hallway, and went into the first classroom. It was empty except for a pile of shackles and a single stone carving of Pol Pot. It was eerie, as if the Khmer Rouge had just been there.

I entered the second room and was startled again. Slouching against the far wall was what looked like a body. As I approached, I discovered with some relief that it was a decomposing, wire-framed mannequin. Heaped on the floor around it were Khmer Rouge infantry hats, boots, a bowl, an ammo box, and mosquito netting. The dummy's head hung morosely as though it knew something that I did not. When I looked to my left, I saw a skull peering at me from a green wooden box on the floor and two large yellow ceramic figurines standing about five feet apart, each holding an urn. At some point they had been badly broken and crudely pieced back together. Between the two large figures was a smaller Buddha with a shattered face, seated in the lotus position atop a concrete pedestal. In front of the makeshift shrine sat another green wooden box, brimming with skulls and bones. Sopheara later explained that these remains came out of the yards of people who lived near Tuol Sleng. He was waiting to inter them in a proper Buddhist ceremony; until he could pay for one, the bones sat in front of the shrine.

A few nights later, Norris, Riley, and I were in a café eating dinner and watching cable television. Suddenly the screen was filled with Rwandan refugees streaming into the Congo by the hundreds of thousands. We all knew that something horrifying if not genocidal must be happening. "Next stop Rwanda," Riley said. Although the United States, the UN, and NATO had halfheartedly intervened in the Yugoslavian civil war, the Rwandans had so far been left free to slaughter one another with no outside interference. We would soon find out that this was one of the most specific examples of genocide of the twentieth century: 700,000 to 900,000 dead in less than three months, mostly neighbors killing neighbors. Alison Des Forges, one of the few westerners in Rwanda at the time, wrote: "When they saw they could get away with that kind of violence in Kigali with no reaction from the U.N. troops . . . it encouraged them to go ahead with the larger operation." It was obvious that some lives counted more than others. Cambodians already knew this, and it was a lesson that I was learning; the western powers' "season of cowardice" was well under way.

BOX OF SKULLS AND SHRINE, TUOL SLENG MUSEUM
AUTHOR

The following week, Riley and I returned to the museum and stopped in to say hello to Sopheara Chey. The director greeted me and said that he had arranged an interview with Im Chan, one of S-21's survivors. I felt a bit tense. The time had come to face in real life what I had only theorized about in academic work. In Germany, the Nazis had been crushed militarily, but in Cambodia things were much more ambiguous: the Khmer Rouge lived on, and the question of war crimes guilt and punishment remained unresolved. Though I didn't realize it at the time, I was trying to bridge the gap between my academic and Chan's and other survivors' empirical understanding of atrocities and accountability. I did not yet know that this was an impossible goal. As David Rieff already had discovered, "history is never the fairy-tale of innocent victims, oppressive gunmen, and caring outsiders that the humanitarian narrative so often presents."[12]

Riley, Sopheara, and I walked out the Tuol Sleng gates and along the dirt road that bordered the museum grounds. We stopped at a traditional Cambodian house that was a stone's throw from the wall of the former prison. Sopheara called to a child, who ran into the house. In the yard we saw more children, babies, dogs, cats, a rooster, and a hen with her chicks. Im Chan soon emerged from the house, wearing only a traditional red-checkered *krama* (scarf) wrapped like a sarong. Wiry and clear-eyed, he was probably fifty. We sat around his outdoor work table and I rested my tape recorder near an etching that was half complete.

iii

Im Chan was a sculptor trained at the Cambodian Fine Arts Academy. He had worked in the Royal Palace workshop carving wood doors and panels for the king. He was sent to Siem Reap to repair the temple carvings at Angkor Wat in 1967. Chan had not been in Phnom Penh when the Khmer Rouge rolled into the city in 1975. During the civil war, he had fled to the Kulen Mountains and remained there because he "disliked war." However, the Khmer Rouge soon identified him as "Sihanouk's carver" and sent Chan to a factory in Phnom Penh, where he made metal frames and taught teenagers to sculpt.

After about six months, Khmer Rouge officials asked Chan's students if they had learned all that the carver knew. When they replied affirmatively, the carver was arrested and sent to be "re-educated." When I asked what he was charged with, Chan bristled at what seemed to him an incredibly stupid question. "When they arrest you there are no charges, they just say, 'You have known modern life. You used to go to the cinema, the restaurants, the bars. If we leave you, then you will tell the youth stories and they will want some!'" His wife was also arrested; they were sent to Pray Sar prison, where they were kept shackled for nearly a month. Chan and his wife were loaded into a jeep and driven to Tuol Sleng after he was captured trying to escape in February 1978. In Chan's S-21 photograph, dated February 16, he is hand-cuffed to another man. "That's my friend. He was beaten to death during in-terrogation." His wife was sent to a different room, and Chan heard her scream, "'What have I done wrong? What mistake have I made? Have pity, I haven't got anybody else, I only live with my husband.' I didn't hear any more of her."

Once inside the gates of S-21, Im Chan resigned himself to death: "One hundred percent, I thought that I would die." Tortured and interrogated, sometimes three times a day, he still "feels in his head" the residual effects of the electric shocks. For twenty-six days, he was asked the same questions over and over: "Do you work for the CIA?" "Do you work for the KGB?"

Im Chan was scheduled to be executed. But after reviewing his file, Brother Duch, the Tuol Sleng prison commandant, changed his mind and or-dered him to carve effigies of Pol Pot. He was moved into a room with other "useful" prisoners. Although they were more comfortable than the rest of the S-21 population, Chan remained convinced that he would die: "They tried to console me because they wanted their statues. They knew if they treated me badly they would not get their statues." He recalled a conversation with a guard: "One day a guard said to me, 'Do you know that one day, when you finish the sculpture you will be killed.'" The only sign of change came in early 1979 when the Khmer Rouge began to move prisoners out of S-21. When their convoy came under Vietnamese attack, Im Chan and a handful of others es-caped in the chaos of battle.

About forty minutes into the interview, I tried to get the carver to talk more specifically about the individuals who ran S-21. I asked him about the infamous Brother Duch. Again he seemed irritated, and his response sur-prised me: "I have a bad memory of Mr. Duch. I do not want to slander Mr. Duch, I just want to tell the international community that I do not want the Khmer Rouge to come back because I have very bad memories about that." Im Chan was a reluctant witness, especially compared with Holocaust sur-vivors I had interviewed. When he spoke of Brother Duch, he inverted the Nuremberg defense, arguing that the S-21 commandant "only issued the or-ders"—implying that because Duch was not a torturer, he was above the law. Chan made it clear that he believed a vindictive settlement would be a mistake.

THE AUTHOR AND IM CHAN
CHRIS RILEY

Besides the larger geopolitical problems posed by war crimes accountability, there were also important cultural considerations. Cambodia is a Buddhist country where retribution comes in different forms. The Buddha did not teach "an eye for an eye"; he, like Im Chan, transcended the simple desire for revenge. Put simply, Buddhists believe that one must break the cycle of vengeance in order to survive. When I inquired as to the whereabouts of the interrogators and torturers, Chan replied, "Some of them have come back, and I would not like to meet them because I would really like to kill them. I would like to see them punished." Then he paused and reconsidered: "But truly I cannot do like that because I am a Buddhist—no revenge." The carver said that he was very angry and would like to say something to Pol Pot, "but I would not know what to say. The words would be difficult to find to express my anger."[13]

After Im Chan returned to Phnom Penh in 1979, foreign journalists interviewed him and the other survivors. For a few months he worked at Tuol Sleng Museum, but the strain grew too great, so he quit. "The prison still makes me feel very bad. When I see it every day, I remember my ordeal," Chan explained. I asked the carver if he thought the Tuol Sleng Museum of Genocide was an important memorial for the Cambodian people. Did it keep the memory of their national tragedy alive? Chan's answer shocked me: "I do not want to have a museum like this. For the people who lived through the Khmer Rouge it is all right, but for the young generation it is bad because they will want revenge and again it will be Khmer against Khmer. I do not want a museum that keeps anger and bad memories alive—Khmers will be against Khmers."

Talking about his memories was not easy for Im Chan, but he was very lucid as he described the pain that the recent past continued to cause him: "Every year during national celebration they invited me to the microphone to make a speech about the bad memories. I did it every year for a while." Again he paused; it was obvious that my questioning had taken him back to a troubling place. His next line was nearly his last: "But every time I went [to speak] I lost some of my life—I shortened my life. At the time I felt very bad that it was shortening my life. I would like to forget all of this; I do not want to remember. I would like to forget, so I never wrote my story. Many journalists came to meet me, but I never wanted to meet them. I only did it this time because of the museum director."[14]

I turned off the tape recorder. We thanked Mr. Chan and quietly left. Back at the museum gate, Riley and I thanked Sopheara Chey and said good-bye; then we got on Riley's motorcycle and headed back into the incongruous chaos of Phnom Penh. As we entered a major roundabout, a traffic cop standing in the center pointed his white baton, blew his whistle, and motioned for Riley to pull over. As we got close, the traffic cop's partner also motioned for us to pull over. Riley backed off the throttle as if he were slowing to stop, then cracked it wide open. I grabbed the seat with both hands and ducked my head into my shoulder as the 100 cc Honda groaned and the sound of whistles faded into the din of traffic. A few blocks beyond, a crowd was rushing off the sidewalk next to a Japanese sedan stopped in the middle of the street, all four doors left open, as if in haste. Ten yards from the car, some men were wading purposefully into the heart of a departing crowd. Were they brandishing weapons? I couldn't tell, we were moving too fast.

Walking from the AFP villa to my hotel, just as I was approaching the gate, I heard tires screech and then a loud crash. A pile-up of motorcycles and bodies in the middle of the street was now snarling traffic. Most of the people picked up their bikes, dusted themselves off, and continued on. One heavy-set woman with a freshly shaven head wailed in pain. She resisted the efforts of a man who tried to lift her onto a motorcycle. When he finally got her halfway on, he popped the clutch. The bike lunged forward and then keeled over. Both passengers hit the pavement with a slapping thud and the crunch of breaking plastic and mirror. Now traffic on Samdech Sothearos Boulevard was stopped in both directions. Although the guards from the Royal Palace came over to look, they made no effort to help. As the woman continued to wail, the crowd grew larger. Finally, a van arrived and six men lifted the screaming woman and put her inside. The hotel guard later told me that the woman was inconsolable over the death of her husband.

The next day I returned to the AFP villa. Riley and Perkins were drinking iced coffee at the café across the street. At the table next to them, a pack of local beggar kids were devouring bowls of noodle soup that Riley had bought them. None of the boys had shoes, one wore a track suit top as pants, and another was stark naked. All of them seemed feral and fearless. I was already feeling overwhelmed, and that sensation only increased until I left Cambodia. I'd finally shifted from theoretical speculation to real-life investigation, but I was having a difficult time making sense of what I had experienced. This first trip had raised as many questions as it had answered.

Had Americans during the 1990s grown so profligate that we were trying to remake the world according to our own politically correct vision while disregarding conditions on the ground? The UN woman was right. Talking to Cambodians certainly was confusing. But wasn't confusion the first stage on the way to comprehension? I certainly had a less benign view of nongovernmental organizations and the United Nations now that I'd seen the results of their billion-dollar efforts firsthand. Both the UN and many NGOs have a vested interest in the "success story." Both groups had bills to pay, and by the 1990s human rights was an industry. Many of these outside interests were beginning to look as colonial to me as the multinational corporations and rubber planters. In truth, I was just as guilty: part of another wave of young, idealistic Americans abroad wagging our collective finger at the natives, telling them how the world should be and how they should live. Previous generations of westerners brought soap and Bibles. My generation brought diverse and often competitive ideologies: human rights, evangelical Christianity, Mormonism, and women's liberation, to name only a few. My most serious doubts were reserved for human rights slogans like "no justice, no peace." Were justice and reconciliation even compatible? Im Chan didn't seem to think so. When I returned to the United States, I read *The Teaching of*

Im Chan's Tuol Sleng portrait
Chris Riley

Buddha, and Chan's attitude began to make more sense. The Buddha taught that "Blood stains cannot be removed by more blood; resentment cannot be removed by more resentment; resentment can only be removed by forgetting it."[15]

One morning I opened the newspaper to read that the Khmer Rouge had recaptured Pailin. Then the bodies of Kellie Wilkinson, Dominic Chappell, and Tina Dominy, the trio kidnapped outside of Sihanoukville, were found in a shallow grave. The autopsy showed that they had been killed almost immediately; the ransom games had been designed to extort money from their families.[16] A few months later, Khmer Rouge spies in Phnom Penh alerted their commander that a train carrying western backpackers Mark Slater, David Wilson, and Jean Michel Braquet was headed for Kampot. Trains were so regularly ambushed in 1994 that soldiers rode behind sandbags on the roof and an empty flat car traveled in front of each locomotive to lessen the sting of land mines on the rails. Khmer Rouge forces, disguised in government army uniforms, blew up the tracks and marched the three western tourists into the jungle. Their leaders in Anlong Veng radioed the soldiers holding the hostages and instructed them: "Keep the three long-noses quiet and in good condition." The Khmer Rouge planned "to use these guys to scare foreign governments."[17]

Another series of ransom negotiations began, and when a media frenzy descended on Kampot, the Khmer Rouge leaders saw an opportunity. The original demand of $50,000 per hostage began to grow proportionally with the news coverage. The guerrillas' clandestine radio broadcast announced on August 16 that they would release the hostages if the westerners' governments stopped supporting "the two-headed government" of Hun Sen.[18] The prime minister refused to negotiate, kicked all journalists out of the area, and ordered the Cambodian army to launch artillery assaults. A correspondent from *The London Times* spoke to hostage Mark Slater via radio in the second week of August 1994. Slater warned: "Every bomb we hear is like a nail in the coffin. We are already inside the coffin, since we were told we were going to be executed a week or two ago."[19] A few weeks later, the Cambodian National Army found the westerners' bodies not far from Phnom Vour. Khmer Rouge radio claimed responsibility for the killings: "They were acting on behalf of the communist You'en [Vietnamese] to kill Cambodians. They were war criminals." Hun Sen declared the Khmer Rouge an "international terrorist" organization and vowed to bring them to justice.[20]

I had returned to the United States with much work to do. First, I had to trace the roots of the Cambodian tragedy. I soon found them as deep and tangled as those of a banyan tree. There is no way to make sense of Cambodia's three decades of strife without stepping back to an earlier time, when Cambodia was ruled by a sax-playing prince and his harem. . . .

2

"*Do not kill any living creature, with the exception of the enemy.*"

i

A single cannon shot marked the dawn of April 17, 1975 and the surrender of Cambodia's capital, Phnom Penh, to Pol Pot's Khmer Rouge forces. The rebels controlled most of the country, and Phnom Penh's population had grown to two million as rural peasants sought refuge from the fighting in the countryside. Fallen Prime Minister Long Boret and Deputy Prime Minister Prince Sirik Matak never imagined their American patrons leaving them to face the same battle-hardened soldiers the United States had failed to bomb into submission. Since 1970, the U.S.-backed Lon Nol regime had waged a brutal war against the Cambodian communists. After Congress learned of the secret American bombing of Cambodia, American aid was abruptly suspended. While the Cambodians would fight on bravely, April 17, 1975 marked the end of the civil war. Cambodians would face the consequences alone. Phnom Penh's residents could only await their fate as long, single files of teenaged Khmer Rouge soldiers streamed into the capital all morning. These barefoot teens, some clad in black rags, others in Chinese olive green fatigues, were all well armed and glowering with malicious intent.

The five-year Cambodian civil war had already cost at least 250,000 Cambodian lives, and the worst was yet to come. The dean of the Southeast

17 April 1975

KHMER ROUGE SOLDIERS MARCH INTO PHNOM PENH, APRIL 17, 1975.
AL ROCKOFF

Asian war correspondents, Neil Davis, described the Khmer Rouge as a "xeno-phobic clique of disenchanted, radical so-called intellectuals" with a "vitriolic hatred" for the Cambodian people. Though it sounded clichéd, even he pre-dicted a "bloodbath" if the Khmer Rouge ever took power.[1] The three-year, eight-month, and twenty-day experiment in "Stone Age" communism that now began would cost over a million more lives and prove to be one of the most radically destructive social experiments of the twentieth century. While executions were commonplace under the brutal regime, the majority of Cambodians who died succumbed to starvation, exhaustion, and disease.

One of the few American reporters to remain in Phnom Penh on April 17, 1975, photographer Al Rockoff, captured the takeover on film. One Rockoff por-trait of a barefoot teenaged rebel soldier speaks volumes: a war booty M-16 resting casually on his hip, a grenade on his belt, a cigarette in his hand—Mao's Red Brigade meets *Lord of the Flies*. According to historian David Chandler, the Khmer Rouge "made virtues of inexperience and ignorance, preferring young people, who were, in Mao's phrase, 'poor and blank.'"[2] Pol Pot would later cred-it "class and national hatred" for the success of his revolution.

Cambodian peasants and others who had supported it were called "Old People." The two million residents of Phnom Penh, known as "New People" or "April 17thists," would undergo the ultimate Darwinian experiment. After being forced into the countryside, most faced a simple choice: work or die.[3] As one young Khmer Rouge soldier later admitted, the rule was that "Old People and New People must clearly be kept apart. Townsfolk are New People. They are to be killed."[4] It didn't take one "New Person" long to realize that "we were under custody of the revolution, not a part of it." Many recall a common refrain from the period: "Keeping [you] is no gain. Losing [you] is no loss."[5] However, on April 17, 1975, after five years of civil war, many Cambodians believed that the revolutionary army would keep their promise of "peace and reconciliation." One Phnom Penh resident recalled the day that the young soldiers marched into town: "Our joy was enormous. We all be-lieved that the war was now over for us, happiness would return to us again."[6]

The Cambodian civil war had been especially dangerous for western re-porters: "almost every journalist, photographer, television correspondent, and cameraman to fall into the hands of the Khmer Rouge was killed."[7] Those who remained in Phnom Penh were now holed up in the French embassy. French photographer Roland Neveu left the compound to photograph the first live Khmer Rouge soldiers he had ever seen, but by mid-morning, "the mood turned sour." Neveu made his way back to the French embassy, noting along the way Khmer Rouge soldiers on three-wheeled motorcycle carts with public address systems. They announced: "Angkar had been alerted that Americans and their lackeys had prepared to attack our city by bigger fighter planes. Be prepared for moving out of the city for a period of time, maybe three days."[8]

By noon, the young soldiers had turned their guns on Phnom Penh's inhabitants. The capital was divided into zones with numerous checkpoints where soldiers and government officials were culled from the human herd. The son of a Lon Nol officer, Sopheara Chey had much to fear that day: "I saw one of Lon Nol's soldiers carrying his gun, pulling back, so I asked him, 'Why have you stopped fighting?' and he said he received orders to stop fighting." When Sopheara arrived home, his father was shedding his uniform. "His face looked ugly; he was wearing civilian clothes. He told me that if the Khmer Rouge caught a Lon Nol officer, he would be killed." Eleven-year-old Aun Pheap searched for his mother and watched "Khmer Rouge soldiers, who did not know how to drive, run over people in military jeeps they had just captured." Aun Pheap did not find her.[9]

Journalists Jon Swain, Al Rockoff, and Sydney Schanberg were pulled from their car at gunpoint by Khmer Rouge soldiers. "They were boys, some perhaps twelve years old, hardly taller than their tightly held AK-47 rifles. Their ignorance and fanaticism made them super deadly," Swain recalled. The western reporters would survive, but their Cambodian colleagues would not be so fortunate. Cambodian Associated Press reporter Mean Leang wrote in his final dispatch: "I feel rather trembling. Do not know how to file stories. How quiet the streets. Every minute changes." He added, "Maybe last cable today and forever."[10]

Most shocking and difficult for western Khmer Rouge supporters to explain away later was the regime's decision to evict Phnom Penh's 20,000 hospital patients from their beds and force them on a death march out of the city.[11] "What the Khmer Rouge are doing is pure and simple genocide. They will kill more people this way than if there had been fighting," Fernand Scheller, chief of the UN Development Project (UNDP) in Phnom Penh, said as he watched hospital patients roll by, many still in their beds, some with IV bottles attached. Catholic priest François Ponchaud later described the procession as "a hallucinatory spectacle," and added, "I shall never forget one cripple who had neither hands nor feet, writhing along the ground like a severed worm."[12]

Sopheara Chey recalled his flight from the capital: "On the road we saw very young Khmer Rouge soldiers. They would take a hand grenade and take the pin out of it to see the look on our faces. They were trying to see who was

17 April 1975

FRENCH EMBASSY GATE
AL ROCKOFF

GOVERNMENT SOLDIERS SURRENDER THEIR WEAPONS.
AL ROCKOFF

a soldier and who was not a soldier. My father knew they were looking for him."[13] Young Aun Pheap left Phnom Penh with his older sister and uncle and remembered passing "many dismembered bodies of soldiers. Heads and limbs were scattered everywhere. The smell was very bad." Another Cambodian survivor recalled her sad exodus: "Wounded people … begged for help. But there was nobody there who could help them. Many pregnant women who gave birth on the way died, and many old women starved."[14]

The remaining westerners in the French embassy could only wonder about their chances of survival as they listened to the *opéra bouffe* unfolding just outside the gates. Khmer Rouge boy soldiers played bumper cars with abandoned Mercedes and Peugeots, grinding gears and smashing anything that dared to get in their way. "Few knew how to drive: the crash of gearboxes was the prevailing sound. In other circumstances, their efforts would have been hilarious; now they were grotesque: the peasant boys with death at their fingertips were behaving like spoiled brats," Jon Swain wrote later.[15] "The Glorious April 17th," the ghoulish national anthem of "Democratic Kampuchea," as the Khmer Rouge had renamed their country, now played on the radio and provided a hint of things to come:

> The red, red blood splatters the cities and the plains of the Cambodian
>   fatherland,
> The sublime blood of the workers and peasants,
> The blood of revolutionary combatants of both sexes.
> The blood spills out into great indignation and a resolute urge to fight.
> 17 April, that day under the revolutionary flag,
> The blood certainly liberates us from slavery.[16]

Cambodia's ousted deputy prime minister, Prince Sirik Matak, first sought refuge at Hotel Le Phnom, which was now serving as a Red Cross sanctuary. The Cambodian leader had refused asylum in the United States and accused the Americans of "heartbreaking betrayal." Sirik Matak warned of "terrible carnage" to come and cryptically added, "I lay on the American conscience all Khmer deaths, present and future." Because Matak had been named by the Khmer Rouge as one of the "Seven Traitors," agents of the American-backed government sentenced to death, the Red Cross turned him away, unwilling to risk the lives of the Cambodian civilians who'd taken shelter at Le Phnom. Before leaving to seek asylum at the French embassy, Matak talked to reporters and handed out copies of a final letter he had given to U.S. Ambassador John Dean on April 12, the day of his departure:

Dear Excellency and Friend:

I thank you very sincerely for your letter and for your offer to transport me towards freedom. I cannot, alas, leave in such a cowardly fashion. As for you, and in particular for your great country, I never believed for a moment that you would have this sentiment of abandoning a people which has chosen liberty. You have refused us your protection, and we can do nothing about it. You leave us and it is my wish that you and your country will find happiness under the sky. But, mark it well, that if I shall die here on the spot and in my country that I love, it is too bad because we all are born and must die one day. I have only committed this mistake of believing in you, the Americans. Please accept, excellency, my dear friend, my faithful and friendly sentiments.[17]

Sirik Matak was allowed into the French embassy, but when the Khmer Rouge demanded all the Cambodians inside, they were surrendered by French *chargé d'affaires* Jean Dyrac. The sad task of informing the deputy prime minister of his fate fell to anthropologist François Bizot, who was acting as the embassy's translator: "'Excellency,' I eventually said, after a ghastly silence. 'The Khmer Rouges are at the gate. They are fully aware of your presence here. They are asking for you.' 'I know what I have to do,' replied the prince decisively." As all the Cambodians filed out of the embassy and climbed into trucks, Bizot noticed a banner hanging outside the gate: DEATH TO THE TRAITOR SIRIK MATAK.[18] Sirik Matak and Long Boret were taken to the nearby International Youth Club and decapitated on the tennis court.[19] Khmer Rouge radio announced shortly thereafter that most of the former Cambodian leaders had been killed: "Some have fled the country but most have had their heads cut off."

"What hurts, is the way the United States used us. You marched into our country, you promised us aid, you encouraged us to keep fighting, you told us you were our friends, and now you drop us," Cambodian diplomat Abdulgaffar Peang Meth said as he agonized over the fate of his country from his Washington, D.C. office. He harshly echoed Sirik Matak's feelings of betrayal in an interview with *The New York Times*: "A prostitute at least gets paid. For us, our lives, our blood, our country, is ended because we helped the United States when it wanted to get its troops out. So your sons and daughters are home and our people are left to die." The Cambodian ended the interview by quoting Patrick Henry from memory: "Is life so dear or peace so sweet as to be purchased at the price of chains and slavery? Forbid it, Almighty God. I know not what course others may take—."[20]

U.S. MARINES EVACUATE THE U.S. EMBASSY IN PHNOM PENH, APRIL 12, 1975.
AL ROCKOFF

"When joy and happiness are so deep, one cannot say anything," King Norodom Sihanouk gushed from Beijing shortly after the Khmer Rouge capture of Phnom Penh. He claimed that the Khmer Rouge were not communists and only wanted to install "a people's democracy." Sihanouk said that his lifelong dream of "the total and irreversible liberation of Cambodia and the restoration of its independence and nonalignment" had been achieved.[21] In his long, colorful political life that had already stretched sixty years, no foreign interests—the French, the Americans, or the Japanese—manipulated the king as successfully as did the Khmer Rouge.

ii

The only child of King Norodom Suramart, Prince Norodom Sihanouk was born in 1922. Appointed king by the French in 1941, Sihanouk would outlast both the Japanese and the French occupiers and ultimately negotiate Cambodian independence in 1954. Soon after, he abdicated the throne and attempted to lead Cambodia down the path of neutrality. U.S. Secretary of State John Foster Dulles had warned against this and told him plainly in 1958, "You cannot be neutral. You have to choose between the free world and the Communist camp." Many years later, Norodom Sihanouk would reflect, "John Foster Dulles was right. There is no nonalignment." In 1965, during the Vietnam War, he broke off relations with the United States after repeated American incursions into Cambodia and later predicted: "At present, they are planning to kill Cambodia. Under the pretext of chasing the Viet Cong, they will enter our country to wreak destruction and death."[22] Once the North Vietnamese presence in eastern Cambodia grew, Sihanouk reestablished relations with the United States in July 1969. When Sihanouk left for an overseas trip in 1970, he was ousted by his pro–American military chief Lon Nol and his cousin Prince Sirik Matak in a bloodless parliamentary coup on March 20, 1970. The king had already departed in January for France and would soon be living in exile in China. Once firmly in control, Lon Nol began to step up attacks against the Vietnamese sanctuaries.[23]

Instead of returning to Phnom Penh after April 17, 1975, the king traveled to Beijing and announced that he had allied himself with the Cambodian communists whom he had previously dubbed the "Khmer Rouge." Sihanouk urged all Cambodians to join the fight against the U.S.–backed Lon Nol regime. In accordance with tradition, the king embodied divine as well as earthly authority: he was a deity in the eyes of the 80 percent of Cambodians who lived in rural areas. So his announcement that he would lead the resistance transformed the obscure Cambodian communist movement into a viable threat to the government in Phnom Penh.[24] Although Sihanouk was attempting to use the Khmer Rouge to regain power, he did not yet know what they had planned for Cambodia.

While the extent of the U.S. role in Sihanouk's ouster is still debated, there is no doubt that with him out of the way, the White House could greatly expand the Vietnam War into Cambodia. President Nixon announced a massive U.S. invasion of Cambodia on April 30, 1970.[25] Nixon and National Security Advisor Henry Kissinger hoped that Cambodian and South Vietnamese soldiers could cover the American exit from Southeast Asia. Although there would be casualties, most would not be American—or so went the unspoken logic of the "Nixon Doctrine." Historian John Ranelagh best described the policy, as "containment 'on the cheap.'"[26] President Nixon announced, "We have stopped the bombing of North Vietnam," but said nothing about bombing Cambodia. By early 1971, William Stubbs at the U.S. embassy already believed that due to the damage and loss of life caused by this American intervention, "popular support" for the Lon Nol army was "waning."[27]

Back in the United States, the invasion of Cambodia sparked the most intense round of student protests of the Vietnam War yet. ROTC buildings were burned on several campuses, and after National Guard soldiers shot and killed four protestors at Kent State University on May 4, 1970, students at five hundred American universities went on strike. The massive reaction stateside forced the White House to consider more clandestine options. While publicly President Nixon promised that he "would not expand the war into Cambodia," Henry Kissinger and his aide Alexander Haig were busy coordinating a secret bombing campaign from American bases in Guam and Thailand. Many State Department officials were kept in the dark. Kissinger privately told colleagues that the United States was "bombing the bejesus out of Cambodia."[28]

Probably the greatest liability for the U.S. policy in Cambodia was Lon Nol himself. The new Cambodian ruler encouraged followers to call him "Black Pappa" and considered his dark skin evidence of "his untainted Khmer lineage."[29] The CIA had considerably less faith in Lon Nol than the White House and described him as a "fantasist" dependent on religious advisors.[30] After Lon Nol had a stroke in 1971, the Cambodian civil war grew increasingly brutal and bizarre as the battlefield crept closer to Phnom Penh. Lon Nol ordered his army's helicopters to sprinkle magic sand at key strategic points throughout the city, rendering them "safe from attack." Pieces of "magic plants" were distributed to soldiers, along with amulets and white scarves to protect them in battle.[31] Lon Nol ordered the following preparations in 1971:

1. Cutting of the skin in order to allow Buddha to enter the body and bring strength, or sewing precious stones or ivory statues of Buddha into the incisions for greater power

2. Making of clothing or scarves with holy inscriptions

3. Securing the blessing of a *kru* [traditional magician/priest]

4. Making creation of the illusion of many soldiers when only a few exist

5. The transformation of leaves of grass into soldiers

6. Strict adherence to the five basic principles of Buddhism. . . . Do not kill any living creature, with the exception of the enemy.

The massive influx of American military and financial aid led to wholesale corruption among the Lon Nol army. While government soldiers were fighting bravely on the battlefield, their generals could often be found in Phnom Penh, drunk by noon on whiskey and soda. As Elizabeth Becker of the *Washington Post* points out, Lon Nol's faith in "magic shirts" was considerably less absurd than his "belief that the U.S. commitment to the war effort was a blank check."[32]

Now disentangled from Vietnam, the American air forces focused their massive firepower on Cambodia. Between February and July 1973, they dropped more than 250,000 tons of bombs in what the Khmer Rouge leaders would later call the "200 nights of bombing." In the end, U.S. bombers launched 3,630 raids along the Cambodian border and dropped a total of 15,000 pounds of explosives for every square mile of Cambodian territory.[33] The secret campaign became public in August 1973 after errant American bombs killed 137 Cambodian civilians at Neak Luong. While U.S. Ambassador Emory Swank traveled to the village and handed out $100 bills to the survivors, the damage stateside was incalculable.[34] The news of a secret bombing campaign was the final straw for many of the Democrats in Congress, who exacted their revenge on the White House and by association, the Lon Nol regime. Today, it remains difficult to estimate how many were killed by American bombs in Cambodia; estimates range from 5,000 to 500,000. Two facts remain certain: the U.S. bombing campaign pushed the Vietnamese deeper into Cambodian territory, and most important, turned many uprooted Cambodian peasants into zealous revolutionaries.[35]

U.S. intelligence knew next to nothing about the Khmer Rouge when CIA analyst Sam Adams began to study the situation in 1971. Adams estimated Cambodian communist troop strength to be ten to thirty times higher than the U.S. government's official estimate. He also made the key observation that the Khmer Rouge were not simply an extension of North Vietnamese power and predicted that the "ancient hatred" between Cambodia and Vietnam could reemerge "in the trappings of the communist dialectic."[36]

Meanwhile, King Sihanouk was winning the hearts and minds of the Cambodian peasantry for the Khmer Rouge. The shadowy Khmer Rouge leaders "used the King with a mastery and subtlety seldom seen in modern political history," writes political scientist Craig Etcheson. The king's well-choreographed propaganda campaign culminated with his visit to the Khmer Rouge "liberated zone" in 1973. Described as "the most mysterious of the world's successful revolutionary movements" by *Time* magazine, the Red Khmer were led by a small handful of western-educated Cambodians who disclosed little about their methods, objectives, and identities.[37] A 1973 Khmer Rouge propaganda film showed the rebels' public leader, Khieu Samphan, warmly embracing Sihanouk; all present are clad in trademark black clothes with traditional checkered Cambodian *kramas* around their necks. One unidentified man smiles broadly at the king, pressing his palms together in an especially deferential *sompea* (bow). He is none other than Khmer Rouge supreme leader Saloth Sar.[38]

Better known by his *nom de guerre*, Pol Pot, Saloth Sar preferred to live in secret and to work behind the scenes while his trusted functionaries served as frontmen. The rebel leader had studied in France during the 1950s and been heavily influenced by Marxist politics. Although Pol Pot claimed to be a great fan of Yugoslavian leader Tito, his true political inspiration came from Mao's China. During a 1966 visit to Beijing, the future Cambodian leader met K'ang Sheng, the Soviet-trained head of Mao's secret police. Pol Pot would remain friends with "the claw of the dragon" until Sheng's death in 1975.[39]

Pol Pot would serve as Khmer Rouge "Brother Number One" for three decades. Khieu Samphan and Pol Pot's brother-in-law, Ieng Sary, would handle much of the diplomatic and public relations duties, while Son Sen, Nuon Chea, and Ta Mok handled security and military affairs. Pol Pot and Ieng Sary were married to sisters Khieu Ponnary and Khieu Thirith. Both women had studied in France and played important roles within the ruling circle of the Khmer Rouge. According to Henry Kamm, the revolutionary leaders "secured their places at the summit in the murderous power struggles that made Stalin's elimination of all imagined rivals seem like a civilized political process."[40] Although a handful of them were educated and well versed in Marxist theory, their rank-and-file soldiers or "cadres" were ignorant young peasants. They knew only what they were fighting against, not what they were fighting for: "They told us we were the king's army," one former Khmer Rouge soldier recalled.[41]

After President Nixon's resignation in 1974, Congress cut off all military aid to the Lon Nol government. President Gerald Ford predicted that America's allies would be slaughtered after their imminent defeat and warned, "No one should think for a moment that we can walk away from that without a deep sense of shame."[42] Although the new U.S. ambassador to Cambodia urged the White House to negotiate a truce with the king, Kissinger was not a fan of Sihanouk and insisted on holding out for better terms.[43] Ambassador John Dean believed that because American policy had helped to create the political situation in Cambodia, the United States had a "moral obligation" to "work out a controlled solution to the Cambodian drama." Once again, he encouraged the White House to contact Sihanouk in Beijing: "Dean said that the Prince wants to talk to the Americans and believes the solution to the Cambodian problem lies in Washington." The ambassador did little to conceal his frustration with Kissinger's secretive policy-making style: "I would like to help in any way I can to carry out the Dept's policy but in order to do so, I need to know what that policy is."[44] "I don't want to hear about any Laos-type compromises," Kissinger replied. "Your job is to strengthen the military position so we can negotiate from strength."[45]

The architect of Nixon's foreign policy sensed that the ambassador in Phnom Penh would not go down with this sinking ship. Kissinger wrote to the State Department on February 18, 1975: "I am willing to listen to any recommendation that is consistent with that objective. But the frenzied approach which Dean seems to have adopted will solve nothing."[46] According to former CIA agent Frank Snepp, Kissinger despised King Sihanouk and believed "that withdrawal of U.S. backing for the Lon Nol regime would be seen in Peking and other foreign capitals as a sign of American weakness."[47] Later that year, former CIA official Ray Cline harshly criticized Nixon's foreign policy in general and Kissinger in particular: "A single policy-maker [Kissinger] ended up controlling dissemination and analyzing of intelligence, and yet intelligence provides the only possible basis for judging the wisdom of the policy."[48]

Sihanouk portrayed the Khmer Rouge in the kindest light and told reporters in March 1975 that they did not plan to take Phnom Penh. U.S. antiwar activist Tom Hayden and his actress wife Jane Fonda publicized a telegram they received from Sihanouk in early 1975: "If the U.S. does not put a rapid and radical end to the sending of arms and munitions, and to financial aid to the Lon Nol group, our national front and our Armed Forces of National Liberation will not be able to accept any contacts with the Americans or with France or with the United States," Sihanouk said. Khieu Samphan, the rebels' prime minister, would later express his deep gratitude

NEIL DAVIS CARRIES A WOUNDED CAMBODIAN.
AL ROCKOFF

to the "peace and justice loving American people and to high-ranking American personalities who have aided and supported our struggle."[49]

The chances of a peaceful transfer of power in Cambodia were slim to none, as the civil war had been brutal long before 1975. American military advisors were often horrified by local martial traditions. One group of western journalists watched as Lon Nol soldiers killed and butchered a paymaster in front of them: "They then fell on his body with knives, cutting open his chest and abdomen, and tore out his heart, liver, and lungs. They also carved out his biceps and calf muscles." The soldiers proceeded to cook, serve, and eat the "man soup" in front of the reporters. Cannibalism was "an act Cambodian soldiers of both the government and Communist sides often commit against the foe, but rarely, if ever, on their own comrades," wrote Neil Davis. These cannibal soldiers were an especially tough bunch: they had survived a nine-month Khmer Rouge siege of Kompong Seila. Ten thousand men, women, and children lived in an underground maze of bunkers dug into a valley one kilometer long and half as wide. After four months, their food ran out, so they established hunting parties and survived on the flesh of Khmer Rouge soldiers. "We got thirty in one night!" one of the hunters bragged to Davis.[50]

Brutality was not limited to the soldiers of the Lon Nol army. American diplomat Kenneth Quinn described life and death in the Khmer Rouge "liberated zones" in a 1974 report: "Death sentences are relatively common although public executions are not the rule. Usually people are arrested and simply never show up again, or are given six months in jail and then die there." Quinn described the charge of "espionage" as an all-purpose "canard under which a multitude of other offenses are grouped."[51] Ith Sarin joined the revolution for nine months in 1972 and lived to tell his tale. Ith Sarin left impressed by their "iron discipline," but terrified by their "Know-nothingism and anti-intellectualism." He correctly identified the Khmer Rouge leaders as Saloth Sar, Ieng Sary, Son Sen, and Khieu Samphan and pointed out that "Sihanouk had no importance inside the movement."[52] Captured by the Khmer Rouge in 1971, anthropologist François Bizot survived three months of interrogations. Upon release, he translated a Khmer Rouge propaganda tract entitled, "Political Programme of the United National Front of Kampuchea" for the French embassy. According to Bizot, "Its contents foreshadowed the horror: already there was mention of the evacuation of towns and the establishment of a state-controlled collectivism based on a reduced population."[53]

The Khmer Rouge continued to close the circle around Phnom Penh and by early 1975, CIA director William Colby concluded that "an orderly surrender is the best that can be hoped for."[54] During the second week of April, Ambassador Dean folded up the stars and stripes and American diplomats prepared to abandon the U.S. embassy. "One day Henry Kissinger will retire, and he will write his memoirs. And you will buy them and I will buy them. And I will write a footnote on every page," Robert Keeley, deputy chief of the U.S. Mission in Phnom Penh, said as 300 Marines secured the U.S. embassy grounds on April 12. CH-53 helicopters ferried 276 Americans and Cambodians to the aircraft carriers U.S.S. *Okinawa* and *Hancock* waiting in the South China Sea. When journalist Neil Davis boarded an American helicopter, he left behind an apartment in Phnom Penh, most of his personal possessions, and a beloved white Mercedes sedan.[55] Pol Pot later called the U.S. evacuation "a great event clearly demonstrating to the world that small Cambodia with a small population was extremely brave and could force U.S. imperialism to flee in a most shameful manner."[56]

iii

"We are turning our society upside down," one Khmer Rouge officer told a *Newsweek* reporter in the weeks after the revolution. "The people of Phnom Penh will grow rice," he said, and almost as an afterthought added, "They will work or starve."[57] By early May 1975, the Khmer Rouge were implementing one of the most radical political plans of the twentieth century, a peasant revolution with a punitive edge. Buddhist monks were made to plow fields; pagodas were turned into killing centers; Cham Muslims, a religious minority, were force-fed pork; Cambodia's National Library was converted into a pigsty. In Pol Pot's Democratic Kampuchea, books were used to start fires. "It was more about revenge," recalled one Cambodian.[58]

   All private property, even money, was abolished in this "ultra Great Leap Forward." Although King Sihanouk claimed that the Khmer Rouge sought to establish a democratic and nonaligned government, radio messages deciphered by U.S. intelligence told a different, more ominous story: "Eliminate all high-ranking military officials, government officials. Do this secretly. Also get provincial officers who owe the communist party a blood debt." While Cambodia's ousted leader, Lon Nol, accepted cash and exile in the Honolulu suburbs and the king watched events play out from Beijing, Sirik Matak, Long Boret, the Lon Nol soldiers, the loyal Montagnards army, and even a handful of U.S. Marines left behind on a lonely Cambodian island in May 1975 paid with their lives.[59] For the United States, the war was over, but for most Cambodians the horror had just begun.

The early accounts of life under the Khmer Rouge came from Cambodian refugees who escaped to Thailand. At first they sounded too bizarre to be true, as if George Orwell had written them to satirize life under a dictatorship of the proletariat: a place where parents feared their children and civilians were slaughtered in numbers and for reasons unimagined since Stalin's purges or Hitler's Third Reich. Survivors described a system of slave labor communes where men, women, and children toiled like human water buffalo under the watchful eye of the mysterious and all-powerful leadership cabal known only as "Angkar."[60] They lived in perpetual fear.

The regime's supporters in the West dismissed the rapidly growing number of horror stories about life in Pol Pot's Democratic Kampuchea as "CIA propaganda." Khmer Rouge foreign minister Ieng Sary was among the first to cast a shadow of doubt on these accounts of life in Cambodia: "You should not believe the refugees who came to Thailand, because these people have committed crimes."[61] However, a May 1976 State Department report entitled "Life Inside Cambodia" turned out to be extremely accurate. It described a network of rice plantations where young and old from all backgrounds worked from dawn to dusk as members of a "production cooperative." The Khmer Rouge were also overturning traditional Cambodian society by separating families: "In several instances the family unit is being destroyed with children permanently separated from their parents and husbands and wives placed in separate work groups." The CIA held little hope for America's former allies and educated Cambodians: "Executions are reported widespread and in many cases members of the entire family of former government officials or soldiers are executed along with the heads of the family. Almost all executions occur in the same manner: several Communist cadres beat the person to death with hoe handles or other blunt instruments."[62]

Not only did the Khmer Rouge eliminate family life, they made sex before marriage a capital offense. Khmer Rouge survivor Youk Chhang remembered watching two young lovers beaten to death in front of his entire commune.[63] "In a larger sense, the Khmer Rouge were threatened by all expressions of love—between husband and wife, parents and children, friends and colleagues," observes Elizabeth Becker. One Khmer Rouge survivor is still haunted by his mother's final words, "You have to learn how to live without me."[64] Ieng Thirith, Khmer Rouge Minister of Culture and Social Affairs, stated: "Only children can purely serve the revolution and eliminate reactionism, since they are young, obedient, loyal, and active." Samondara Vuthi Ros described her time in a children's mobile unit as a "vagrant life, like that of a plant floating in the ocean." Each child was responsible for building fifty meters of dike or three cubic meters of dam each day. If this quota was not met, his or her food rations would be reduced.[65]

Although the majority of the Khmer Rouge victims were simply worked to death, public executions were not uncommon. "Killing happened every day, in the morning, in the evening—every day. Sometimes they would kill people in front of the Children's Center. All the children watched. They wanted the children to watch, so they didn't send them out to the fields. They wanted to provide an example to the children. If they knew a child was a relative of the prisoners, they would kill the child, too," one survivor wrote.[66] A young Khmer Rouge soldier later admitted to foreign journalists that he was "a revolutionary who killed people." Another told the same reporter that his security group "planted rice and killed people" and boasted about his skill: "I hit them. Here on the neck. One blow with the pick."[67]

Henry Kissinger was among the first to describe the Khmer Rouge takeover as a "bloodbath" and "an atrocity of major proportions." He expressed his *schadenfreude* over much of the Left's misreading of Khmer Rouge intentions: "I think that it is fair to say that in the six years of war, not ten percent of the people had been killed in Cambodia than had been killed in one year of Communist rule."[68] Many of the same academics who had vigilantly drawn attention to American atrocities during the Vietnam War tied themselves into rhetorical knots in an attempt to dismiss the Cambodian refugee accounts of Khmer Rouge atrocities. A combination of distrust of the U.S. government and solidarity with the ideals purportedly held by the revolutionary regime led many to close one eye to some of the worst atrocities of the twentieth century.

Australian academic Ben Kiernan portrayed the refugees as disgruntled oppressors: "After interviewing many refugees I have found, as others have, that each one's view of the revolution depends to a great extent on their class background. This is natural, the revolution is decidedly biased in favor of the poor, in particular the peasantry. Most Kampuchean refugees are from wealthy, urban, educated, and often military backgrounds. In general, their experience of the revolution does not match those of workers and peasants." Kiernan went on to compare favorably the life of a Cambodian under the Khmer Rouge to the life of an Australian factory worker. Even Amnesty International, in a 1975–76 International Report, maintained that "it remains hard to assess the human rights situation in the absence of independent inquiries."[69]

The irreconcilable views of life in Pol Pot's Democratic Kampuchea clashed in May 1977 before a U.S. House of Representatives International Relations Committee, led by New York Representative Steven Solarz, convened to gather information about living conditions in Pol Pot's Cambodia. Historian David Chandler, a Khmer-speaking former U.S. Foreign Service Officer in Cambodia, believed that "bloodbath" was an accurate description of the situation and by no means an exaggeration. Chandler was one of the few who did not divorce the Khmer Rouge from the previous Cambodian civil war. He believed that the regime was the bastard child of a flawed American foreign policy: "We bombed Cambodia without knowing why, without taking note of the people we destroyed. We might have thought things through. Instead, we killed thousands of people who had done nothing to us, thousands of people we had never met. And at that last moment we walked away from our friends."[70]

Next to testify before the House committee was Gareth Porter of the Institute for Policy Studies, who dismissed the cries of a Khmer Rouge "bloodbath" as "hysterical." Porter charged the refugees with offering "the darkest possible picture of the country they fled," providing "fertile ground for wild exaggeration and wholesale falsehood about the government and its policies." Porter rejected "the suggestion, now rapidly hardening into conviction, that 1 to 2 million Cambodians have been the victims of a regime led by genocidal maniacs." To support his views, he cited the writings of Ben Kiernan.[71]

Representative Solarz began to ridicule Porter before he had even finished speaking, calling his testimony "cowardly and contemptible." Solarz compared Porter to "those who are still publishing books contesting whether 6 million Jews were killed by Hitler." When Porter attempted to respond, "I came here on the assumption that the committee was interested in hearing views on the fact of the matter, rather than—," the New York congressman would have none of it: "How anybody can deny it is beyond me." Gareth Porter tried to justify the Khmer Rouge evacuation of Phnom Penh's hospitals as "a reasonable alternative to move the patients as fast as possible to locations outside the cities where there were in fact other facilities." Solarz interrupted: "This isn't some kind of put-on where you are playing a role? I mean you actually believe that what you have said is true."[72] The hearing dragged on into the evening, and by the end nobody was any closer to understanding life under the Khmer Rouge. If anything, the testimony had only served to harden preexisting views.

The most ardent Khmer Rouge defenders in the United States were based at the prominent left-wing think tank, the Indochina Resource Center, in Washington, D.C. Cambodian historian Sophal Ear described the institute as "the Khmer Rouge's most effective apologists in the West." Resident scholars Gareth Porter and George Hildebrand painted an extremely positive portrait of the Khmer Rouge regime in their 1976 book, *Cambodia: Starvation and*

Revolution.[73] Noam Chomsky and Edward Herman praised the work in a 1977 *Nation* review, calling it "a carefully documented study of the destructive American impact on Cambodia and the success of the Cambodian revolutionaries in overcoming it, giving a very favorable picture of their programs and policies, based on a wide range of sources."[74] Hildebrand and Porter argued that the evacuation of Phnom Penh was a humane triage decision by the Khmer Rouge leadership that prevented widespread famine. Chomsky also attacked the refugee accounts of killings and starvation: "The sources of the stories are suspect, and their failure to convince those with the most at stake tells heavily against the credibility of the reports. It must also be suggested that, however unsuccessfully, the stories were placed in circulation with the aim of discouraging trained Cambodians from assisting in the reconstruction of their devastated country." Chomsky and Herman charged that the "mass media are not grateful for Hildebrand and Porter's message and have shielded the general public from such perceptions of Cambodia."[75]

Chomsky, a world-class linguist, then as today, was careful to cover himself with a caveat: "We do not pretend to know where the truth lies amidst these sharply conflicting assessments; rather, we again want to emphasize some crucial points." For the next decade, he played the role of hit man: any magazine that published a negative article about the Khmer Rouge found itself inundated with letters from Chomsky and his followers challenging its veracity.[76] There was only one problem: Ponchaud and many others whose scholarly ethics Chomsky was so quick to malign have been proved right. Today, Hildebrand and Porter's *Cambodia* reads like Walter Duranty's *New York Times* stories praising Stalinist Russia at the height of the famines.[77]

iv

Pol Pot did not emerge publicly until late September 1977, when he was received in Beijing by Chairman of the Chinese Communist Party Hua Guofeng and Vice Chairman Deng Xiaoping as the Prime Minister of Cambodia. Pol Pot blamed the revolution's shortcomings on an "infamous handful of reactionary elements" in a five-hour speech that signaled the start of even more killings.[78] Not only would Brother Number One carry out widespread purges of the most paranoid sort, he would antagonize his most obvious and immediate threat: Vietnam. After a series of border clashes in late December, the Khmer Rouge broke all relations. The increased tension led to even more purges, of both civilians and hundreds of thousands of Khmer Rouge in the eastern zone on the Vietnamese border. Some, like the Khmer Rouge regimental commander

Hun Sen, defected to Vietnam when ordered to attack the better-trained, equipped, and armed Vietnamese.[79]

By 1978, Chinese leaders were having to defend the Khmer Rouge internationally, so they orchestrated a public relations campaign complete with documentary films like *Democratic Kampuchea Is Moving Forward* and accompanying glossy magazines. The Khmer Rouge put their best foot forward in 1978, with Ieng Sary serving as the regime's public face at the UN in New York.[80] He distributed these magazines to his UN colleagues and even screened the Chinese propaganda film. When asked if the Khmer Rouge were carrying out genocide, Ieng Sary replied, "Absolutely not." Sympathetic delegations from Asian and European countries were invited to travel to Cambodia throughout 1978. The visits followed a set script: sightseeing at the temples of Angkor, a visit to a model agricultural cooperative, and finally, an interview with Ieng Sary or Khieu Samphan. A select few like Elizabeth Becker were even allowed to interview Pol Pot.[81]

Nuon Chea bragged to sympathetic Danish communists in a July 1978 interview that the spirit of the young Khmer Rouge cadres "has to be clean, uncorrupted and without entangling contacts with the enemy. We investigate life histories and class backgrounds both before and after they join the revolution. We do this to prevent infiltration by, for example, CIA, KGB, or Vietnamese agents." He maintained that secret work remained "fundamental. We no longer use the terms 'legal' and 'illegal'; we use the terms 'secret' and 'open.'" Then, Nuon Chea suddenly stopped making sense: "It is more widely known that the USA planned to seize power from us six months after liberation. The plan involved joint action on the part of the USA, the KGB and Vietnam. There was to be combined struggle from inside and outside. But we smashed the plan." One can sense the confusion in the Danish journalist's follow-up question, almost hoping that Nuon Chea had been mistranslated: "Is it co-operation between the CIA and KGB or is it rivalry for control of Kampuchea?" "Both," Nuon Chea explained. "On the one hand they co-operate; on the other; they are rivals."[82]

Four Americans from an obscure left-wing magazine, *The Call*, visited Democratic Kampuchea in April 1978. Like Noam Chomsky, these Americans believed that the real culprit was not the Khmer Rouge but the western media: "Without a doubt, Kampuchea is today the most maligned nation on the face of the earth. 'Genocide,' 'forced labor,' 'starvation,' 'mass executions'—these are just a few of the favorite code words used by the Western press to describe life in Kampuchea today." The Americans flatly rejected the idea that the Khmer Rouge were killing Cambodians on a massive scale: "Everyone we talked to denied the existence of widespread killings and we saw no evidence of 'mass executions' ourselves. If people had been killed in the numbers suggested by the press, surely there would have been some signs, either as physical evidence or in diminished popular support for the government. This was simply not the case." After an eight-day guided tour that took them through six provinces, the visitors concluded that conditions in "Democratic Kampuchea" were "very good" and that "The new government is strong and enjoys broad popular support." On their final day, they were given an audience with Ieng Sary, who vowed "to continue to carry out the socialist revolution by rooting out the remnants of the old exploitative social relations." In October, Sary, responding to the international outcries about life in Cambodia, announced, "We have nothing to hide," and invited UN Secretary-General Kurt Waldheim to visit Cambodia to "see with his own eyes the truth of the human rights charges against the Communist government."[83]

At roughly the same time, another group of Americans were experiencing an altogether different side of Democratic Kampuchea. James Clark and Lance McNamara were sailing off the Cambodian coast in their 38-foot fiberglass sloop *Mary K* when a wooden fishing boat appeared in the distance and opened fire. The boat pulled alongside, and several young men with AK-47s boarded the *Mary K*. Clark and McNamara were tied up and blindfolded, then taken to Kompong Som, a coastal village. From there, they were driven inland, northward toward Phnom Penh. Just south of the capital, the truck turned down a dusty road and stopped at the barbed-wire, reinforced gates of what had once been Tuol Svay Pray High School. The truck drove under a banner that read FORTIFY THE SPIRIT OF THE REVOLUTION! BE ON YOUR GUARD AGAINST THE STRATEGY AND TACTICS OF THE ENEMY, IN ORDER TO DEFEND THE COUNTRY, THE REVOLUTION, THE PEOPLE AND THE PARTY RELIABILITY and into the former school's courtyard.[84] The Khmer Rouge had renamed the former high school S-21 in 1976, when they turned it into an interrogation, torture, and execution center. Historian David Chandler described S-21, also referred to as Tuol Sleng, as "the nerve center" of Pol Pot's "system of terror." Ung Pech, one of the prison's survivors, recalled hearing one of the American prisoners cry out in pain as a teenaged guard dragged him across the courtyard by his beard. "Those Americans brought here will be executed after interrogation," Pech overheard one guard tell another. S-21 was the end of the road: between 14,000 and 20,000 people entered; fewer than a dozen survivors have been discovered. The Americans are not among them.[85]

3

"THE ANGKAR IS MORE IMPORTANT TO ME THAN MY FATHER AND MOTHER."

i

The head of S-21 prison was another former academic named Kang Keck Ieu, better known as Brother Duch. According to David Chandler, "Duch became one of the half dozen most important leaders in the country." He ran a tight ship on which both guards and inmates feared for their lives. The torturers, guards, and other staff at S-21 numbered around 1,500 young men and women between the ages of 15 and 19, all recruited from what their intellectual leaders considered "pure" or "clean" peasant backgrounds.[1]

Most of the young cadres at S-21 would not see their families for years; many would not live to see them again. "It was pointless to know where my son was going or what kind of work he would be doing, because there was nothing I could do. There was no other choice for me," recalled one father who lost his son to Angkar forever. The future S-21 "staffers" were subjected to months of harsh military training at a camp outside Phnom Penh, where they were ordered to forget about their parents and to think only of the revolution. Their rations consisted of little more than banana stalks, papaya roots, and bugs. Slight rule infractions were severely punished, and those who openly disobeyed were executed. One former S-21 cadre recalled his hardening indoctrination process: "At that time, the Khmer Rouge taught us to hate our parents and not to call them 'Pok' and 'Me' [Mom and Dad] because our parents did not deserve to be 'Pok Me.' Only Angkar deserved to be children's parents [Pok Me]. We believed what they said, and step by step they slowly made us crazy." "The Angkar is more important to me than my father and mother," another S-21 guard wrote in a "self-criticism."[2]

While these self-righteous teens served as the praetorian guards of Pol Pot's revolution, like those of the prisoners, their lives were insecure. According to S-21 records, 563 guards and other members of the prison staff were killed between 1976 and 1979, supporting the claim of survivors that whether or not to disobey orders was a life-or-death decision. One of the most striking things about the prison was the all-pervasive culture of paranoia—every ally was also a potential enemy. David Chandler points out that friendship "provided little or no security, and patronage could be withdrawn at any moment. Every act could be construed as political." Former S-21 head guard Him Huy admitted years later, "We were all spying on each other."[3]

Duch told his staff at a 1976 meeting that "Kindness is misplaced. You must beat for national reasons, class reasons, and international reasons." According to Brother Duch, torture helped to loosen a prisoner's memories: "Beat until he tells everything, beat him to get at the deep things." Interrogators were carefully trained to extract inmates' torture-induced personal histories: "They must write confessions in their own voice, clearly, using their own sentences, their own ideas. We should avoid telling them what to write. When they have finished telling their story or writing it down, only then can we raise their weak points, press them to explain why they did things, why they are lying, concealing, abbreviating things."[4] An interrogator named Pon sent this ominous message to his victim, Mr. Doeun, after one interrogation session: "Your tape has already been sent to Angkar. Based on the historical analysis by Angkar, the content of the tape is not authentic." Pon warned that "Such inventions will cost you your eyeballs." Although the confession was long and detailed, the S-21 interrogator charged that it was "full of falsehood. It will not do. Be careful with your eyeballs."[5]

Torture for its own sake was not the objective, Brother Duch explained: "You must be aware that doing politics is very important and necessary, whereas doing torture is subsidiary to politics. Politics always takes the lead." A Khmer Rouge document left behind at S-21 discouraged torture until death, what it called "a loss of mastery." The objective was "to do politics," to extract all the information possible before killing the prisoner.[6] Some confessions voice a sense of revolutionary betrayal, while others are a testament to man's remarkable creativity under extreme duress. Americans James Clark and Lance McNamara were charged with working for the CIA. After weeks, even months of torture and interrogations, Clark broke down and claimed to be working for the CIA and using drug smuggling as cover for intelligence work. Shortly thereafter, Clark and McNamara were executed; the only record is a photograph of Clark, lying on his back with his hands folded over his chest, his open and unfocused eyes staring into the distance—he is dead.[7]

The prison workers were divided among three main departments: interrogation, documentation, and security. The interrogators worked in three-man teams composed of a torturer, an interrogator, and a transcriber. Different teams specialized in "mild," "hot," or "rabid" forms of interrogation. Many of the questions asked revolved around charges of sedition. Individuals were accused of being agents of "C" or "K," shorthand for the CIA and the KGB, respectively. Typically, the victim was asked a battery of questions that had no correct answer. Torture came in a variety of forms: beatings with fists, feet, sticks, or electric wire; cigarette burns; electric shock; force-feeding feces; needle jabbings; ripping out fingernails; suffocation with a plastic bag; and a variety of water tortures.[8]

This interrogator's note to Duch recounts a typical session: "In the afternoon and evening of 21.7.77 I pressured him again, using electric cord and shit. On this occasion he insulted the person who was beating him: 'You people who are beating me will kill me,' he said. He was given 2–3 spoonfuls of shit to eat, and after that he was able to answer questions about the contemptible Hing, Chau, Sac, Va, etc. That night I beat him with electric cord again." Some prisoners, like Suy Chheng Huot, simply asked to be killed: "I no longer wish to live, make no protests to the Organization, by way of seeking justice. But I must declare that in my heart I have not betrayed the Organization at all. I declare my guilt … because I am dying. Long live the glorious revolution! Long live the Revolutionary Organization!"[9]

All of the surviving S-21 workers remember the dreaded staff meetings. After a long day of labor, the young cadres were required to assemble and face a unique version of the "prisoners' dilemma": if one surrendered too much information, he would be punished or even killed for his "crimes." If he revealed too little, his colleagues would attack his smallest flaws. One former worker described a typical meeting: "After the group chief finished his speech, each member of the group took turns talking about his mistakes. After talking about yourself, you had to … put yourself up for every member's comments if you have done anything wrong." One S-21 guard was killed for burning a wasp's nest, another for shouting "the house is on fire" in his sleep.[10]

The most feared unit at S-21 prison was the "catchers" unit, responsible for bringing in prisoners. By 1977, there were so many prisoners to kill that every few weeks batches had to be driven in trucks to a mass graveyard 15 kilometers southwest of Phnom Penh. The victims were forced to kneel at the edge of a pit, then clubbed in the back of the neck with iron bars.[11] The climate of fear, paranoia, and distrust at S-21 had few equals during the twentieth century.

ii

Pol Pot's purges did little to increase Democratic Kampuchea's national security. For all their paranoia about internal enemies, the Khmer Rouge continually antagonized their most obvious and immediate external threat: the Vietnamese. In October 1978, Vietnam publicly charged the Khmer Rouge with the deaths of "over two million Cambodians." Nguyen Vo Giap, Vietnam's greatest general, led fourteen divisions supported by planes, tanks, and troops into Cambodia in late December. By the first week of January 1979, Pol Pot and hundreds of thousands of his followers were streaming to the Thailand–Cambodia border. Pol Pot charged the Vietnamese with a "war of genocide" and compared the Khmer Rouge to the Jews under the Third Reich: "Hitler killed the Jews and those who opposed him. Vietnam kills those who oppose it and innocent people who will not join it." Pol Pot called for a "people's war" against "the hated Vietnamese invader."[12]

As for the million or so Cambodians who died between 1975 and 1979, Pol Pot claimed that "Only several thousand Kampucheans might have died [*sic*] due to some mistakes in implementing our policy of providing an affluent life for the people." With their political movement was on the brink of collapse, the once fiercely independent Maoists were now groveling at the feet of the United Nations. Pol Pot would soon drop from sight for almost two decades, leaving his brother-in-law, Vice President and Foreign Minister Ieng Sary, his wife Ieng Thirith, and President Khieu Samphan to do the explaining. While they served as the public faces of Democratic Kampuchea, Pol Pot would remain firmly in control.[13]

The 1978 resumption of U.S.–Chinese diplomatic relations and a similar Vietnamese–Soviet treaty greatly complicated the American response to the Khmer Rouge ouster. Cambodia would test U.S. President Jimmy Carter's commitment to human rights. State Department spokesman Hodding Carter III was coy. While the Carter administration took "great exception" to

Democratic Kampuchea's human rights record, this representative stated that the larger principle was the "unilateral intervention against that regime by a third power."[14] The Chinese denounced Vietnam as "the cat's paw" of Soviet imperialism and began to mass forces along the Vietnamese border.

Vietnamese radio announced the capture of Phnom Penh on January 8 and called for the surrender of Khmer Rouge soldiers.[15] By the second week of 1979, much of Cambodia was under Vietnamese military control. The Vietnamese foreign ministry contacted East German documentary filmmakers Walter Heynowski and Gerhard Scheumann and invited them to travel to Cambodia. The veteran East German reporters had a long history with the Vietnamese. The film crew followed the Vietnamese military and were the first western reporters to arrive in Phnom Penh after the Khmer Rouge defeat. They would later describe the experience in their film, *Kampuchea: Death and Rebirth*, as "a nightmare, something without parallel in history." The crew drove through the empty streets that had been a bustling city of two million inhabitants just four years earlier. In one scene, the cameras roll for more than two minutes, and the only signs of life recorded are three pigeons. The East Germans hoped that their films would highlight several "absurdities"—above all, Chinese, American, and Thai support for the genocidal regime in exile.[16]

A humble King Sihanouk emerged publicly for the first time in three years on January 7, 1979 in Beijing. Like millions of other Cambodians, he sought answers to very basic questions, like the fate of his children: "I don't know where they are, whether they are alive or dead, or under the Vietnamese." Sihanouk had been under Khmer Rouge house arrest since 1976. Accompanied by a Khmer Rouge handler, Democratic Kampuchea's UN representative, Thiounn Prasith, he was en route to New York City, where the king would address the UN General Assembly.[17] Sihanouk appeared nervous and sent mixed messages. Dressed in a Mao-style tunic, he spoke for six hours to the press in the Great Hall of the People. Once again, China and the Khmer Rouge would attempt to use the king to influence international public opinion. What he would actually say or do was anybody's guess. Above all, Sihanouk said, he worried about the "extinction" of his nation and believed that Vietnam was in the process of swallowing Cambodia. There was a new solemnity to the once jovial monarch.[18]

Cambodia would be the ultimate test of American President Jimmy Carter's humanitarian commitment. After all, Carter had called the Khmer Rouge the "worst violator of human rights in the world today." However, in early 1979, the official American position was very difficult to decipher due to ambivalent words from Washington. Cambodia was again little more than a battleground for larger geopolitical disputes, and soon the Khmer Rouge would add the United States to a long list of supporters. In the end, according to the groundbreaking archival research of diplomatic historian Kenton Clymer, the Carter administration "secretly supported Thai and Chinese efforts to provide military assistance" to the Khmer Rouge. While its diplomats and officials hid behind "irrelevant gestures of disdain," the United States would help prop up the Khmer Rouge during the most critical year—1979.[19]

When Sihanouk addressed the UN General Assembly on January 10, he raised the larger question of Cambodia's survival as a country. He did not want his nation to become "a province of the Vietnamese imperialists and their Soviet masters. . . . It is no longer a question of political differences or human rights."[20] The Vietnamese, along with their Soviet and Cuban allies, ridiculed Sihanouk's speech. Ha Van Lau, Vietnam's UN representative, defended the Cambodian invasion on the grounds that Democratic Kampuchea's widespread atrocities had been "condemned by the entire world." Cuba's representative, Rao Kouri, mocked King Sihanouk as "an opera prince" and a political opportunist: "When did the Prince speak out against the family separations, the forced moves to the country, the two million people slain, all by the Pol Pot regime? Perhaps when he strolls with Pol Pot." Sihanouk did not even have the good taste to "incinerate himself like a simple Buddhist monk," Kouri added. Even the Cuban's *ad hominem* attack could not raise the ire of the new, more serious king, who complimented the Cuban's speech as "the best today."[21] He reminded his critics: "I have lost two elder sons, two daughters, and about ten grandchildren in Cambodia." Sihanouk found it laughable that Fidel Castro's representative would call anyone a puppet: "Castro gives speeches in Soviet language, not Cuban language, and when I pointed that out to him, he blushed like a tomato." The king's missives hit their target: the enraged Cuban delegate lost his cool and called Sihanouk "a pipsqueak."[22]

The next day's fight between the Soviet and Chinese UN representatives was described by *The New York Times* as one of "the harshest diplomatic clashes they have ever fought in an open international forum since breaking relations with each other more than two decades ago." Once again, the conflict over Cambodia had little to do with the ongoing suffering of the Cambodian people. Asian and African nations, and even *The New York Times*, were now charging Vietnam with aggression.[23]

At roughly the same time, Khmer Rouge leader Ieng Sary was in a Thai military helicopter flying from the jungles of Poipet in northern Cambodia to

Bangkok, where he boarded a Hong Kong–bound Thai Airways flight. Waiting for him in the first-class cabin were Henry Kamm of *The New York Times* and several western intelligence agents. So soon after his regime's ouster, Sary was contrite and admitted, "In the early days there was certainly much killing." Kamm wrote that it made him feel "queasy" when Sary began to thank him for American support: "We appreciate very much the attitude of President Carter and his principles." Even the seasoned journalist was floored by this political about-face: "To hear the Khmer Rouge leader fawn over the attitude and principles of a president of the United States was as astounding a reversal as I have ever experienced."[24] In the coming year, Ieng Sary would make a clumsy 180-degree political shift, from Maoism to anticommunism. Soon Cambodia officially would be part of America's Cold War alliance.

Ieng Sary told Kamm that he was on a "very delicate" mission to Beijing. Although he did not yet know it, Sary was about to be called onto the carpet by his Chinese mentors. When the Khmer Rouge Foreign Minister arrived, Chinese leader Deng Xiaoping pointed out some unpleasant realities: "World opinion has taken note of several aspects of the purges that are a bit excessive and on a bit too large a scale." He went on to outline the survival strategy that the Khmer Rouge would follow for the next two decades. Although Ieng Sary would vaguely admit "mistakes" that led to deaths, his larger goal was to recast the Khmer Rouge as Cambodia's nationalist fighters against the Vietnamese invaders.

The thousands of bone-filled pits and mass graves throughout the countryside were now to be blamed on the "genocidal" Vietnamese. Deng warned Sary that China would not resume aid until the Khmer Rouge formed a resistance coalition with Prince Sihanouk as the figurehead: "His speech at the United Nations was good, well grounded and firm. When reporters asked him whether the communist party of Kampuchea has committed the crime of genocide, he replied that he hasn't seen the communist party of Kampuchea act in such a fashion, and that the population is happy."[25] Although the Chinese granted the Khmer Rouge request for financial help and a radio transmitter, Sary was warned that its use would be closely monitored: "Your broadcasts will be ridiculed as not reflecting the truth. For now don't talk a lot about the communist party. Talk about patriotism, nationalism, and democracy."[26] The Chinese also would punish the Vietnamese invaders. When Deng Xiaoping visited Washington in late January 1979, he informed the American president of an impending Chinese "punitive strike" against Vietnam. Two weeks later, on February 16, 1979, 170,000 Chinese soldiers supported by tanks and fighter planes attacked key points along the

500-mile border between China and Vietnam.[27] This short, bloody invasion left thousands dead on both sides, and was meant as a reminder to the Vietnamese that for every action there is a reaction.

With his radio transmitter in Beijing and Chinese money, Ieng Sary set about implementing China's plan and announced in May 1979 that Khmer Rouge supreme leader Pol Pot had agreed to enter an anti-Vietnamese coalition with Sihanouk. Like Pol Pot and Khieu Samphan, Ieng Sary admitted "some thousands" had been killed by the Khmer Rouge, but indicated that the Vietnamese were worse: they were carrying out "an ongoing genocide of our race and nation." He claimed that only the Khmer Rouge could prevent a Vietnamese takeover of Cambodia.[28]

Meanwhile, in Cambodia itself, the Vietnamese had established the People's Republic of Kampuchea. The People's Revolutionary Council, largely composed of former Khmer Rouge mid-level officers from Cambodia's eastern border with Vietnam, was headed by Heng Samrin. Although he officially led the People's Republic, the head of Vietnam's Politburo office of Cambodian affairs, Le Duc Tho, was the final authority and kept a close eye on things. Like their Vietnamese mentors, Cambodia's emerging leaders were battle-scarred veterans. The new foreign minister, Hun Sen, had lost an eye on the battlefield. Now, at twenty-seven in 1979, he was the world's youngest foreign minister. With little experience in government, these men saw no separation between politics and war. Singapore's longtime president Lee Kuan Yew, a Khmer Rouge supporter during the 1980s, recalled his first impression of Hun Sen: "He left an impression of strength and ruthlessness. He understood power, that it came from the barrel of a gun, which he was determined to hold."[29]

The Heng Samrin government wasted no time in condemning the Khmer Rouge. The People's Revolutionary Tribunal was established in Phnom Penh in August 1979 to try "the Pol Pot–Ieng Sary clique" for genocide *in absentia*. Five hundred spectators packed Chaktdomuk Hall to hear witnesses testify. A few handpicked foreign lawyers and journalists with Vietnamese-approved credentials were invited to attend. The ten-person jury (each member a "People's Assessor") was a strange mix: one lawyer, several teachers, power plant workers, and diverse others represented a cross-section of the population, if nothing else. The president of the court was Cambodia's new Minister of Information, Keo Chanda.[30] Prosecutor Ros Samy delivered the opening statement: "It is impossible to record fully the genocidal crime committed by the Pol Pot–Ieng Sary clique, a heinous regime, a bunch of henchmen of the Peking reactionary ruling circles, which has defiled the Angkor civilization and has challenged the conscience of progressive mankind." The tribunal heard dramatic and graphic testimony.[31]

Denise Affonço, a secretary from the French embassy, described one atrocity she had witnessed: "The condemned man was tied to a tree, his chest bare and a blindfold over his eyes. Ta Sok the executioner, using a large knife, made a long cut in the stomach of the poor man. In pain, the man screamed like a wild beast. Even today his cries still ring in my ears." Affonço went on to describe acts of ritual cannibalism: "Blood rushed everywhere, his insides were all laid bare, and Ta Sok cut out the liver and cooked it on a little stove that Ta Chea had just heated up. A strange fact to mention is that the human liver, cooking on a stove, made little jerks like frying pancakes. They divided up the liver among them and ate it hungrily."[32]

Several of the S-21 prison survivors also testified. Ung Pech, a former engineer, was told to repair the prison's generator or die. "The head of the prison, Ho, told me that I would be killed if I failed to fix the machine."[33] After two sleepless nights, Pech fixed it and was allowed to live and to work as the prison mechanic. After many days of torture, survivor Im Chan testified that he was prepared to admit anything: "The murderers beat me from morning until 11:00 p.m. My arms and legs were tied to the bed. They covered my face with a piece of cloth on which they poured water to suffocate me. When I would lose consciousness, they would press my stomach to expel the water that I had breathed in from the wet cloth. Then they would pour in more water. I suffered this torture for five successive days. Then they changed the method, using electrical current instead."[34]

History professor Khem Maly Cham testified about Khmer Rouge medical experiments. "Hieng, the leader of the local soldiers, showed the witness gallbladders that he got from dead bodies" and claimed that "the government took those gallbladders to sell in China because they are very good as medicine."[35] Testimony about the Khmer Rouge "doctors," mostly unschooled adolescents, was also unsettling: "It was noticed almost everywhere that before an injection the nurse wiped the needle with his or her fingers to disinfect it. A needle was sometimes used for ten consecutive injections, without disinfection."[36]

Vang Pheap, a S-21 guard later made a prisoner, described the executions: "After being interrogated, all the prisoners, whether they confessed or not, were killed on the spot, either just outside the prison, or in a paddy field in Prey So village, Don Cao district, Kandal province." Pits were dug ahead of time and victims were taken one at a time to the edge, "where they were hit on the neck or on the head with iron bars that were nearly one meter long."[37]

Another witness, Sim Phia, described soldiers feeding prisoners to crocodiles. "The crocodile breeding center is near the site where we were working, but we were not allowed to go there (it was only open to Chinese, Romanians, and Koreans)." One day in 1977, while working nearby, Sim Phia saw trucks arrive. He hid behind a coconut tree and watched soldiers "take nine children from 10 to 13 years of age out of the trucks. The children's arms were tied. The soldiers pulled them up to the bridge over the pool. No matter how much they cried and shouted for help, they were thrown into the pool as prey to the crocodiles."[38]

After the prosecution presented the case, Pol Pot and Ieng Sary's court-appointed attorney, American Hope Stevens, read her opening statement. She offered little in the way of a defense and instead delivered a cliché-filled monologue: "I have not come halfway around the world to give approval to monsterous crime or to ask for mercy for criminals. No! A thousand times no!"[39] Stevens described her own clients as "criminally insane monsters" who were "carrying out a program, the script of which was written elsewhere for them." She wanted to amend the indictment to include not only Pol Pot and Ieng Sary but also "the manipulators of world imperialism, the profiteers of neo-colonialism, the fascist philosophers, the hegemonists, who are supporting Zionism, racism, apartheid, and reactionary regimes in the world, all these would be standing there with the false socialist leaders of fascist China awaiting the verdict and sharing the sentence of your decision." Stevens ended her "defense" with a call for a "revolution of true socialism."[40]

The tribunal found Pol Pot and Ieng Sary guilty *in absentia* of genocide, and sentenced both to death *in absentia* on August 19, 1979. Although the trial had presented a great deal of legitimate evidence, such as the testimony of S-21 survivors Ung Pech and Im Chan, the tone was like the Stalinist show trials of the 1930s. The indictment's strange categories of criminality, the short duration of the trial, and the absurd defense combined to create the impression of primitive political justice. The reaction in the West to the verdict of the People's Revolutionary Tribunal was conspicuous silence—two square inches in the back pages of *The New York Times*.[41] Although he had been sentenced to death, Ieng Sary now served as Democratic Kampuchea's international representative. When asked about the sentence handed down against him in Phnom Penh, Sary laughed: "I read the sentence at the UN, like many other diplomats. They said it was a comedy, not worth watching."[42]

While the U.S. State Department was careful to avoid the word "genocide" when discussing Khmer Rouge atrocities due to "the judicial and diplomatic implications of the Geneva Convention," the moment of truth came in

September 1979, when it was time to decide which regime would represent Cambodia in the UN General Assembly.[43] By a vote of six (including the United States, represented by Secretary of State Cyrus Vance) to three, the UN Credential Committee allowed Pol Pot's Democratic Kampuchea to retain Cambodia's seat in the General Assembly. After the vote, a senior U.S. official told journalist Nayan Chanda, "The choice for us was between moral principles and international law. The scale weighed in favor of law because it served our security interests."[44] The United States and the Association of Southeast Asian Nations (ASEAN) countries like Singapore, Thailand, Malaysia, the Philippines, and Indonesia enjoyed the spectacle of Vietnam's comeuppance. The Chinese-led effort would keep the Khmer Rouge alive and allow them to rebuild throughout the 1980s. Within months, the regime had a permanent mission near the UN in New York City. During the remainder of 1979 and most of 1980, Ieng Thirith traveled the globe as the public face of Democratic Kampuchea, visiting Egypt, Sudan, Somalia, Zaire, Manila, Rome, Geneva, and Vienna during 1980 alone.[45]

iii

A handful of diehard western Khmer Rouge supporters gathered in Stockholm, Sweden to denounce the Vietnamese "war of aggression against Democratic Kampuchea" in November 1979.[46] Marita Wikander, Chairman of the Swedish–Kampuchean Friendship Association, opened the Stockholm International Kampuchea Conference by reading a message from Khieu Samphan, President of Democratic Kampuchea. The Khmer Rouge leader attributed one million Cambodian deaths to the Vietnamese: "During these 11 months of invasion, more than 500,000 Kampucheans have been massacred and more than 500,000 others have died from starvation."[47] The highlight of the Stockholm conference came when Ieng Thirith addressed the small crowd and took the anti-Vietnamese rhetoric to new, gory heights. She described the Vietnamese invasion as "the most cruel and barbarous war" of the twentieth century: "Even seventy or eighty years old women are not spared. As for children, they are killed in a specific way. Small babies in cradles have their body quartered in two by the two legs or thrown upon bayonets. The biggest have their heads dashed against trees." Like Pol Pot, Khieu Samphan, and her husband, Ieng Thirith charged: "This genocidal war is intended to exterminate the people and nation of Kampuchea by massacre and famine, and to make Kampuchea an integral part of Vietnam."[48]

Finally, Ieng Thirith tipped her hat to the UN for their recognition and their demand that Vietnam withdraw from Cambodia. She was the first Khmer Rouge leader to challenge publicly the authenticity of the Tuol Sleng photographs:

> About the pictures. You know that the Vietnamese, they are very cunning about this. They can stage anything. They stick at nothing in order to legalise their aggression. And I admit, as I told you, that there were excesses but those excesses had been ordered from Hanoi. So the Hanoi authorities they are double faced. On the one hand, they order the agents to commit excesses in our country and on the other hand they take these few excesses in order to enlarge into systematic slanderous propaganda against our government so that once they aggress our country public, international public opinion have been already mobilised against us, would legalise the aggression by saying: "Oh very good those Vietnamese, they are no, not aggressors, they are liberators of the Kampuchean people who was the victim of their own government."

Ieng Thirith attempted to clear up the apparent contradiction of the Khmer Rouge's alliance with their former enemy, the United States: "You know that the United States first they are aggressing our country, but now that they are in favour of our independence we consider the United States as our friend."[49]

Another featured speaker at the Stockholm conference was American academic George Hildebrand, coauthor of *Cambodia: Starvation and Revolution*, the sympathetic account of the revolution praised by Noam Chomsky in 1977. Hildebrand followed the new Chinese line and admitted that there were some "extremely serious problems in Cambodia during the period of 1975–1978." He called for "constructive criticism."[50] Even after 1979, Hildebrand, Noam Chomsky, and others continued to argue that the situation in Cambodia was unclear. "War implies propaganda, but here we have a record of mendacity that rivals Dr. Goebbels's, so let us proceed with due caution in trying to understand Cambodia from all that is said about the Cambodians by their enemies, past and present," Hildebrand warned.[51] On the final day, the conference condemned "the brutal occupation of Kampuchea by Vietnam" and called for the immediate and unconditional withdrawal of all Vietnamese troops and the removal of all "Vietnamese settlers introduced into Kampuchea by Vietnam since the invasion." The delegates "warmly" acclaimed the UN for their steadfast support of the Khmer Rouge regime in exile.[52]

By the end of 1979, Chinese pressure on King Sihanouk to cooperate with the Khmer Rouge was so constant that he fled to North Korea. Not everyone within the Carter administration supported the idea of using the king to create another governing coalition that included the Khmer Rouge. Cyrus Vance wrote the president a memo arguing against Sihanouk allying himself "with the Democratic Kampuchea (DK) regime as long as Pol Pot and his Khmer Rouge henchmen continue to control the regime."[53] When the Chinese *chargé d'affaires* in Pyongyang handed Sihanouk a letter from Khieu Samphan asking the king to forget the past and to form a united front by working alongside the Khmer Rouge, Sihanouk was outraged: "This passes the limits! Hitler massacred the Jews and Hitler's collaborators were hanged, but China tells me: 'Prince Sihanouk, do go and greet the Khmer Rouges and even go and serve them.'" The king stated flatly that out of respect for the memories of his dead children, grandchildren, and all Cambodians, he would never join another alliance with the Khmer Rouge. "The new front and the new political programme presented by the Khmer Rouges are incontestably a new deception. Only idiots and imbeciles will fall into the trap of your new delusions."[54]

4

"THE WEAPON OF THE MOUTH"

i

"I encouraged the Chinese to support Pol Pot," Zbigniew Brzezinski, President Jimmy Carter's national security advisor, announced in 1980. Brzezinski seemed to be enjoying the spectacle of inter-communist warfare. After Secretary of State Vance's resignation that year, Brzezinski's views ruled.[1] The remnants of the Khmer Rouge had settled in three main camps on the Thai border: Pailin, Phnom Malai, and Preah Vihear. The largest camp, Site 8, had a population of 50,000 scattered throughout the villages southeast of Aranyaprathet. Pol Pot was rumored to be in a secret jungle military base, dubbed Zone 87 after his Khmer Rouge alias, "87." The Thai army's "Task Force 80" played the key role in resupplying the remnants of Pol Pot's forces, as all foreign aid was now surrendered to and distributed by the Thai military.

The United States gave $85 million to the Khmer Rouge between 1980 and 1986. The Carter administration donated more than half (at least $40 million) during the crucial years of 1979 and 1980.[2] President Carter's ambassador to Thailand, Morton Abramowitz, attempted to justify supporting a genocidal government in exile: "The real question is whether the United States should have bullied the Thais and Peking not to help the Khmer Rouge but to intern them. We never considered this a serious option because (1) we thought the Vietnamese were wrong in Cambodia; (2) the Thais and the Chinese were our friends; (3) they had greater interests in Southeast Asia than we; and (4) we might not have succeeded. What would have happened if we had said to the Thais 'Take the Khmer Rouge weapons away' and then the Khmer Rouge had resisted?" Abramowitz seemed unconvinced by his own rationalizations: "Still, I have asked myself a thousand times whether that is what we should have done."[3]

Established in 1980 by the United States, Thailand, Malaysia, and Singapore, the Kampuchea Emergency Group provided essential nonmilitary aid to the resistance "coalition" from a field office just across the border in Aranyaprathet. From 1979 to 1981, China and the United States pushed King Sihanouk to head an anti-Vietnamese resistance movement that included the Khmer Rouge and rightist Son Sann. The KEG enabled the United States to maintain an arm's-length relationship with the Khmer Rouge while officially assisting Cambodian refugees in border camps. The majority of the Khmer Rouge aid came from China: their soldiers now sported new Chinese olive green fatigues and the telltale Chicom (Chinese communist army–issue) AK-47 magazine pouches on their chests. According to journalist Jacques Bekaert, "The Chinese had their own channel, in direct cooperation with the Royal Thai Army."[4]

Ronald Reagan's election as U.S. President in 1980 meant continued support for the Khmer Rouge as part of his worldwide anticommunist crusade. The new CIA chief, William Casey, according to biographer Bob Woodward, was "willing to dance cautiously with the devil." Casey considered the anticommunist resistance movements in Nicaragua, Afghanistan, Angola, Ethiopia, and Cambodia the vanguard forces of the "Reagan Doctrine" (arming anticommunist resistance forces). Vietnamese general Nguyen Vo Giap best described America's strange new alliance with the Khmer Rouge and China as "an arranged marriage" and quoted a Vietnamese saying about such alliances: "The couple share the same bed but they have different dreams."[5]

A film crew working for Heynowski and Scheumann happened to be in the Khmer Rouge camp, Site 8, when a Thai helicopter landed and former CIA deputy director Ray Cline emerged from it. The film crew ambushed him in a remarkable *60 Minutes*–style interview. When asked why he was in a Khmer Rouge camp, Cline claimed that he was now an academic and produced a card from Georgetown University's Center for Strategic and International Studies: "My trip to Southeast Asia is practically to just restore my own knowledge, to bring it up to date, and naturally I will report my impressions and my finds about the international problems here to the whole group that is going to be suggesting policies to the president-elect." When the East Germans asked, "Do you think that it is still advisable to recognize the Pol Pot regime and to support them?" the senior American spy (who had once asked, "Must the United States respond like a man in a barroom brawl who will fight only according to the Marquis of Queensberry rules?") broke into spontaneous laughter.[6] The new Cambodian government took a dim view of western aid and nongovernmental organizations. Nguyen Con, economic advisor to the People's Republic of Kampuchea government in Phnom Penh, believed that "helping Cambodia is a pretext for helping Pol Pot."[7]

Ieng Sary continued to lead the Khmer Rouge public relations campaign. He broke down the international geopolitical situation for the East Germans in 1980: "First are the aggressors and expansionists headed by the Soviet Union, and the other part is the movement of struggle for independence against the expansionists. It is good that the U.S.A. and China are agreed here. We too are on this team!" Ieng Sary espoused the Reagan Doctrine with a zeal that would have pleased the Gipper himself: "We set our hopes on the Reagan government, that it will implement its declaration to act uncompromisingly with regard to the Soviet Union and only negotiate from a position of strength. That would help us a lot."[8]

From the Khmer Rouge Potemkin village near the Thai border, Ieng Sary warmly greeted western supporters. Khmer Rouge children staged a play for one group, recorded in the East German film *The Jungle War*. Young boys wearing pith helmets, dressed as Vietnamese soldiers, walk down an imaginary jungle trail with toy AK-47s at the ready. Suddenly the "soldiers" are felled by punji sticks. When the three boys sit and begin to remove the arrows, young girls sashay their way behind the wounded soldiers. Once within range, the girls pull hatchets from the folds of their gowns and dispatch the wounded soldiers with single blows to the backs of their necks. The crowd bursts into spontaneous applause. After the performance, when a Canadian Khmer Rouge supporter takes the microphone, he announces breathlessly, "The next time I come to visit you, I think it will be in Phnom Penh."[9]

The Khmer Rouge were soon being treated as a legitimate part of the anti-Vietnamese resistance coalition. For the Reagan administration, the July 1981 UN conference on Cambodia was an opportunity to tell the Soviets that action on Cambodia and Afghanistan could ease strains in their relationship with the United States.[10] Alexander Haig was now the American Secretary of State. Haig, under President Nixon and Secretary of State Kissinger, had once coordinated the secret bombing of Cambodia. He announced that the "international community cannot and will not acquiesce in the eradication of Cambodia's sovereign identity to the aggression of its neighbor."[11] When Ieng Sary, the official Khmer Rouge spokesman, came to the podium, American delegates Haig and Jeane Kirkpatrick, America's UN representative, left the assembly hall. "This bit of theatrics made the front page of the *New York Times*, but behind the scenes, they pressured us to accept the Chinese position," one Asian diplomat recalled.[12] The American statesmen epitomized the hypocrisy of the U.S. policy in Cambodia, doing their best to preserve appearances while propping up a genocidal regime.

China and the United States had finally succeeded in pressuring King Sihanouk into service as a figurehead for the Khmer Rouge-led anti-Vietnamese coalition. "I went to see the Americans, they said one must form a united front with the Red Khmer," Sihanouk explained in an interview with Heynowski and Scheumann. The U.S. ambassador in Beijing, Leonard Woodcock, had said to him "these words in English, 'If you form a united front, it will be easier for friendly countries to help you.'"[13] Neither the handful of royalist soldiers still loyal to the king nor the rightist faction's 2,500 men were a match for the 15,000 battle-hardened Khmer Rouge soldiers under the command of Ta Mok. If there was any fighting, the Khmer Rouge would be doing the majority of it. Sihanouk, Son Sann, and Khieu Samphan officially formed the Coalition Government of Democratic Kampuchea (CGDK) on June 22, 1982, in Beijing. Son Sann described his predicament: "Choosing between the Vietnamese and the Khmer Rouge is like choosing between plague and cholera."

The Cambodian government in Phnom Penh described the new coalition as "cosmetic surgery to make up the face of the Beijing Dracula."[14] The Khmer Rouge used anti-Vietnamese prejudice to recast themselves as national saviors intent on ending the occupation. Propaganda claims about the "Vietnamese genocide," while seemingly absurd to many western observers, were gaining ground in Cambodia by the early 1980s. According to historian Evan Gottesman, "The charges, expressed openly in the border camps and whispered inside Cambodia, were endless: the yuon were colonizing Cambodia; the yuon were taking Cambodian rice and starving the Khmers; more than a million yuon were in Cambodia, with more to come; the yuon were committing a 'genocide' against the Khmers, forcing Khmers to speak their language, even taking Khmer orphans back to Vietnam to turn them into yuon spies."[15] While Khmer Rouge leaders admitted they had made "mistakes," they continued to blame the atrocities on the Vietnamese. Democratic

Kampuchea's UN representative, Thiounn Prasith, claimed that "between 10,000 and 20,000 people were killed, 80 percent of them by Vietnamese agents who infiltrated our government."[16]

Throughout the 1980s, as the evidence of Khmer Rouge atrocities became irrefutable, the number of votes for Pol Pot's Democratic Kampuchea to represent Cambodia in the UN General Assembly increased. While the UN's 1979 resolution on Kampuchea obtained only 91 favorable votes, it gradually gained favor: 97 votes in 1980; 100 in 1981.[17] By the early 1980s, the world knew that Cambodia had been ravaged by a human catastrophe as bad as anything else in the twentieth century, yet political concerns still prevailed over human rights. The leaders who had held power during the genocide stayed on as players in the new Cambodian government, unprosecuted and unpunished. American disdain for the Vietnamese far outweighed any other considerations.[18]

Further complicating matters was the nature of the Vietnamese occupation. Khmer Rouge propaganda complained of Vietnamese genocide and millions of *yuon* settlers flooding the country. Although the reality differed from the official story, there were aspects of the occupation that did not win the hearts and minds of Cambodia's already traumatized population. After nominal Prime Minister Pen Sovan, a Cambodian installed by the Vietnamese, was arrested by the occupying military in December 1981 and sent to Hanoi (where he would spent the next decade imprisoned without charges), many Cambodians began to wonder about their own security under the supposedly benevolent Vietnamese protectorate.

Another controversial aspect of the occupation was Vietnam's secret K-5 plan, designed in the mid-1980s to contain the Khmer Rouge.[19] By 1982, almost 250,000 Cambodians had been impressed to clear jungle, build fortifications, and plant a half million antipersonnel mines along the 500-mile Thai border.[20] One former K-5 worker described the conditions: "There was no shelter, and it was useless to look to build oneself a hut, because we were moved every day." After six-month tours, 80 percent of the K-5 workers returned home with malaria. Even Hun Sen, now deputy prime minister, acknowledged that "there is a lot of malaria," but added, "it is easy to cure." Hun Sen was elected prime minister by the National Assembly in 1985 and had emerged as a force gaining momentum.[21]

While there were isolated revenge killings in the immediate aftermath of the Khmer Rouge collapse, by the early 1980s the People's Republic of Kampuchea allowed former high-ranking Khmer Rouge with dubious histories and "blood debts" to join both the police and the military with little more than a promise not to commit further atrocities.[22] The Cambodian government admitted in a 1985 human rights report that "respect for legality" had never been reestablished in Cambodia after the fall of the Khmer Rouge: "That is to say, the abuses are not committed as a result of a lack of understanding. They are committed intentionally for the purpose of winning more absolute power."[23]

U.S. intelligence obtained "notes" from a meeting led by Pol Pot and Khieu Samphan at their secret Zone 87 compound in December 1986. Reviewing Democratic Kampuchea's "victories and mistakes," Pol Pot admitted that "from top to bottom, we were somewhat excessive," but offered no specific examples. The Cambodian leader described the current Hun Sen government as "the peel of the orange" and the Vietnamese as "the fruit."[24] Khieu Samphan said that the outside world was demanding an end to the Cambodian civil war, but he was "buying time in order to give you comrades the opportunity to carry out all the tasks." Pol Pot made a key point: the Khmer Rouge's ongoing survival would require skillful public relations: "As soon as you arrive in a village, you must use the weapon of the mouth." If the past were not effectively obfuscated, the consequences could be fatal: "Because of past mistakes, if you don't take the weapon of the mouth with you, you will die."[25] Pol Pot described the weapon of the mouth as "the heart of the movement."

As late as 1990, there were still no international efforts to bring the Khmer Rouge leaders to justice or even officially account for their atrocities. Individuals like David Hawk and Gregory Stanton spent much of the 1980s trying unsuccessfully to get any nation to bring genocide charges against the Khmer Rouge in the International Court of Justice at the Hague under Article IX of the UN Genocide Convention.

Cambodian leader Hun Sen called the Khmer Rouge's continued presence in the UN "unjustifiable" and offered a sports metaphor: "It is taking sides. As in football, one should find a neutral and fair referee. We cannot put faith in one who is taking sides."[26] Discussion about the fate of Pol Pot and other Khmer Rouge leaders resumed only after the collapse of the Soviet Union and the end of the Cold War. The five permanent members of the UN Security Council signed a "Comprehensive Political Settlement of the Cambodian Conflict" on October 23, 1991.[27] It called for a massive UN occupation of Cambodia that would culminate with "free and fair" supervised elections. This New Age Marshall Plan stood in stark contrast to the post–World War II occupations and reconstructions of Germany and Japan. It would be led by civilians, and the Khmer Rouge would be treated as one of four legitimate political parties in an effort to create a "neutral political environment."[28] Hun Sen headed the incumbent Cambodian People's Party; Prince Sihanouk's law professor son, Ranariddh, led the royalist FUNCINPEC (United National Front for an Independent, Neutral, Peaceful, and Cooperative Cambodia) Party; Son Sann led the Buddhist Liberal Democratic Party; and Khieu Samphan headed the Khmer Rouge.

The UN's ambitious relief and social engineering project in Cambodia was the organization's largest undertaking to date and the first major test for the paradigm of "expanded peacekeeping" during the 1990s. There was a great deal at stake, as Robert Kaplan pointed out: "What happens in Cambodia hereafter will say much about the long-term value of UN operations. Cambodia's future will be crucial to any historical reckoning of the UN."[29] The end of the Cambodian civil war and the terms of the UN occupation were outlined in the Paris Treaty, signed by nineteen nations and the various Cambodian political factions on October 23, 1991.

By far the most contentious question was whether or not the word "genocide" would appear within the text of the treaty. The final version did not mention war crimes or genocide; it only required Cambodia's oblique vow to recognize "that Cambodia's tragic recent history requires special measures to assure protection of human rights, and the nonreturn to the policies and practices of the past."[30] Elizabeth Becker reflected sagaciously: "There will be unending self-congratulations at the ceremonies Wednesday. But a serious flaw in the plan should give everyone pause. Nowhere is the Khmer Rouge held responsible for genocide; instead, two top Khmer Rouge officials sit on the Cambodian National Council." The sophistry of diplomats and international lawyers did not sway this longtime observer of Cambodian politics. Becker reduced the treaty to its essence: "Diplomats argue that this was the price for China's cooperation. More accurately, it reflects the international community's inability to take human rights as seriously as the sanctity of national borders."[31]

When Khieu Samphan returned to Phnom Penh in 1991 as leader of a UN-sanctioned party, an angry mob, rumored to have been orchestrated by Prime Minister Hun Sen, stormed the villa and overpowered Samphan's bodyguards. Someone hit the Khmer Rouge leader on the head with an iron bar, and a flurry of feet and fists left Khieu Samphan on the floor trying to fend off the blows as blood streamed down his face. After the mob finally retreated, Khieu Samphan was left to stem the blood with a pair of jockey briefs. Hun Sen appeared on the balcony of a house across the street from the melee and tried to calm the crowd through a loudspeaker. He later admitted that he could have ended the protest in ten minutes, but asked: "But can I shoot my own people? I understand their feelings. It shows there is no safe place in Cambodia for this kind of person."[32]

When Cambodia's still-exiled Norodom Sihanouk visited the United States in November 1991, he was asked about the possibility of a war crimes trial for the Khmer Rouge leaders. Not only did he "support 100 percent the idea of setting up an international tribunal," he also asked President Bush for "permission" to borrow "the very famous and the victorious General Schwarzkopf with his army to attack Pol Pot's headquarters and try to catch him." On December 3, fifty-five U.S. senators urged President Bush to support an international tribunal "to bring the perpetrators of genocide in Cambodia to justice."[33]

ii

Initially, the UN had two objectives in Cambodia: to disarm the four factions and to hold "free and fair" elections. Whereas the reconstruction and occupation of postwar Germany had been overseen by a creative and dynamic American general, Lucius Clay, the man in charge of the United Nations Transitional Authority in Cambodia (UNTAC) was a Japanese civilian. A career UN bureaucrat, Yasushi Akashi, was named the head of UNTAC. "The people of Cambodia," Akashi wrote in a statement in the *Phnom Penh Post*, "must believe themselves free from intimidation and violence, a belief that can only come about through the limitation of the military capabilities of the four factions."[34] A strict constructionist when it came to "traditional peacekeeping," Akashi did not believe in the use of force or in taking sides. UNTAC's main purpose, he claimed, was to ensure a "neutral political environment conducive to free and fair elections." "Neutrality" was a sacred principle, so the Khmer Rouge would be treated just like the other three parties. Pol Pot could even run for the National Assembly under the terms of the UN peace plan. But how would a former foe like the Khmer Rouge, still a formidable military force, react to such passivity?

The UN effort in Cambodia brought more than 15,000 UN troops from 11 different countries (the Netherlands, Bangladesh, Pakistan, Uruguay, India, Indonesia, France, Malaysia, Bulgaria, Tunisia, and Ghana) to keep the peace while 5,000 UN civilian advisors established a "transitional government."[35] The UN passed Resolution 28, creating UNTAC, in February 1992, and a year later, its soldiers and civilian employees had transformed Phnom Penh forever.

UN workers received a *per diem* of $150, more than the annual income of many Cambodians. Shortly after UNTAC's arrival, Cambodia's currency, the *riel*, declined so far in value that the U.S. dollar replaced it in all but the smallest transactions. Some UN civilian employees made as much as $3,000 to $4,000 per month, plus their *per diem*. Little of this would benefit Cambodia and its people. According to journalist Carol Livingston, "Of the estimated 1.8 billion US dollars spent during UNTAC—the final amount varied by another billion or so, depending on who did the accounting—a large proportion either never came near, or only temporarily rested in, Cambodia. Salaries paid into Phnom Penh banks for non-Cambodian staff were quickly wired home."[36] Although the handful of French Foreign Legionnaires and Australian Special Air Service soldiers gave UNTAC military forces some claws, a more lasting impression was created by the UNTAC soldiers and civilian workers who viewed the posting as a paid vacation. Brothels began to pop up like toadstools all over the country, and other vice industries expanded right alongside. To add to the tensions, civilians with desk jobs in Phnom Penh were paid a disproportionately higher salary than the soldiers in the jungle facing off with the Khmer Rouge—a telling index of UN priorities during the 1990s.[37]

True to form, the Khmer Rouge negotiated and acted in bad faith. After they refused the UN access to their areas of control and continued to lay land mines, Secretary-General Boutros Boutros-Ghali refused to confront them with force. The UN's most visible humiliation came in May, when UNTAC's top civilian and military leaders, High Commissioner Akashi and Australian Lieutenant General John Sanderson, attempted to drive into Khmer Rouge territory, primarily as a symbolic effort. They were turned back by a handful of young soldiers who blocked the road with bamboo poles.[38] The Khmer Rouge called the peacekeepers' bluff, and they folded. It would prove to be a fitting metaphor for UNTAC's endeavor.

Under the terms of the UNTAC plan, disarmament was supposed to be completed by July 1992. However, by June only 12,000 soldiers had entered the UN's cantonment sites, outposts established according to traditional regional groupings. As a result of this lack of progress, the most elementary aspects of any military occupation, cease-fire and disarmament, were never achieved because the Khmer Rouge, the most potentially dangerous faction, refused to disarm and the UN could not punish them.[39] AFP reporter Sheri Prasso obtained a secret Khmer Rouge memo in 1992 that outlined a very devious plan of political subversion, to "throw the situation into confusion" by launching attacks on Cambodian villages that would divert UN troops and thus weaken the provisional government. Similar to their 1975 strategy, the Khmer Rouge hoped to continue their "strategic offensive in the countryside" before opening "a battlefield in Phnom Penh."[40]

Khmer Rouge soldiers attacked and overran villages in the Preah Vihear and Kompong Thom provinces in July 1992 as artillery shells landed near the provincial governor's house and the residence of UN military observers. Secretary-General Boutros Boutros-Ghali admitted the Khmer Rouge could "jeopardize the whole peace process," but still refused to respond with force.[41] Khmer Rouge leaders continued to demand that 100,000 to 500,000 Vietnamese settlers be removed from Cambodia and that Hun Sen be removed from power before they would cooperate in the peace process. Charles Twining of the U.S. State Department feared that he might see "Vietnamese corpses floating down the Mekong River in Cambodia"; Khieu Samphan told reporter Nate Thayer that if "the Cambodian people cannot see a peaceful resolution to the problem, they will seek other means. So the nightmare that Twining was talking about might become a reality."[42] Although UNTAC head Yasushi Akashi admitted that Khmer Rouge intransigence posed "a threat and challenge to the whole peace process and to the prestige also of the United Nations," he remained "very optimistic" because "there is no other alternative than peace."[43]

While UNTAC's political future and ultimate effectiveness looked uncertain even in 1992, the UN would leave one lasting legacy in Cambodia—AIDS. Cambodia had been isolated from the outside world for many years, and this was reflected in the lack of public health information as well as the scarcity and poor quality of medical treatment. UN workers were neither tested for the HIV virus before arriving in Cambodia nor sent home if they were found to be infected. To bar HIV-positive employees from working there would be to discriminate—so went the UN's tortured logic during the 1990s. Swiss UN doctor Beat Richter wanted the organization to test soldiers before sending them to Cambodia, but his request was ignored: "He [Akashi] told people, 'Everybody has the right, even the soldiers, to enjoy the young ladies, and we cannot discriminate the HIV positive soldiers.'" UN chief medical officer Dr. Peter Fraps believed that all UN workers should have been tested and those who came up positive sent home. To Fraps, public health concerns outweighed civil liberties: "We have soldiers in the mission area from countries where HIV is epidemic; therefore it's absolutely likely that soldiers coming from these countries contributed to the contamination in the area." Fraps said he "asked specifically what to do with HIV positives here in the mission area and I did it twice and I never received an answer."[44] When Richard Holbrooke, former Assistant U.S. Secretary of State, visited Cambodia in 1992, he observed, "It was like the last scene in *The Deer Hunter*. . . . It was absolutely clear that these guys were going to both spread AIDS and take AIDS home with them."[45]

By 1992, AIDS had arrived in Cambodia. Sixty-five people tested HIV positive that year. The National Centre for Blood Transfusions added another 35 to this number when it began to screen blood donors. Prostitutes, the group most vulnerable to infection, could get only half of their customers to wear condoms. A 1992 Cambodian Ministry of Health survey made more shocking discoveries: 1 in 5 Cambodians did not know what AIDS was, and 72 percent of Cambodian men had never used a condom. Even more alarming, the number of prostitutes in Phnom Penh had jumped from 1,500 in 1990 to 6,000 in 1991 and to 20,000 in 1992.[46] Although health care workers had had some success in getting prostitutes to force their customers to wear condoms, drunken soldiers did pretty much as they pleased.

Many Cambodians still believed that traditional medicine could cure and even inoculate against the AIDS virus. Charlatan doctors offered AIDS prevention shots and Cambodian newspapers advertised any number of witches' brews sold as "cures." Dr. Tea Phalla, chief of Cambodia's national AIDS committee, pointed to the largest obstacle to prevention—denial: "People feel terrible accepting the disease has come into their community, so instead they try to adapt their beliefs to the situation—deluding themselves it is just kind of a latent syphilis and not a new disease." Cambodian journalist Moeun Chhean Nariddh recalled a conversation he had overheard: "My AIDS is gone and my swollen neck is also disappearing. There's no such disease as AIDS, it's just the worst state of syphilis."[47] While 47 UNTAC workers tested HIV positive in Cambodia, UNTAC doctors treated over 5,000 cases of sexually transmitted diseases among UN workers. The UN's state of denial was no different than the Cambodian population's, and the disease thrived.

Akashi outraged many foreigners working in Cambodia when he dismissed their complaints about UNTAC staff frequenting the brothels with a flippant, "Boys will be boys." An open letter said to represent "the community of women living in Phnom Penh" complained that they were the "victims of stereotyping," "inappropriate behavior," and "sexual harassment." The group called for education in "gender awareness" and an official UNTAC code of conduct, and complained about the lack of women in high-level UNTAC jobs. Almost as an afterthought, they requested that an effort be made to educate Cambodians about sexually transmitted diseases like AIDS.[48]

By 1993 it was clear that the UN's military occupation and disarmament program had failed. UNTAC succeeded in repatriating more than 300,000 Cambodians, but the UN's original mandate was being redefined. The entire stated purpose of the exercise was to create peace and stability in Cambodia for the first time in twenty years, but this was never achieved. The Khmer

Rouge launched attacks throughout November and even shot down a UNTAC helicopter near Siem Reap.[49] Because the UN military components were not allowed to fight back, their leaders grew dispirited and the rift between UNTAC civilian and military contingents widened. Troops like the French Foreign Legion's Rapid Reaction Force saw fighting as a job and reprisals as the rule of this particular stretch of jungle. French General Frank Michel resigned, "frustrated by my inability to implement the U.N. mandate."[50] The UN's Deputy Force Commander, French Brigadier General Rideau, also believed that "some decisions should have been made to rediscuss or to do something. It could have been from a military point of view. But we went on whatever the incident."[51]

In April, Bulgarian soldiers invited their Khmer Rouge counterparts to dinner in the UNTAC compound in Kompong Speu. After enjoying a home-cooked meal, the Khmer Rouge guests gunned down their hosts. Once again, High Commissioner Akashi "condemned the treacherous and cowardly act in the strongest terms," but there were no reprisals.[52] Cambodian Prime Minister Hun Sen chided the UN for its unwillingness to fight: "Right now everyone seems to be too scared from my point of view. Of course, the Khmer Rouge will try to disrupt the elections." He suggested that "Mr. Khieu Samphan be arrested and prosecuted for the crime of genocide." To Hun Sen, it was a clear case: "He is the boss. He has given orders to his soldiers to commit these crimes."[53] UN Secretary-General Boutros Boutros-Ghali still favored a nonconfrontational approach and argued that "patient diplomacy" was the best way to get the "peace process back on track."[54]

UNTAC now attempted to salvage its reputation by going ahead with "democratic" elections, scheduled for May 23–27, 1993. While it encouraged Cambodians to participate in the electoral process, it could not protect them from the unpleasant side effects. Joining a political party, much less running for office, would prove to be a life-and-death decision in Cambodia throughout the 1990s. Former Cambodian leader Pen Sovan best described the situation: "Cambodian politics has the head of a chicken, but the arse of a duck. They speak about democracy and multiple political parties, but they practice communist ways." The election had the potential to rekindle the civil war. King Sihanouk had written to UNTAC leader Akashi on January 4, announcing that he would no longer work with UNTAC or members of Hun Sen's ruling Cambodian People's Party because of an ongoing, orchestrated campaign of violence against members of his son Prince Ranariddh's royalist FUNCINPEC Party. Sihanouk had lost faith in the UN and predicted "the situation will get more unstable, more insecure, more confusing."[55]

The heroes of the UNTAC election were the Cambodian people, as more than 90 percent of those registered turned out to vote. The actual polling ran smoothly with only isolated incidents of violence. When High Commissioner Akashi declared the polling "free and fair" on May 29, even the candidates briefly concurred. However, when the election results began to indicate a victory for Prince Ranariddh and his FUNCINPEC Party, that changed. According to the UN's final tally, the prince defeated Hun Sen, 1,824,188 to 1,533,471. When the UN declared Prince Ranariddh the winner (FUNCINPEC would get 58 seats in the National Assembly and the CPP only 51), Hun Sen charged that the UN and the West were conspiring to steal the election from him.[56] While UNTAC officials rejected Hun Sen's claims out of hand, it quickly became clear that upholding the results of their election would require the threat of force. After tense behind-the-scenes negotiations went nowhere, King Sihanouk pushed the UN and the election results aside and announced that the country would be ruled by both Prince Ranariddh and Hun Sen as First and Second Prime Ministers.[57]

UNTAC's elections in Cambodia did not result in an accepted victory and a peaceful transfer of power. Instead, the loser refused to honor the outcome and was appeased out of political and military necessity. Historian Richard Hofstadter points out that the amazing and novel thing about American democracy is the ability to hold hotly contested elections and then peacefully transition to a new government. This was not possible in Cambodia. After King Sihanouk's stopgap solution, Singapore Premier Lee Kuan Yew warned Prince Ranariddh that a coalition with Hun Sen was "a precarious arrangement"; being called prime minister "was of little value when the officers and troops were loyal to Hun Sen."[58]

Cambodians from all walks of life had been abandoned by westerners before; the feelings of disappointment and betrayal were all too familiar. But this time, Cambodians would tax them. An open season was declared on UNTAC's vast material resources as the UN began to pull out. One well-run auto theft ring even specialized in the UN's prized Toyota Land Cruisers.[59] When UNTAC officials raided the house of a Cambodian politician suspected of having a stolen Land Cruiser, they were held at gunpoint for seven hours. "The investigations will continue but nothing will happen. This is ridiculous, the way things are disappearing here," said one disgusted official.[60]

By August 1993, the UN had already lost 160 cars to thieves, and it would only get worse. After the UN's human rights office had five cars stolen in one day, mostly at gunpoint, it threatened to suspend operations. One NGO employee blamed UNTAC, "because they did nothing but add each stolen car onto their list. Cambodians are just laughing at UNTAC and it's too late. If they had stated at the beginning they would not accept this, maybe it would have never gotten to this point." UN headquarters responded with more threats, but in truth was in headlong retreat.

When UNTAC leaders Sanderson and Akashi finally left Cambodia in late September, Khmer Rouge radio announced that UNTAC had brought nothing but AIDS, and urged Cambodians to "throw feces" at Akashi.[61] In a fitting conclusion to the debacle, the Russian crew of the UN cargo ship *Vladimir Vasaysev* held an impromptu dockside auction of UNTAC cars, motorcycles, and refrigerators before weighing anchor.[62] The stolen vehicles were a metaphor for UNTAC's tenure in Cambodia, or so reporter Henry Kamm seemed to think: "Their continued presence in Cambodia may be the most lasting heritage of the two-billion-dollar international enterprise." Kamm was wrong, though: AIDS would outlast even the venerable Toyota Land Cruisers. The rate of new HIV-positive cases in Phnom Penh had leaped by 150 percent in 1994,[63] and that was the tip of the iceberg: the only Cambodians tested regularly were blood donors, and their HIV-positive ranks had multiplied twentyfold since 1991. The World Health Organization estimated that the true number of HIV-positive Cambodians was much higher. When the WHO's regional head, Dr. Sand Tae Han, visited Phnom Penh's Tuol Kork red light district, he spoke with prostitutes who had never even heard of the AIDS virus. By 1994, Dr. Krury Sunlay predicted that AIDS would be Cambodia's "second killing fields."[64]

The Khmer Rouge continued their strategy of terror into 1994; they burned six villages in one January raid and began to kidnap westerners.[65] Despite this graphic evidence and the inability—or unwillingness—of the "democratic" government to stop the violence, the UN refused to admit the UNTAC operation and "expanded peacekeeping" paradigm were flawed. Instead, UNTAC was hailed by many diplomats as "a model and a shining example for other U.N. member states." Instead of being fired for failing to implement the terms of the Paris Treaty, Yasushi Akashi was in effect promoted, sent to former Yugoslavia to replicate the paradigm and achieve even more tragic results.[66]

Given the absence of any form of accountability for past war crimes and the ongoing political and military resistance during the UNTAC occupation of Cambodia, it was ironic that war crimes accountability would be so central an issue in other UN occupations during the 1990s. Because there had been no war crimes investigations or trials, the battles over interpretation of Cambodian history were especially fierce and showed no signs of cessation, even as late as 1993. Since my first visit to Cambodia, I had learned that a Vietnamese colonel named Mai Lam and a group of "East German experts" had turned S-21 prison into the Tuol Sleng Genocide Museum and constructed the skull pagoda memorial at Choeung Ek. Colonel Lam had previously curated the American war crimes museum in Saigon, and was ordered to turn the former prison into a museum in 1979. Although he left most of Tuol Sleng as the Vietnamese army had found it, Mai Lam added the map of Cambodia constructed of human skulls, in which the nation's lakes and rivers were painted blood red. While the museum occupied a central role in the anti–Khmer Rouge propaganda of the Vietnamese, it was not without controversy.[67] Much like the German reaction to American reform efforts after World War II, many vanquished Cambodians rejected the heavy-handed historicizations of their occupiers.

French scholar Serge Thion had spent 1968–69 teaching at Tuol Svay Pray High School, and he believed that East German–trained North Vietnamese "experts" had turned Tuol Sleng into "a propaganda machine": "In 1991, the map made of skulls could not be seen anywhere. The huge pile of clothes, deliberately reminiscent of WW II concentration camps [*sic*] photographs had disappeared." Thion believed that the Tuol Sleng Museum had been created to suit the tastes of a western audience "by equating in a subdue [*sic*] way, the 1975–79 massacres to the Jewish drama during the Nazi period. The use of the word 'Genocide' is further proof of it. This is cheap propaganda. It did not stop the West, and particularly the U.S. government, to support Pol Pot until quite recently." He scoffed at the notion that education and awareness could prevent future atrocities: "Keeping monuments to educate for the future is an illusion. The keeping of Auschwitz did not prevent Tuol Sleng. Tuol Sleng does not prevent Sarajevo. Politics is not rooted in memory but in the thirst for power. And memory in itself is not strongly related to justice." Most important, Thion added, he did not "believe that Cambodians really accept this kind of institution."[68]

5

"ONLY THE THIRD PERSON KNOWS."

i

After my first trip to Cambodia, I became interested in interviewing more Tuol Sleng guards, staff, and survivors—above all, the Tuol Sleng photographer, if he was even alive. Legitimate war crimes trials seemed so beyond the limits of the possible in 1994 that I turned my attention to the more practical tasks of historical accountability. Only about 6,000 of approximately 14,000 Tuol Sleng negatives had been recovered. My most reliable contacts continued to steer me toward the Vietnamese colonel who had created the Tuol Sleng Museum. During the Vietnamese occupation of Cambodia, Colonel Mai Lam served as Vietnam's "Cambodian criminology expert" and was responsible for collecting documentary and photographic evidence for the 1979 trial of Pol Pot and Ieng Sary. Later, he turned S-21 prison into what would be known thereafter as the Tuol Sleng Museum of Genocide. I had no proof that the colonel had made off with the missing archives, but he was a logical place to start.

In November 1994, I met Chris Riley in Hong Kong and we traveled to Saigon together. He had done most of the legwork and felt confident that he could find Mai Lam's house. At first glance, Saigon, now officially renamed Ho Chi Minh City, was a welcome relief from Cambodia. We walked down Dong

Khoi Boulevard past colorful markets and residential areas. Although the adults more or less ignored us, a pack of small children began to stalk us. If it had been war, we would have been dead.

SSSSSting, sting, sting, sting, sting, the first barrage hit me squarely in the face and neck. It was extremely painful and disorienting, as I could not see my attackers and thought for a moment that I was being stung by wasps. When the second volley hit, again in the face, I saw them—about a dozen children, armed with peashooters and mouths full of fruit seeds. Riley aggressively advanced and I covered him with a volley of gravel I'd quickly scooped up from the street. All of the kids scrambled except for one girl who seemed so shocked by Riley screaming like a crazed white ape that she froze. Riley pretended to take her prisoner and she began to cry. Most of the adults watching the spectacle were doubled over with laughter, but one old lady scowled and half-heartedly threw a rock that landed at my feet. We continued to a restaurant, where we sat on small wooden stools at a low table. There was no meat, but here the alternative was ten different kinds of mushrooms. After we finished our meal, I filled my pockets with gravel, but we made it back to the hotel without incident.

The next morning we drove in a cab down a crowded boulevard near the city's center to find Mai Lam. BMWs, pedicabs, cars, trucks, and buses all converged on impossibly narrow streets. The air was thick with dust and the smoky, blue exhaust of two-stroke engines. Our driver pushed forward with a hand on the horn and a heavy foot on the gas. After several passes of the target area, a seemingly middle-class residential neighborhood, we stopped the cab and continued on foot. We asked some residents about Mai Lam, and they pointed to a half-completed structure obscuring a smaller house behind it. We approached the gate and asked one of the workmen in the yard if this was the house of Mai Lam. He responded affirmatively. Then a woman came out and asked us what we wanted. We told her that we would like to speak with Colonel Mai Lam. She opened the gate and led us down a pathway to the door of the smaller house. We removed our shoes and went inside.

On one wall of the living room into which she led us was a photograph of Ho Chi Minh; on the opposite wall, a shrine of ancestral photographs. After a minute or two, Mai Lam entered the room. Although he was in his seventies, he looked very healthy, with penetrating blue eyes and a shock of white hair. I wondered where the blue eyes came from. In my broken high school French, I told him that we would like to ask him about the transformation of S-21 prison in Phnom Penh into the Tuol Sleng Museum of Genocide. Mai Lam smiled coyly and replied in French, "I would like to speak with you, I have many interesting things to tell you. But first you must get the permission of the Cambodian embassy and the Vietnamese Ministry of Information." We thanked him and headed back out into the city.

Our cab driver took us to the Cambodian embassy. We already had a letter from the Cambodian Ministry of Culture explaining the purpose of our research, so the staff were very accommodating and it took only fifteen minutes to complete the necessary paperwork. Next, at Vietnam's Ministry of Information, we were escorted into a side office. The official who greeted us, Madame Phan, was probably in her forties and spoke English well, but with a distinct Russian accent. We would later learn that she was a graduate of Moscow University. Riley handed her his card and my curriculum vitae. "What is the purpose of your investigation?" she asked. Riley told her that we were trying to get more information on the missing Tuol Sleng negatives. The entire exchange was very businesslike. Then she disappeared. Fifteen minutes later she returned with the letter we needed.

Excited by our success so far, we returned to Mai Lam's house that afternoon. The colonel led us inside and Riley handed him the letters. He moved to his chair, sat down, and put on his glasses. He read only part of the Vietnamese letter, then handed it back to Riley. "The letter says that I can speak with you if I like." Mai Lam smiled and said, "I would like a letter saying that the government would like me to speak with you."

Returning to the Ministry of Information, we told Madame Phan about our dilemma. Fortunately, she said that she would speak to Mai Lam on our behalf. We could do nothing but wait, so we walked to the Rex Hotel nearby, where a previous generation of Americans had plotted the strategy of the Vietnam War over cocktails at the rooftop bar.

In the tourist area near the hotel, we encountered a young boy with such a severe harelip that he had no nose. He liked to sneak up on foreigners and pop into their faces when they least expected it. The tourists would usually recoil in horror when he touched them and throw money just to get him to go away. When he snuck up on me, I shuddered visibly at the sight of the dirty, ulcerous holes where his nose should have been. He knew the look and tried to grab my pant leg. "Give me one dollar, one dollar," he said. I refused, so he followed me, shouting, "Give me one dollar." Next we literally stumbled over a three-foot-tall boy with deformed, pincherlike hands and feet, perched on a rolling cart. His strategy was to wheel himself in front of passing tourists and cling to their legs until they either surrendered a dollar or kicked him off. As I wondered if these deformities were the result of American defoliants, an old man approached us from the shadows. He thrust out an official-looking photo ID with a picture of him, much younger. "I worked very hard for your country, now I am a marked man. I can get no job, nothing—I am on a list. Please, just one dollar." We shook our heads until he finally gave up and moved on.

The next morning, having heard nothing from Madame Phan, we decided to visit the other museum Mai Lam had created, The Exhibition House of Aggression War Crimes, housed in a series of old colonial-style buildings. The large courtyard was filled with American military hardware: Huey helicopters, tanks, armored "flamethrowers," bombs, bulldozers, and more. Each had a descriptive sign, such as: ONE OF THE PUPPETS' ARMORED CARS SEIZED ON THE 9TH HIGHWAY SOUTHERN LAOS FRONT 1971.[1] The main "exhibition" was a house of horrors specially designed to evoke American self-loathing and guilt. The brochure describing it had a photo on the cover of three American soldiers marching, carrying the American flag, under the boldface headline: CRIMES IN AGGRESSION WAR IN VIETNAM. The accompanying text read: "In 1965, with a gigantic force involving 6 million turns of soldiers, the United States began launching a war of aggression against Vietnam. . . . For years US planes dropped 7,850,000 tons of bombs, and sprayed 75 million liters of lethal chemicals on villages, ricefields and forests of South Vietnam." The pamphlet contained gruesome photographs of bullet-riddled corpses—the victims of the Son Mai Massacre, the Binh Duong Massacre, phosphorous bombs, steel-pellet bombs, and Napalm—and finally, a B-52 opening its bomb bay. The majority of the photos illustrated American atrocities: a soldier setting fire to a hut; a tank dragging a body; two black soldiers leading two captured Vietnamese women out of the jungle, under the caption "Molesting and arresting women."[2]

Colonel Mai Lam had not pulled any punches. Inside the exhibition hall were more disturbing images: four American commandos kneeling behind two headless corpses, probably Viet Cong, severed heads sitting on the grass in the foreground; the soldiers smile as if they have just bagged a ten-point buck at their deer-hunting camp in the Adirondacks. Finally and climactically, a two-headed Vietnamese baby bobbed peacefully in a large green glass apothecary jar full of formaldehyde. Although The Exhibition House of Aggression War Crimes offered graphic examples of atrocities, the experience was like visiting Disneyland's Haunted House. Colonel Mai Lam was not a subtle fellow; Tuol Sleng was subdued compared to this propaganda-filled horror show. When we returned to the hotel, there was a message from the Ministry of Information: Mai Lam would meet with us, and Madame Phan would serve as our translator.

The next morning we picked up Madame Phan and drove to Mai Lam's house. The same woman escorted us into the living room. Mai Lam was elegant in a pair of white pants and a white silk shirt. "Before answering your questions, I would like to know the purpose of your interview and the purpose of your work," he said. Riley told him about his restorative work at Tuol Sleng and my background in war crimes. "That is very interesting, my career is related to that topic," Mai Lam said to me. "The first time I went to Cambodia was in 1946. At that moment I was the leader of the Vietnamese voluntary army and stayed until 1954."[3]

The colonel was one of the early Vietnamese communists who helped export the revolutionary ideology to neighboring Cambodia. Mai Lam produced a battered manila envelope from which he extracted several photos. He sorted through them until he came to one of three people. "Her name is Mem Won, she was a great Cambodian patriot. The man next to her is the chairman of the Khmer Liberation Front. The other person you can guess, that is me. I was twenty-five years old." He came to another photograph, of a formidable-looking young soldier in a military uniform. "Here I was in uniform, a soldier of General Giap," he said proudly. Mai Lam said that he hated the French and decided to join the army. "I left my family, my parents did not know. I was sent to the south of Vietnam in 1946. They also sent us as a voluntary force against the French in Cambodia."

After Mai Lam was a soldier, he became a lawyer and supervised the implementation of the Geneva Agreement. "I also researched in international law, especially the implementation of agreements." He was appointed to investigate war crimes in North Vietnam in 1967, and that became his specialty. After the Vietnamese defeat of the Khmer Rouge in 1979, he was sent to Phnom Penh "to help the Cambodians collect the necessary information about the crimes of Pol Pot–Ieng Sary"; a later assignment was to establish the Tuol Sleng Museum. Lam made a conditional offer to help us search for the missing photo negatives and track down prison survivors: "If I contribute to this, I want to make it a real good work. I think that to make the work go better, I might go back to Phnom Penh and meet my friends." When Mai Lam said, "Normal people don't care. I contributed nearly 2,000 pictures to Tuol Sleng Museum," Riley could not contain himself and asked him directly what had happened to the approximately 9,000 missing negatives.

Mai Lam paused before responding. "It was difficult to collect documents in Phnom Penh. Pol Pot tried to destroy information; it was very difficult to collect. I went to all corners of Cambodia to collect those pictures, negatives, and all that information." He continued to be coy: "I may go back to

Cambodia to collect information about that period. There are some other things that are out of our hands that only the third person knows." I asked who the third person was and what "the other things" were. Mai Lam grinned; his blue eyes flashed. "You may think about it. Do you agree with me that there is a third person who knows much better? The third person knows about pictures, negatives, prisoners—and knows much better than us."

I asked if the third person was the Khmer Rouge? The Chinese? Mai Lam replied, "Don't force me to answer that question, I leave that question for you." According to him, Tuol Sleng was just a small part of that period's history: "Each province in Cambodia has their own stories about the crimes of Pol Pot and Ieng Sary." The colonel seemed to be making an offer of sorts: "You can meet the witnesses who lived in the prison during Pol Pot–Ieng Sary. You can also meet the murderers. Many resources of information in Cambodia—not Vietnam, Cambodia. You can meet the killers. I met the killers." When I asked how he found them, he said only, "I did my homework, my way," and that it was "easy" for him because "I dressed like this, no uniform, and spoke Khmer."

When asked if he could verify the rumor that Chinese advisors had traveled to Cambodia in 1976 or 1977 to teach the Khmer Rouge cadres the latest Maoist interrogation techniques, he shrugged. "It is difficult for me to answer that question." When I pressed him, Mai Lam sighed. "If I don't answer you, of course you will feel unsatisfied." He urged me to be patient and said, "Time will answer your questions."

I was growing more and more dissatisfied with the old man's roundabout answers. Riley's question about the missing negatives had obviously made Mai Lam defensive. The interview was going south fast and I doubted that there would be another, so I pressed him nonetheless: "Do you believe that the Khmer Rouge had their own agenda? Or were they working on behalf of the Chinese with a Chinese agenda?" Again, Mai Lam smiled mysteriously and said, "Time will answer your question."

Given that Colonel Lam was one of Vietnam's foremost war crimes experts, I tried a slightly different tack, attempting to draw out his professional opinion on contemporary events: "There is much debate over the United Nations Genocide Convention. Did the Khmer Rouge commit genocide? If these expanded laws of war cannot punish, then what are they worth? What are your views on the laws of war in light of Rwanda and Bosnia?"

But Mai Lam continued to bob and weave. "Opinions differ," he said. "I think they are guilty of genocide crimes, they killed massively. You don't have time to discuss and debate because opinions differ." I asked if I could return to ask him a broader set of questions about the laws of war and war crimes when I returned from a research trip to Hanoi. He remained noncommittal. "I must repeat, I only specialized in war crimes," he replied.

Mai Lam was beginning to wear me down. "So do I! And that is what I want to talk about!" I exclaimed.

The colonel sighed. "I think that your book is good and the topic interests me, too. It has been my research for forty years, but I must prepare. Next time. Have a good trip and if you meet General Giap, tell him that you met his old soldier."

We walked out of the house and to the car. When my turn came to shake Mai Lam's hand, he grasped it firmly, looked me sternly in the eye, and said, "Do not make bad propaganda." It dawned on me in the car as we drove away—"propaganda." Even the phrase "war crimes" fit neatly into the cliché-ridden lexicon of the Vietnamese, who had used evidence of Khmer Rouge atrocities to justify their 1979 invasion. But they were not the only ones trying to reduce Cambodia to a political battleground. Perhaps Mai Lam was more intellectually honest than many in the West, who had proclaimed the dawn of a new era in international law even while genocidal civil wars raged around them.[4]

ii

I returned to the United States with more questions than answers. Above all, I wondered who Mai Lam's "third person" was. I had heard a rumor that an East German documentary film crew had followed the Vietnamese into Cambodia weeks after the collapse of the Khmer Rouge in 1979. The film-makers were supposedly the first westerners inside of S-21 prison and were rumored to have interviewed guards, interrogators, and all seven survivors. According to Mai Lam, much of the S-21 archive had been sent to the German Democratic Republic so that it could be included in a documentary film. Had the film crew borrowed the negatives and simply not returned them? Perhaps they were the "East German experts" and the "third person" to whom the colonel had referred.

An odd combination of coincidences put me on the trail of these "East Germans" during the summer of 1995. Chronos Films in Berlin had hired me to serve as a historical advisor for a documentary film on the Nuremberg trials. One of the largest private documentary film collections in the world, Chronos is owned and operated by Bengt von zur Mühlen. He proved unusually well connected, as demonstrated by the fact that former East German spy Marcus Wolf, Luise Jodl (wife of General Alfred Jodl), and others who had never before been interviewed appeared in our project, *Nuremberg: A Courtroom Drama*. My boss, thirty-five-year-old Michael Kloft, was one of Germany's outstanding documentary producers.

The German historical advisor, Jörg Friedrich, was the author of *Das Gesetz Des Kriegs* (*The Law of War*) and one of the world's foremost war crimes experts. We met for the first time in Kloft's apartment. Friedrich sneered when I told him that Kloft and I had been up late the night before at a rock concert. After I made some lame attempts at small talk, the historian made it clear that he had not come to chat and drew first blood: "Tssso Peta, do you know that the sentences of *ALL* the allied war crimes tribunals were never accepted as legally valid in Germany? Look at the world around you! What do you think of your Nuremberg principles now?"

Friedrich was right. The Balkan war was in full swing, and there was an unspoken consensus: the United Nations, the United States, and the much-vaunted European Community would let it rage. Once again, the prevailing concept of "neutrality" had a paralyzing effect on the West's ability to react, even when they had troops on the ground and jets in the sky. As early as 1994, reporter Ed Vulliamy was calling bullshit on the "international community." According to Vulliamy's "new rules" of post–Cold War statecraft, atrocities were tolerated, accommodated, and eventually rewarded because they "provided the basis for new frontiers."[5] During one of the breaks from the Chronos filming, I traveled to The Hague to see the opening sessions of the first international war crimes tribunal since Nuremberg. Despite the setbacks on the battlefield, Hague prosecutor Richard Goldstone barreled on. The South African Supreme Court justice was emerging as an interesting and autonomous political actor, exactly the type of media-savvy, independent war crimes prosecutor most feared by the United States.[6] The UN's International Criminal Tribunal for former Yugoslavia was up and running in the summer of 1995, even as atrocities were still being carried out. The court heard motions in the case of Dusan Tadic, said to be a particularly sadistic prison guard. He was alleged to have forced prisoners to bite off one another's testicles.

Thirty-five feet and two glass partitions stood between me and Tadic. The five judges sat on an elevated platform to his left. The defendant and his two guards were enclosed in a glass booth resembling a hockey penalty box. Dressed in a double-breasted, navy-blue suit with an open-collared pink shirt, Tadic was short and stout. After a few days, the pretrial maneuvering began to look farcical to me.[7] All day long I listened to the world's international legal luminaries split hairs in this case of a garden-variety war criminal; then at night I watched Serb forces close in on the UN "safe haven" of Srebrenica on live television. Vulliamy wrote that Srebrenica "presented the West with its final chance to rescue a battered credibility in Bosnia."[8] If the UN wouldn't dig in and fight to protect what they themselves had declared "safe," would they ever fight?

Yasushi Akashi was once again at the center of the action and once again, he was pushing the envelope of neutrality as the UN Secretary-General's special representative for Yugoslavia. "Playing for time, avoiding confrontation, and constantly supporting more negotiations no matter how bad the situation were Akashi's hallmarks," wrote journalist David Rhode.[9] While Rhode was referring to the diplomat's performance in former Yugoslavia, it was an act that Akashi had tuned finely during his tenure in Cambodia. Like the French generals Loridan and Rideau in Cambodia, NATO's military chiefs in former Yugoslavia were growing dispirited under the no-reprisals policy imposed by the UN. One of them, American Admiral Leighton Smith Jr., was quick to remind his critics that the decision not to use force was made "by political leaders not NATO officers."[10]

Heedless of the stern words of the UN, the Serbs were pushing forward with the most brazen phase of their "ethnic cleansing" campaign. When Serb forces led by Ratko Mladic captured Srebrenica on July 15, 1995, UN soldiers did not fire a single shot and NATO planes did not drop a single bomb. Captured Dutch UN commander Tom Karremans was even forced to drink a humiliating toast after his surrender to the Serb military leader. The most ominous footage was of Muslim men being loaded onto European tour buses to be driven to their certain deaths. No incident caused the UN a more public loss of face during the 1990s than the Serb capture of Srebrenica.[11]

iii

Cambodia was very far from my mind when I returned to Berlin to resume work on the Nuremberg documentary. One afternoon I casually asked the cameraman, a former East German named Gunther, if he knew anything about an East German documentary on the Khmer Rouge. Although my German is bad, even I understood when he said, "*Ya, Ya, 'Die Angkar.' Ich war die Kamaramann fur Heynowski und Scheumann.*" Not only did he know of the film, he had done the camera work! Three films had been made by Heynowski and Scheumann Studios, East Germany's only private documentary film company, and one was devoted entirely to S-21 prison. The next day Gunther brought me the phone number of the films' producer, Gerhard

Scheumann. I called him at his home and asked point blank if he had taken any negatives from S-21. He snapped, "I HAVE NO CELLULOID!" When I asked for an interview, Scheumann told me to have Bengt von zur Mühlen call him. During my final week in Berlin, Gerhard Scheumann agreed to be interviewed on the condition that von zur Mühlen serve as my interpreter.

It was a cold, gray Friday when I met the owner at the Chronos studios in the suburbs of Berlin. From there we drove east for about an hour, to a rural area dotted with small lakes. When we pulled into the driveway of one of the lakeside houses, an older man with an Abe Lincoln beard came out of the house and greeted Bengt von zur Mühlen warmly. We went inside and convened around a coffee table. Gerhard Scheumann had collaborated with the North Vietnamese on one of the most famous films of the Vietnam War, *Pilots in Pajamas*. It featured interviews with ten American pilots or "air pirates" shot down and captured in Vietnam. The four-hour documentary was screened in East Germany on four consecutive nights. A condensed one-hour version was translated into English, French, Russian, and Vietnamese and shown all over the world. One U.S. MIA organization recently called *Pilots in Pajamas* "one of the major propaganda coups of the war."[12] In fact, it was a sobering reminder of American powerlessness in Southeast Asia during the Vietnam conflict and beyond.

The Vietnamese, through negotiations with the East German government, invited Heynowski and Scheumann, prominent communist-bloc documentary filmmakers with a relationship with Vietnam, to be the first western camera team into Cambodia after the 1979 invasion. The East Germans were especially disturbed by the fact that the killings in Cambodia "had been carried out under the hammer and sickle." Scheumann felt strongly that this "cannot be casually passed over by those of our generation, for whom the hammer-and-sickle flag raised over the Reichstag in Berlin in the last days of the war marked a turning point in life." It was his intention "to tear that symbol away from them, so to say." Above all, he believed that the Khmer Rouge had "dragged the Communist Party in the dirt, so that it lost respect in which it was held by the people."[13]

Scheumann and his five-man crew drove in jeeps from Saigon to Phnom Penh in January 1979: "We started early in the morning and arrived in Phnom Penh in the evening. I have a specific memory of this trip. Back where we stored the camera and audio equipment, we had six or seven live chickens tied up. Every day we would butcher one of the chickens." Scheumann said Cambodia was so denuded that "nothing existed in the country, not even coconuts were hanging on the trees."[14] When they finally arrived in Phnom

Penh it was completely deserted, "a ghost town." The opening scene of his first film (*Kampuchea: Death and Rebirth*) shows a completely deserted yet strangely intact capital city. The apartments the film crew enters look as if the owners are away for a long weekend: beds left unmade and personal photos still in frames. The producer's memories are strange, still-frame snap-shots of a city coming back to life: water faucets running that had not been shut off four years before; a shoe store with all of its merchandise still in the street. "There were grotesque impressions," Scheumann recalled.

The Vietnamese army even provided the East German camera crew with captured S-21 guards to interview. I asked about their condition. "They were prisoners; if they were charged and sentenced, it goes beyond my knowl-edge." I asked if these were gunpoint interviews—were the Khmer Rouge forced to sit before his camera? Scheumann made an important point that I would soon understand through my own experience: "It is difficult to say; in such situations, you have to hide your feelings. I wanted to find things out from them, and not argue with them."

Gerhard Scheumann left the room and came back with a book of story-boards from two of his Cambodian films, *Kampuchea: Death and Rebirth* and *The Angkar*. They had still-frame images and complete transcripts of the nar-ration and interviews. "We had to deal with this question," he explained. "Over here was a mound of skulls and here above it, the symbol of the ham-mer and sickle." Like most of the participants in the struggle over Cambodian history, Scheumann clearly had a political agenda. Unlike so many of the other players, he was refreshingly straightforward. Not impressed by the Khmer Rouge's "Stone Age communism," he considered it "a totally confused theory of communism. The Khmer Rouge distinction between 'old' and 'new' people is nowhere to be read in Marx and Engels. Naturally, nothing of the sort exists." Scheumann added derisively that such ideas were "the out-growth of Sorbonne intellectuals."

Next he made an important point about the Khmer Rouge leaders educat-ed in France: "They came back from France and carried out their theories with one eye on the Chinese Cultural Revolution. They wanted to surpass the Cultural Revolution, however. It is recorded that Chou Enlai in his last years spoke with the Cambodian leaders and warned them not to go beyond the goals set by the Chinese. But they said, 'He's an old man, we'll do it even better than the Chinese.'" I asked Scheumann if he was surprised that western leftists had so adamantly denied the refugee accounts of Khmer Rouge atrocities. "They did not want to believe it partly because of the relations to China. China was something of a symbol back then. Personally, for me, it was incomprehensible, this reserve in the judgment of the conditions inside Khmer Rouge–ruled Cambodia. There were refugee accounts in the mainstream media!"

I asked if the East German government had forced Scheumann to pursue a particular political agenda in his films. He explained that initially there had been no pressure, but when his discoveries began to implicate the Chinese, things changed. "I'll divulge a secret here," Scheumann said. "Our first film, *Kampuchea: Death and Rebirth*. In the original form it begins the following way: we had a helicopter fly above Phnom Penh, we gradually zoomed in on the former Chinese embassy. The first narration text read: 'Our thinking about Kampuchea has to start here, at the former Chinese embassy in Phnom Penh.' We were talked out of it, as it was not in line with the reigning foreign policy." He shrugged and said with a laugh, "Here the foreign political interests outweighed the subjective impressions of filmmakers which we had gathered in Cambodia." When I asked if he had censored himself, he laughed again. "It is the destiny of the filmmaker to be told at home what it is he has experienced. I believe that it doesn't only go that way with the GDR, but that it goes that way elsewhere." Did this pressure increase over time? "Yes, it continued to play a role. For example, we had pictures of the Red Khmers with their weapons and the weapons had engravings of Chinese characters on them. That was sometimes problematic." Scheumann conceded, "We were half pulled down and half fell down, as it is said."

The filmmaker opened the book again and pointed to a photograph for which he had personally recovered the negative from S-21. Above all, Scheumann said, he had been struck by the professional quality of the photographs. "I found the negative on the floor of an abandoned house in which photographs were made." When he first visited the prison, most of the negatives were carefully catalogued: "They were in these bags, a professional photographer must have worked there. He had thousands of these bags that you use to preserve passport photos." I had not seen many of these images, like the one of a young woman handcuffed to another woman carrying a baby in her arms. The unfamiliar photos were definitely not among the 5,000 in the Tuol Sleng archive and were lost, probably forever.

Flipping through the pages of the storyboard book, Scheumann stopped and pointed to another Tuol Sleng photo that I had never seen. I told him that two thirds of S-21's photographic archive was still missing. "I found one negative in one of those houses, but otherwise the photos were in the care of Ung Pech," he replied. "We took some of the photos from him and back to Germany at the conclusion of the shoot. When we had the negatives and positives, we drove back to Cambodia with the completed films. We did not keep a single piece of it here in the GDR." Ung Pech was the S-21 survivor who served as the first Tuol Sleng Museum director. He had retired in the early 1990s and was now ill and had been unwilling to talk to either Niven or Riley.

When I told Gerhard Scheumann that people like journalist William Shawcross had criticized the "East German" influence on the Tuol Sleng Museum and that some Cambodians even considered the museum Vietnamese propaganda, he roared, "Fantastic! Fantastic! Absurd! Ieng Sary naturally said the same thing, that it was the Vietnamese! We filmed him in Singapore, he was then the official representative of Democratic Kampuchea in the UN." Scheumann had sent a camera crew to the Khmer Rouge camps on the Thai border in 1980. "Back then, our people were still able to enter into the front lines to where the Pol Pot people had their headquarters. They were able to go into the camps and film. They got very close to Pol Pot, and spoke to Ieng Sary and Khieu Samphan."

Scheumann chided the western nations for their hypocrisy and pointed out that even after Rwanda and Bosnia, many still refused to face the uncomfortable truth that they had failed to protect human rights because geopolitical concerns took precedence: "One has to be mindful of the following political phenomenon: as long as Pol Pot and Ieng Sary ruled in Cambodia, it was, in the eyes of the West, the worst, most wayward form of communism. When the Vietnamese came and chased the Khmer Rouge out, the Vietnamese were suddenly the aggressors. That was then the foreign policy of the western world. That is why the mass murderers were representatives in the UN." Unlike the majority of individuals debating about the Khmer Rouge, Scheumann wore his political ideology on his sleeve, and though it didn't accord with the preferences or opinions of some policy makers and scholars, his analysis of the situation in Cambodia between 1975 and 1979 was correct. Gerhard Scheumann was a refreshing leftist compared to Noam Chomsky, who for all his verbal dexterity was simply wrong and refused to admit it. The filmmaker had backed his ideological commitment with a kind of empirical inquiry that simply could not be done from a studio office or a university campus.

That night, after I returned to Berlin, I called Jörg Friedrich to tell him about my interview and to invite him to the concert of "a great American icon," Johnny Cash. When I asked Jörg if he had heard of him, he said, "No Peta, I think that tonight I should stay in my flat and put on the phonograph the record of a great German icon, his name is LUDWIG VON BEETHOVEN, HAVE YOU HEARD OF HIM?" I responded in my best Californiaese, "Ya, wasn't he, like, that dude in *Clockwork Orange*?"

The next day, over tea and plum cake, Jörg and I had a more somber farewell meeting. He handed back the draft of an article that I had written about Cambodia, the UN, and war crimes accountability. "This article is so shaded, there are no . . ." Friedrich thought for a moment. "You don't judge. In the beginning you say I am a young writer and I am acquainted with those many Nuremberg Principles and now I come to reality and nothing fits together! Then all those figures like the UN worker." Jörg began to laugh, then became serious. "Understand that this article has no answer and can never have an answer. . . . There is nothing firm to hold onto. There are the principles: 'We shall do, we must do.' But there is no one interested in what you feel or what should be. When you stop you are helpless and desperate, and now it all starts again." He pointed to a grim truth: "If you get to the essence of the problem, you come to conclusions that you can't say and that you are not prepared to say." Just as in the article, I didn't know how to respond and didn't want to admit it. Finally he sighed. "It [the question of accountability] is too black and it is too exotic. What I would really say is that Hitler won the war by making everyone into Hitlers."[15]

In just a few months, my employer, Michael Kloft, had given me a great opportunity to apply and extend my academic experience in real time and in the real world. Friedrich, who'd become a friend, had also taught me a great deal about distinguishing between the way things seemed and the way they really were. On the flight home, I read the storyboards from the East German films, which Scheumann had lent me. On the cover was a photograph of Khmer Rouge Foreign Minister Ieng Sary superimposed on a background of S-21 photographs. Pol Pot's brother-in-law would prove himself the most ruthless Khmer Rouge opportunist. Sihanouk had always despised Ieng Sary. The king said, "Do you know that after World War II the Nuremberg tribunal sentenced Hitler's closest assistants? You would never assume that Marshall Göering, Marshall Keitel, Himmler, and the others were innocent and Hitler the only guilty man. Pol Pot is guilty, but just as guilty, like Himmler, is Ieng Sary. He is the big guilty man number two after Pol Pot."[16]

iv

As Democratic Kampuchea's Foreign Minister from 1975 to 1979, Ieng Sary oversaw the country's limited contact with the outside world. His signature atrocity began as a documentary film made with the help of the Chinese and shown to Cambodian expatriates in Paris and other European cities. The film featured long shots of the idyllic Cambodian countryside and Tonle Sap Lake:

"How beautiful, our liberated home, shining in all your grace. Your beauty, beloved, conquers every heart. Oh Tonle Sap, you greatest of all lakes in the world!" Sary screened the film in Paris in August 1975 and told the audience that the evacuated residents of Phnom Penh had returned to their homes. The Khmer Rouge leader promised this group of mostly middle- and upper-class professionals and intellectuals that if they returned to Democratic Kampuchea, they could work in their areas of expertise.[17]

Approximately 1,000 Cambodians living in France, Eastern Europe, and the United States returned to Cambodia between 1975 and 1978. Most sold everything they owned and donated the proceeds to the government of Democratic Kampuchea. One group of 127 French expatriates issued this declaration on the eve of their May 26, 1976 departure: "We—students, trainees, officials, soldiers, former 'forced refugees' expatriated to the United States, Canada, and Europe in the context of the U.S. war of aggression against our country—are going to return this very week to our dear native land, Democratic Kampuchea." They said that their decision was not a result of outside pressure or ignorance, but a belief in the "political, economic, social—accomplishments that were realized in the new society of Democratic Kampuchea, notably after the total liberation of 17 April 1975." The statement flatly denied the atrocity stories that were widespread by 1976. "How can the success obtained by our people in all fields be explained if there were so many hundreds of thousands of massacres? How can it be believed that such a people, who so obstinately fought all the injustices, all the inequalities, all the tribulations, could, once in power, institute or tolerate the same evils?"[18]

Most of the intellectuals who arrived in Phnom Penh were sent to the old Khmer–Soviet Friendship Technical Institute to be "reeducated" by Khmer Rouge leader Khieu Samphan. One of the survivors, Keo Bunthouk, recalled: "We arrived at the airport and the people who knew us didn't dare to say hello. They were all dressed in black and didn't say anything." The new recruits got a sense of what was to come when young Khmer Rouge cadres told them, "Let us say clearly that we do not need you; we need people who know how to work the land, and that is all." Most of them were sent to rural communes to work. Those with suspicious confessions were sent straight to S-21 prison and killed. Of the thousand Cambodians who returned to Democratic Kampuchea from abroad after 1975, only 150 were alive in 1979.[19]

One of the S-21 interrogators recorded this account of his "questioning" of a returnee: "I questioned this bitch who came back from France; my activity was that I set fire to her ass until it became a burned-out mess and then beat her to the point that she was so turned around I couldn't get any answer out of her; the enemy then croaked, ending her answers." The French-Khmer women appear to have been singled out for acts of sexual sadism. Another interrogator wrote: "Separately, I had interrogated the woman returned from France by burning deeply into her vagina until she died without giving any answer." Another administered similar treatment: "I tortured two women who came from France until they were undressed. In the same way, I deeply burned their vaginas."[20]

When Heynowski and Scheumann interviewed Ieng Sary in 1980, he presented himself as a staunch ally of the United States. When asked about the importance of the hammer and sickle, Ieng Sary replied, "We never used this symbol. Because the hammer and sickle has no importance for us." When it came to the million or so dead Cambodians, he said coolly: "Insofar as we were lazy, the leaders bear responsibility. But the murderers were Vietnamese agents, that's as plain as day." By 1980, the public leader of the Khmer Rouge was confident that he had backing of both his Chinese patrons and their American allies: "We are firmly convinced that the Chinese government will always help us in the struggle for independence and preservation of the nation—until final victory."[21]

Even though Ieng Sary used "the weapon of the mouth" better than most, he showed a political naïveté common to all of the Khmer Rouge leaders. It might have been touching, had their regime not committed genocide: "We weren't aware of life at the grassroots; that is the way murders are able to happen. To that extent, we leaders bear responsibility." Ieng Sary was the first Khmer Rouge leader to admit that he had heard of Tuol Sleng prison. He claimed that he "thought it was a reeducation center, and after reeducation people would be sent back. But later I noticed they didn't come back. I knew people were accused there without justification." Sary also implicated Democratic Kampuchea's Deputy Prime Minister Nuon Chea: "Only two people knew for certain, because they must have been there: Nuon Chea, who was responsible in the party for security, and Son Sen, who was responsible for state security."[22]

During the late 1980s and early 1990s, Ieng Sary had fallen out of favor with the hard-liners like Pol Pot, Ta Mok, and Nuon Chea, due to what historian Stephen Heder described as "his non-proletarian political style" and his lack of military background. What had long been an academic question of historical accountability was radically transformed into an urgent issue on August 8, 1996, when Pol Pot's Khmer Rouge radio denounced Sary as "a piece of excrement" who had "unmasked himself as an enemy of the nation." Sary was accused of profiteering and Khmer Rouge radio called for his death. Very soon the debate over war crimes would become a seminar on realpolitik led by Prime Minister Hun Sen.[23]

When Pol Pot rejected diplomacy and continued to wage guerrilla warfare after UNTAC's departure in 1993, his regime's leadership underwent a shake-up. Ieng Sary and his wife Ieng Thirith, long the public faces of the Khmer Rouge operation, were falling out of favor with Pol Pot and his henchman, Ta Mok. Sary's business acumen had won him large contracts with Thai businessmen, but it had also earned him Pol Pot's distrust. This decision to continue waging war sparked a great deal of dissension among Khmer Rouge rank and file, many of whom had spent their entire lives fighting. As ineffective as UNTAC might have been at implementing the Paris Treaty, the influx of westerners and aid had provided many in the Khmer Rouge with a glimpse of a very different type of life.

Ieng Sary was rumored to be meeting with Cambodian officials in Bangkok, making some kind of deal for his Democratic National Union Movement (DNUM) Party's collaboration. While the UN-sponsored Cambodian government was managing to destroy the Khmer Rouge and ending the civil war, they were also integrating battle-hardened Khmer Rouge soldiers into the national army with little more than a handshake and a change of uniform. It was one thing for Hun Sen to pardon the cadres, but what about the leaders of a regime that had left over a million Cambodians dead? Ieng Sary still considered himself a legitimate leader and had a laundry list of demands that included an insurance policy. He would announce his conditions for cooperation with the new government in late summer 1996. First was an amnesty from the 1979 Vietnamese tribunal's death sentence. Once the Cambodian government "officially and clearly" determined his legal status, Sary and his followers would continue the negotiations. Although the soldiers in Pailin and Phnom Malai would wear the green fatigues of the Cambodian National Army, they would be under Sary and his son Ieng Vuth's *de facto* control.[24]

I not only believed that Ieng Sary was a key Khmer Rouge leader, I also considered him one of the smartest. He had obviously seen the writing on the wall and introduced his faction to the more lucrative aspects of globalism. Strip mining, clear cutting, and artifact theft had made many former Khmer Rouge rich and loyal to him. Decades of isolation in the jungle had left Pol Pot ill with malaria and deluded, unaware of the machinations of other interests in Cambodia. Nothing had changed for Pol Pot: "It is black and white. Those who implement the guidance are with us and those who do not are against us."[25]

Hun Sen exacerbated this divide by offering Khmer Rouge officers amnesty and their equivalent rank in the national army if they defected. Even Chouk Rin, the Khmer Rouge commander who had orchestrated the 1994 train attack and kidnapping of the three western backpackers, went over to the government with 147 loyal soldiers in October 1996. Tattooed with bullet holes and shrapnel divots, Rin was also missing part of a foot from a land mine explosion. The self-proclaimed "famous Khmer Rouge commander" said that he was "tired of war." Chouk Rin was made a colonel in the Cambodian army and his wife was given a day at the hairdresser in Phnom Penh.[26]

The amnesty for Ieng Sary and other Khmer Rouge defectors was extremely successful on a political level: of the 6,624 Khmer Rouge soldiers who joined with the Cambodian government, almost 3,000 received positions in the Cambodian army (among them three brigadier generals, nine colonels, and thirty lieutenant colonels).[27] The government's amnesty program was doing something that both the Vietnamese and the UN had tried and failed to accomplish—break the back of the Khmer Rouge. Would this combination of clean slate and special rewards be the explicit price of peace? One human rights official admitted that in this case there was "a contradiction between sound policy and international law."[28] Things were changing so fast in Cambodia that even reporters I knew in Phnom Penh were divided about what was really happening. People were still speculating about Pol Pot's fate: was he even alive? It seemed incredible that so many would defect if he were still in control.

Hun Sen made a surprise television appearance in August to announce the defection of two full Khmer Rouge divisions, numbers 450 and 415, to the government.[29] Now that they'd switched sides, the question arose: who would command the new recruits, Hun Sen or Prince Ranariddh? In Pailin and Phnom Malai, 10,000 ex–Khmer Rouge soldiers were now up for grabs; they had the potential to be a significant, even deciding factor in any internal conflict. "The Khmer Rouge are now like the Foreign Legion in France. Everyone wants them because they are good fighters," an Asian diplomat explained to Seth Mydans of *The New York Times*.[30]

After Pol Pot, Ieng Sary was the most important test case for the Cambodian government because he had been tried *in absentia* and sentenced to death in 1979. King Sihanouk declared adamantly that amnesty for such Khmer Rouge leaders was unacceptable and described Sary as a "pirate thirsting for riches."[31] By now, Prince Ranariddh and Hun Sen were trying to broker separate amnesty deals. Hun Sen had the inside track and made the first move on August 15, 1996, when he pledged to protect the Khmer Rouge leader.[32]

Borrowing from Sun Tzu, Hun Sen argued, "Whatever we do, we must not push them in a corner." To him, the collapse of the Khmer Rouge and the end of the civil war justified ignoring the immediate demands of justice: "If we do not allow him to come, he has no choice. What can he do? He has to lead his forces to fight to the end."[33] Ultimately, Hun Sen was a bloody-nosed realist—to him there was no separation between politics and war. The fragile coalition government created by the UN was beginning to buckle under the strain of the Khmer Rouge breakup.

Ieng Sary called the charges against him "unreasonable slander" in a fax to the press on August 15, after Hun Sen's pledge of protection: "Slandering, telling lies, are the methods that . . . Pol Pot has been using for a long time during the period of historical struggle." Sary also made an interesting, preemptive accusation, charging Pol Pot with the killings of the Cambodians he had recruited from France: "Pol Pot decided to destroy intellectuals from abroad—those whose goodwill is to join the reconstruction of the nation—accusing them of being CIA agents, or KGB agents of countries from which they gained knowledge." Sary claimed that his Democratic National Union Movement had broken away "from the fascism and cruelty of Pol Pot's regime."[34]

Ieng Sary's first press conference after his defection took place in a safe house near Phnom Malai on August 28, 1996. Flanked by the commanders of the Pailin and Phnom Malai regions, the former Khmer Rouge leader said that he had decided to break away from "the dictatorial group of Pol Pot, Ta Mok, and Son Sen" to end the decades of war. He and his followers hoped to "realize national reconciliation under a democratic regime." When it came to the key question of amnesty, Ieng Sary stated confidently, "I have [made] no mistakes for them to excuse me."[35] Finally, one reporter asked the question everyone had been stepping around: "You were said to be Mr. Pol Pot's right-hand man during the Pol Pot regime, where so many people died from massacres or starvation or something like that. Do you take that kind of responsibility?" "I am not the right hand of Pol Pot," Sary fired back. It was obvious that he had rehearsed his defense.

Once again, Ieng Sary brought up the Cambodians he had lured back from France. He admitted that he was "very regretful for the intellectuals because I was the one who gathered them to come to help build the country," but still proclaimed his innocence. "Why did I not talk about this since the beginning?" Ieng Sary offered rhetorically, then answered his own question: "Because it was the reason of solidarity in the period of struggle. Now they've accused me of being a traitor and I must make everything clear."[36]

Ieng Sary finished the interview by claiming he was a supporter of limited democracy, like that practiced in Singapore, Thailand, and Japan. His new-found contrition seemed too good to be true, yet another tactical move. If he had proven one thing over the course of his thirty-year political career, it was that he was an opportunist. His 1979–1980 transformation from Maoist revolutionary to Reaganite Cold Warrior had been one of the most rapid and dramatic political about-faces of the twentieth century. Phnom Penh journalist Hurley Skroggins renamed Ieng Sary's DNUM the "I was only giving the orders" Party.[37]

Ieng Sary's public relations effort shifted into high gear when he opened the Khmer Rouge stronghold of Phnom Malai to journalists on September 9. Before the press conference, Sary distributed a ten-page, typed document entitled, "True Facts About Pol Pot's Dictatorial Regime, 1975–1978." The report proclaimed its objective was to "help people know who the true murderers are in order to get them tried and punished accordingly." It blamed the Khmer Rouge atrocities on Pol Pot and his "secret security committee" run by Nuon Chea, Son Sen and his wife Yun Yat, and Ta Mok—these were the real "mass murderers of Cambodia." According to Sary, Pol Pot "made all decisions according to his own will and did not worry at all about universally upheld principles, law or rules."

Again, Ieng Sary's naïveté would have been touching had his intentions not been so obviously self-interested. Sary continued to maintain that he was completely innocent because he played no direct role in any killings: "I have no remorse because I never killed anyone, nor did I ever make a decision or suggestion to Angkar to do so—never at all. Neither did I suggest the arrest for execution." After the press conference, Khmer Rouge radio broke from their standard playlist of Vietnamese conspiracy theories to refute this statement, announcing that the former foreign minister alone had lured the Cambodians back from France: "We want to assure that Ieng Sary was responsible for the [intellectuals]."[38]

Human rights organizations were outraged by the soft treatment Ieng Sary was receiving from the Cambodian government. Amnesty International wrote an open plea to King Sihanouk urging him to prevent Ieng Sary's amnesty: "It is important that all those engaged in the quest for national reconciliation in the interest of Cambodia's future don't lose sight of the need to uncover the truth about Cambodia's past." The human rights group warned of the long-term effects: "Amnesties which have the effect of preventing the emergence of the truth and subsequent accountability before the law should not be acceptable." Under extreme pressure from Hun Sen and Prince Ranariddh, Sihanouk issued Ieng Sary a tersely worded amnesty that nullified the 1979 death sentence. Further confusing matters, the day the king granted the amnesty, he pledged to support the judgment of any future court that might try Ieng Sary or any other Khmer Rouge leaders. Prince Ranariddh told a reporter from the *Phnom Penh Post* that this amnesty would not stand in the way of future prosecution.[39]

"Probably there is a different sense of justice between West and East," one ASEAN diplomat explained to Seth Mydans of *The New York Times*. The diplomat considered the amnesty "a reward for bringing peace and reconciliation. One has to know the magnitude of this break-away movement. This is practically the beginning of the collapse of the Khmer Rouge."[40] Although it seemed like a hefty price to many western human rights activists, the decision to divide and conquer the Khmer Rouge this way would end a thirty-year civil war. Moreover, peace was the basic precondition for any postwar reconstruction, and neither the UN nor the West had delivered it despite their vast outlay of money, energy, and resources. Western diplomats in Phnom Penh commented off the record that they were disappointed by the news of Ieng Sary's pardon, but the U.S. ambassador abdicated any responsibility, describing the decision as a "Cambodian affair."[41]

The defections continued throughout September 1996. A unit of twenty crack Khmer Rouge soldiers sent from Anlong Veng to assassinate the defectors decided to defect instead.[42] Hun Sen's divide-and-conquer strategy was decimating the Khmer Rouge as a military force, but accountability was an altogether different matter. The prime minister, himself former Khmer Rouge, was candid when he answered reporters' questions about Ieng Sary's pardon on September 27.[43] He made his primary goal very clear: "You can then ask why I should provide a pardon? My answer would be the same—it's for peace." Hun Sen admitted that Sary's repeated claims of innocence were absurd: "I don't believe him because it took a long period of time [for him to defect]. They have been together since the '6os until the late '9os; if there was a real split, it would have been long before this."[44]

When a western reporter asked Hun Sen to respond to those who would criticize him for making a deal at the expense of justice, he pointed with justifiable bitterness to the West: "They did not recognize the 1979 verdict. After he was sentenced in Phnom Penh, he went to New York to deliver speeches. What does that mean? He delivered a speech at the [UN] General Assembly in 1979, '80, '81—three years. Why did Interpol or the New York police not arrest him and send him back to us?" Remaining vague about the terms of the pardon, he said it "does not mean that we put an end to the trial for the crime of genocide in Cambodia."[45] Hun Sen's candor was refreshing, in a way; he admitted plainly that Ieng Sary's fate was a political question, a perfect example of the West's two-faced relationship with international law: "What is the reality then? It has to be changed according to the political situation.... When there is political demand for support of Ieng Sary, they say Ieng Sary did not commit any crime. Then they say the other way, in different circumstances."[46]

Ieng Sary's protestations of innocence were attacked by his former employee Laurence Picq, ex-wife of his aide, Suong Sikeoun. Picq, one of the few westerners to live in Cambodia during the Khmer Rouge years, joined her husband after the regime took power in 1975 and worked in Ieng Sary's Ministry of Foreign Affairs. This first-hand witness claimed that Ieng Sary was an expert manipulator who had been carefully rewriting his personal history since 1979. Picq called the ministry an "ante-chamber of death, this fiefdom of Ieng Sary."[47] She ridiculed his newfound contrition: "Ieng Sary was one of those responsible for the Khmer Rouge genocide. And that is not all. He was a master liar, able to distort both the facts and common sense values." Picq brought up a very obvious and uncomfortable question: "For him we prepare the red carpet and forget all the abominable crimes. All shame is gone. Some say in the name of peace. What kind of peace for Cambodia? A Khmer Rouge peace? A peace in the blood of genocide? A peace in a lie? A peace in shame?"[48]

Prince Ranariddh traveled to Pailin on October 11 in a last-ditch attempt to woo Ieng Sary and his followers into his royalist party. When asked whether he felt the amnesty issued by King Sihanouk would protect him, Sary replied confidently, "I have no worries about any future prosecution, both nationally and internationally. But if domestically they want to prosecute me, they will have to abolish the monarchy first because the king was the one who granted me amnesty. And the court's verdict in 1979, I'm asking you, was the [Vietnamese] court's verdict at that time recognized by the international community or not?"[49]

6

"I AM EXCELLENT SURVIVOR."

i

All of the clamor over Ieng Sary's amnesty overshadowed the defection of many of the men who had carried out his orders. One who emerged from the nameless, faceless ranks was an elite Khmer Rouge propaganda officer named Nhem En. In the predawn hours of November 15, 1995, En had slipped into the jungle armed with an AK-47, a walkie-talkie, and a videotape of the terrain surrounding the last Khmer Rouge stronghold of Anlong Veng. He claimed to have been one of the leaders of a secret, pro-democracy movement. When Ta Mok heard of this, he sent a team of twenty men after En with orders to kill.[1]

Nhem En had decided to break from the favored ranks of a movement that he had served with distinction for more than twenty-seven years. He had taken the Khmer Rouge mantra, "You are only responsible for the hair on your head," to heart and left his wife and five children behind.[2] He crisscrossed Cambodia on a decrepit motorcycle for the next few months, visiting family he had not seen in decades and trying to rally opposition against Pol Pot and the Khmer Rouge hardliners in Anlong Veng. Finally En showed up at the Associated Press office in Phnom Penh, looking for work as a photographer. When he cited as experience the fact that he had been a photographer for the Khmer Rouge, reporter Robin McDowell put two and two together and realized that he must be the Tuol Sleng photographer.[3]

Doug Niven and David Chandler did the first in-depth interviews with En in early 1997, and the results convinced me that McDowell was right.[4] Niven invited me to conduct a longer, oral history–type interview if I could get to Cambodia in nine days. En had returned to Anlong Veng and was rumored to be working against Pol Pot and Ta Mok. It would be difficult; I had just finished the semester teaching at both of my alma maters. They had extended an academic version of welfare to me after my Nuremberg book manuscript had been twice reviewed by major publishers and twice rejected. By 1997, war crimes was a booming field. I was often struck by the evangelical tone and the many false assumptions of recent initiates. However, my views on international law and conflict were too dark, too pessimistic; American popular opinion saw the glass half full, while I saw the glass half empty.

I had not been back to Cambodia since 1994 and was eager to see how it had changed in three years. My flight to Bangkok arrived at 11 p.m.; I met Niven, who was living there at the time, sometime after midnight in a Patpong bar that reeked of beer, puke, sweat, smoke, and cheap perfume. He explained our mission: "You don't know how lucky we are. Sok Sin saw our man Nhem En; he is back in Phnom Penh, and we should be able to start interviewing him Monday or Tuesday." I was apprehensive—it sounded too easy. Niven continued, "We are also going to see Van Nath. He is another S-21 survivor. I plan to show him Nhem En's photo and see if he remembers En." The next morning I boarded my flight to Phnom Penh; Niven would join me a day later. Compared to the half-filled plane of aid workers and journalists that I had taken three years previously, this flight was packed. The khaki-clad NGO types had been replaced with honest-to-God tourists.

When I disembarked at Phnom Penh's Pochentong Airport, it was immediately clear that over the last three years, there had been some major upgrades. There was now a large air-conditioned customs and reception hall with an orderly visa processing center to handle the tourists. I cleared customs and the pneumatic doors opened, releasing me into what, last time around, had been a seething, brawling mass of soldiers, cab drivers, and beggars. By comparison, it now seemed much more sedate. A dozen guys shouting in unison formed a strange chorus: "You take my car okay? My car okay?"

I stopped in the crowd of taxi drivers, dropped my duffel bag, and shouted, "Sok Sin! Sok Sin!" When I yelled "Sok Sin" a third time, the cabbies looked at one another dejectedly, mumbled, "Sok Sin," and magically parted. I had never met Sok Sin, so I did not know what he looked like. Then, from the end of the human column, a slightly built Chinese-Khmer man with two sparkling gold incisors began talking at me: "Nhem En is not at the guesthouse, maybe go out of town." Though it was our first face-to-face meeting, he did not introduce himself and wasted no time with small talk. "I see Nhem En's motorbike at guesthouse where he stay. I see him, Friday, but he no call, maybe go out of city."

This was my "fixer," the dirty little secret of Cambodian journalism: the key middleman between foreign journalists and their sources. Sok Sin was one of the best in this, and many other businesses. That nonintroduction was the start of a partnership that brought many contacts, interviews, and unexpected adventures.[5]

When Sok Sin was drafted into the Lon Nol army in 1974, his mother sold her jewelry and bought his freedom. She took him home and apologized before chaining him to the bedpost. "Son, I like you very much," she said, "but right now I buy a chain with a lock." Sok Sin said that "she spent all of her money to bribe … me out of the camp, and so I make her happy and let her lock my foot."[6] When the Khmer Rouge came to power the following year, they sent Sok Sin to Kompong Chom, where he worked on a giant rice farm. He claimed that he worked harder than anyone else and sang "revolutionary songs all day like a crazy man! It just say about feudalism, capitalism, about the poor people who own the property—we work for our own selves—like that." Accused of "betraying Angkar" and put on the Khmer Rouge blacklist many times, Sok Sin managed to buy his life back with bribes of liquor, jewelry, and even women. When anyone asked how he had outlasted the regime, he would reply proudly, "I am excellent survivor."[7] Shortly after the Khmer Rouge collapse in 1979, Sok Sin was captured by the Vietnamese and imprisoned for twenty-three days before returning to Phnom Penh. For the next three years, Sok Sin struggled to feed his wife and young son. His big break came in 1983 when he was able to lease land, grow a crop of mushrooms, and use the proceeds from selling it to buy a pedicab, or *cyclo*—a leg-powered, three-wheeled taxi.[8]

One western photographer remembered that in 1985, Sok Sin was clearly the most enterprising cyclo driver in Phnom Penh: "He slept in his cyclo, but he had business cards."[9] A succession of vehicles followed the pedicab, each bigger and better than the last: a motorbike, the white Toyota sedan that became his trademark, and later a beat-up Isuzu Trooper. Because he spoke several Chinese dialects, pidgin English, French, Khmer, and Vietnamese, Sok Sin was a natural to work as a press fixer. His blunt English, partial interpretations, and refusal to translate my more pointed questions made him more of a collaborator. While he regularly frustrated me with his mistranslations and retranslations, without him, there would have been no interviews. Sok Sin's greatest skill was his ability to locate people and win their trust in a very brief time.[10] This was a precious gift in a country where trust was in short supply.

I was fortunate to meet one of Cambodia's leading journalists, Moeun Chhean Nariddh, in 1996. A teacher at the Cambodian Communication Institute, he became my trusted translator of hours of audiotaped interviews. When I told him that Sok Sin had been my interpreter for most of them, Nariddh rolled his eyes. When the transcripts were finished, I understood why. They showed me another side of Sok Sin: cajoling, coaching, leading, threatening—in short, breaking every rule in the journalists' rule book. Subjective, unprofessional, but not uncommon behavior. Sok Sin's interpretations often yielded more than direct translations of my staid academic inquiries would have—though I often cringed when reading them in the transcripts. Nariddh told me many times, "Sok Sin is not asking your questions."[11]

Sok Sin's ambition knew no limits. In addition to his work as a fixer, he was building an apartment house near the French embassy. We drove around Phnom Penh that first afternoon and talked about a variety of subjects. Because he had worked with the majority of journalists and scholars who focused on Cambodia, he knew all about them. His accounts gave the expression "brutally honest" new meaning. Sok Sin broke down the journalists into different categories: he viewed the "high-profile" types as blow-dried sheep sent by the Buddha to pay for the construction of his guesthouse. Sok Sin would serve them all the same stale subjects for interviews. Some journalists were mocked for physical weakness: "Soft like woman." Others were ridiculed for their lack of discipline: "Ohhh! This guy drink all night sleep all day!" and still others condemned for their lack of professionalism: "This guy, he take no notes, no tapes, and he quote Sok Sin!" His ultimate and irredeemable condemnation, strangely reminiscent of Khmer Rouge rhetoric, was: "He is very lazy." Fortunately, Sok Sin considered me a "researcher," a different, low-rent breed, and for whatever reason, he enjoyed this grim hunt as much as I did.

Sok Sin was leading four lives at once, making up for lost time. He believed that he had been robbed of his youth. "When I was twenty, Khmer Rouge bombed all over Phnom Penh. Cannot go to learn, cannot go anywhere, just sit in the shelter. Khmer Rouge come at twenty-four, after Khmer Rouge twenty-seven already, twenty-eight! At that time everybody was starving and so we had to solve [that] very big problem. After the big problem I was more than thirty!" He admitted that even so much later, when he saw a young couple in love, he was saddened: "It makes me, oh! Very bad! Bad idea—very bad

Sok Sin, 2001
Nic Dunlop

remorse, remorse!" In Sok Sinese, that meant that the memories it evoked were too painful to bear: "So why I tell you I am not happy with my life, never be happy." While he had been lucky in business, Sok Sin had been unlucky in love. He had many children, but he also had many ex-wives.[12]

The day after my arrival, we headed to lunch at the Foreign Correspondents Club. Doug Niven, Sok Sin, and I were discussing our interview strategy on the second-floor balcony overlooking the river, a perfect perch from which to observe the goings-on in the riverbank park across the street. When a woman wearing a large straw hat exchanged loud insults with a lady in a green polyester shirt, I grew tense. Public displays of anger were often followed by horrific acts of violence in Cambodia. Shootings, "choppings," grenade and acid attacks were all regularly used by civilians to settle scores. A recent story about a man at a noodle stand was all too common. He complained that his noodles were cold and the proprietor shot him in the head. Each week the *Phnom Penh Post*'s police blotter ran down a litany of gruesome and violent crimes committed by Cambodians against Cambodians. This type of explosive, homicidal brutality was increasingly common, and most were numb to it.

Suddenly there was noise and commotion on the street. The woman in the hat had reached into the cart pushed by the woman in the green shirt and taken out a small hatchet. Once she walked back to the safety of her own cart, she started shouting insults and waving the hatchet in a threatening manner. Then, in classic Cambodian style, the lady in green snapped and began to rifle through her cart. I was sickly curious; what would she bring to the fight? I expected a knife, but instead she produced a softball-sized block of concrete, which she quickly and expertly wrapped in her scarf and began swinging over her head, like David taking aim at Goliath. Niven and the reporter sitting next to me on the balcony continued to talk and had not noticed the action. Finally, too distracted to keep up my end of the conversation, I turned to him and pointed down. "Looks like we might witness a homicide. Watch Greeny—she's got a piece of concrete in her *krama* and is closing the distance on the lady with the hatchet." At ten yards, the Hat Lady lost her stomach for the fight and tried to bolt. It was too late, though: Greeny chased her around her cart until they finally squared off directly beneath us. Niven sighed and pushed his chair back from the balustrade. "I've seen this too many times, I'm not watching another." Like the morbid child in the famous Weegee photograph, I leaned over the rail. Greeny tried to swing her sling, but the Hat Lady was very defensive. She grabbed both of her attacker's wrists and the pair twirled in an awkward *pas de deux*. Hat Lady knew all too well that Greeny would kill her if she got the chance. Finally, the motorbike taxi drivers by the FCC entrance separated the pair; violence was bad for business. The Hat Lady hastily pushed her cart away, dropping a trail of plastic bottles and other scavenged valuables as she went, not daring to stop and retrieve them.

Later that afternoon, Sok Sin told us that he thought Nhem En was out of town because it had been two days since his motorbike had moved from his guesthouse. So we decided to go ahead and visit our other prospect, Van Nath, another S-21 survivor, who had been kept alive because he, too, could paint portraits of Pol Pot. Unlike Im Chan, Van Nath, though pained by bad memories, felt an obligation to serve as living testimony. The next day, Sok Sin drove us to his home. We walked through a restaurant to an apartment tucked behind steel gates. Peeking through a crack in the gates, I saw Van Nath sitting cross-legged about two feet away from a television set, zapping aliens in a video game of some sort. Where the Carver had a tense, drawn disposition, Nath was very open. He turned off the game, greeted us warmly, and gestured for us to sit down while he fixed a pot of tea.

Niven pulled out a photo of Nhem En; it was a close-up of En holding his S-21 identity card. Van Nath looked at it and broke into a broad, spontaneous grin. "Oh yeah! That was taken when he was young." Nath said that he had arrived at the prison blindfolded and shackled to another prisoner. When the blindfold was removed, he was staring into the lens of En's camera. "He was the one who took my photo!" Nath said excitedly. I was dumbfounded. Van Nath was growing positively upbeat, recounting memories of the Tuol Sleng photographer. He did not hand back the photo, but continued to hold it and look at it. Nath said that En had visited his prison painting studio. "Once he came to my room with a full glass of ice in his hand. He drank some, then he left it in my room without saying anything. As you might already understand, at that time there was no ice in the prison, and I just got the feeling that it was a present from En when he left a glass of ice in my room." Nath drank the ice water gratefully. "He was a fine young man, very gentle, not cruel like the others."

During one of these visits, En told Nath that he must fit into the system if he was to survive. "'You have to lower yourself more than everyone else. You have to be gentle, respectful.' He also told me to call everyone who worked in the prison 'Big Brother.' It didn't matter if he or she was older or younger than me."[13] Van Nath really came to know En when he was ordered to teach him to paint. Although Nath was careful not to talk about "anything outside of painting," he said that he noticed "En was a very smart guy and treated me as an equal. I knew he felt sorry for me."

NHEM EN AND HIS TUOL SLENG ID PHOTO
DOUG NIVEN

According to Nath, En was a highly trusted and important cog in the S-21 machinery because he was "an expert or professional photographer, and his business was separate from the others." En had both technical ability and a certain meticulousness that contributed greatly to his success: "When he got the assignment, [if] he was ordered to make ten photos a day he made ten, if he was ordered to make twenty he made twenty. I think because he didn't have any bad marks, he was able to move around the city freely." Van Nath talked about the elite Patriotic Youth group that Nhem En belonged to and described how the Khmer Rouge nurtured their young elite: "They put all those children who were classified as Patriotic Youth in one separate center. Because their background record didn't have any bad marks, it meant they were from the poor family, farmers, peasants, not from the rich, capitalists. They were evaluated on their job performance." Nath continued, "If they were not lazy they would have been selected." The word that kept coming up, in regard to both Nhem En and the Khmer Rouge, was "lazy." To Van Nath, En was an obvious choice for a responsible position because he was "a hard worker, very motivated."

When I asked Nath if all of S-21's "seven survivors" were authentic, he rolled his eyes, took a puff of his cigarette, exhaled through his nose, and shook his head. "I want to tell you a story: I really want to see this French guy. He had the same idea as you [that some survivors might have been pretenders]. That Frenchman thought I might be a Vietnamese spy that was sent into Tuol Sleng and to break up Pol Pot's activities." Thus Nath dismissed the charge, and I was embarrassed to have asked the question. I did not know then that a French researcher had recently accused Van Nath of being a Vietnamese spy. "But whatever he thinks is wrong. He just accused me; I think he now may work for the French embassy, I'm not sure. This guy said I was a Vietnamese puppet, that the Vietnamese sent me to tell about the bad things about Pol Pot during the communist regime." Van Nath was getting riled up. "I responded to him by saying this: 'I don't ask you to trust me, to believe me, but this is my story. Whoever comes to ask my story I have to tell them.'"

Van Nath had been contacted by a French documentary crew and asked to appear in a film on S-21 prison. What they did not tell him was that the former S-21 head guard, one of the reputed killers, Him Huy, had also been brought to the Tuol Sleng Museum to appear in the film. "When I got out of my car at Tuol Sleng I didn't recognize Huy until the people who worked there told me it was him. I was standing next to him." Nath noticed my surprise as Sok Sin translated the story and perked up: "Yeah, that's right! At that time I

was really scared to even look at his face. When he claimed he was not a killer!" Nath drew from his cigarette again, exhaled, and shook his head. "This is not true. He had his own group at Choeung Ek, under his command!" he said, referring to the killing fields near the prison. When Vann Nath realized who he was standing next to, he felt faint: "I couldn't stand up anymore. My energy was gone, I felt empty. While I was sitting down, I was thinking, how should I talk to him?" Van Nath paused. It was clear that Huy had tested the limits of his forgiveness. "It took me a little while for my soul to come back; then I got up and walked around. When I walked close to him I noticed his body was not the same as before. Now he looks like a very poor farmer, very skinny. Now when I saw him this time I felt sorry for him. I couldn't raise my hand to kill him right now. This is what he received from his previous acts, bad karma," he said. However, karma alone was not sufficient: "For what he has done, he should be punished. If the government or the court decides on his case because he used to be a killer and must be executed, I'm not against that."

Van Nath did not believe that Khmer Rouge leaders like Ieng Sary deserved amnesty: "I didn't agree with it, but what can I say, I'm just a regular civilian. I don't like them at all. In that system there are only three who ran the system: Pol Pot, Khieu Samphan, and Ieng Sary. Those three killed Cambodians." Although Nath conceded that this was "government business," he added, "personally, I would give him nothing at all." I asked if the amnesty had come as a surprise. "Yeah, it was unbelievable, when I heard Ieng Sary was pardoned. This is the government's business."

I asked broader questions about what Van Nath thought of the western-led effort to uplift, civilize, and in some cases Christianize Cambodia. He conceded that when UNTAC came, the Cambodian standard of living improved. However, the key political questions were left unresolved: "I'll tell you this: before UNTAC there were no shootings, kidnappings, or robbery on the street. Now there is a lot of conflict and tension and everything's a big mess." He did not fault the UN for a lack of effort; rather, he believed that "the result we have now is not equal to what they paid for." Above all, Nath wondered why the United States was unwilling to help Cambodians punish the Khmer Rouge leaders, yet continued to pursue war criminals in other countries. "According to the news I've read recently, the Americans have captured criminals in Somalia and Serbia, so what about Cambodia? I really don't understand why Pol Pot is untouchable. He's still alive right now."

I asked Van Nath if he remembered seeing the American prisoners at S-21. He did and described them: "Long noses, brown hair. I saw them from a few meters away when they were being escorted by my painting room. I remember the first day they were brought to the prison; they had no clothes on, only underwear. They were blindfolded. There were two of them. They were both handcuffed separately. Both had beards." Van Nath got up and left the room. He returned with a surprise: a picture of two Americans, probably taken in Hawaii in the late 1970s. The man on the left, hiding behind large shades, bushy hair, and a moustache, was wearing a T-shirt and OP brand corduroy shorts. "His relative told me this photograph was taken before he left for Cambodia." Van Nath sat down and said, "This is Scott. One of his relatives came to meet me and left this photograph in 1990. I didn't recognize him by looking at this photo, but his relative told me that he was the guy at the prison." It was Californian Michael Scott Deeds, who'd been captured in a small sailboat off the Cambodian coast in 1978. After torture and interrogation, he claimed to be taking pictures for the CIA. "I think he's 100 percent dead by now," Nath said. "I can't remember exactly how long they were held in the prison, but I think maybe three or four months."

We thanked Van Nath and left his apartment in a collective state of shock. Not only had he known En, but he had liked him and considered him an ally!

Once again, Cambodia and its people were confusing me. As we were walking toward the car, Van Nath yelled something to Sok Sin. "He say, if we find Nhem En, come and get him, he would like to see him."

Sok Sin had noted my fascination with Him Huy, the S-21 executioner. "I can get him. Very poor, live in house like chicken coop," the fixer said, studying my eyes in the rearview mirror.

ii

The next day I happened to be in the hotel lobby when Sok Sin called. "I am with Nhem En, I think it would be very good for first interview this afternoon at your hotel. Get Doug, tell him five o'clock." It was already past 4:45. A few minutes later, Sok Sin and Nhem En came into my room. En was very short and sturdy with very dark skin. He had perfect posture, the carriage of a former athlete. Only 5'4", he spoke in forceful but high-pitched Khmer. He had been born in Kampong Leng, Kampong Chhnang province, in 1961 to poor, uneducated farmers. En was first exposed to the political ideology of the Khmer Rouge after the Lon Nol coup in 1970. The National Front promised to liberate the farmers and the poor from the capitalists and landowners. "I liked these ideas," En recalled. "Not only myself, but all the farmers in the country felt like myself." The old National Front slogans rolled easily off his tongue: "Long live the National Front! We have to fight against the American imperialists, the capitalists, and the Lon Nol regime!" When En's three older brothers joined the Khmer Rouge, he followed them.[14]

En's primary training at this point was not in politics or war, it was in propaganda. The ten-year-old became one of the Khmer Rouge's three "beloved leading children" who were part of the Patriotic Youth group. This group of one hundred boys and girls danced and sang at victory celebrations in the "liberated" zones and also entertained visiting delegations of leaders. En acted in propaganda skits geared to draw recruits to the Khmer Rouge. "These plays were also used for teaching the Cambodians to understand that these were the real Cambodian plays, which were not like western plays with their hugging and dancing—these were the real, conservative Cambodian plays."

Nhem En also served as a rearguard soldier for the National Front and was issued his first gun at age twelve. I asked him what the Khmer Rouge strategy was in those days. He replied that they used as little ammunition as possible: "One for one: one bullet for one target." En reflected on the defeat of the American-backed Lon Nol army with visible pride: "I understood the Lon

Nol army were backed by the Americans, and they had more weapons and ammunition, fighter airplanes, B-52s, F-111. They bombed us, they shot at us, but they could not hit us! We were not in danger! We were the guerrilla fighters, we were invisible! We were mobile! Nobody knew where we were! They didn't know our strategy! And we were the real resistance! All of these facts made us win the war." En stopped and beamed a confident smile before reciting more revolutionary slogans: "We beat the Americans because our fighting unit was secretive, confidential, flexible, skillful, cautious, and had solidarity. These were our military strategies. If we had all of these, we would succeed. We didn't copy anyone else's fighting strategy; we learned and practiced by ourselves."

At an age when I thought only of surfing and Little League Baseball, Nhem En was carrying weapons and food to front-line soldiers in pitched battles against the Lon Nol army and their American air wing. "I had a lot of memories during the fight with Americans." En paused and shook his head. "Everyone knew about the B-52 bombings, but this was all in the past. Now, even I have almost forgotten about it, and only your questions brought back the memories. I almost forgot about it, but since you asked this question now I feel like my shadow is chasing me." He was not impressed by the U.S. campaign: "The American bombing was unsuccessful. They bombed only already evacuated and empty villages, the trees, the jungle, sometimes the rice fields. There were not many casualties, I might say only one in a thousand were hurt."

By the age of fourteen, En had served with distinction and been made the chief of a battle group. He and his men heard over the radio that Phnom Penh had fallen on April 17, 1975. "Our country is small, our population is also small, but we can still beat the Americans, the superpower. This is why we were so proud of ourselves." As En and his comrades approached Phnom Penh, they saw the residents of the capital crowding along Route 5, the main artery leading out of the city. "They looked different from us," he recalled. "We always wore black uniforms, and they wore many different colors."

En claimed that he did not hate the "New People," he simply obeyed Pol Pot's orders to divide "the classes between people." Even though he was only a teenager, En was one of the "Old People," thanks to both his "clean" peasant background and his years of revolutionary service. After he arrived in Phnom Penh, he was sent to study at a technical school. En was again promoted to another elite children's unit and noticed that their progress was being closely monitored: "They started to choose the children from that group by looking at who was a hard worker, who was careful on the job, and they kept the lazy children separate from us." Angkar selected Nhem En to be one of a very select few sent to China for advanced training in 1976. After the students arrived in Shanghai, they were divided: some were selected to train in naval affairs, others in military strategy. En would study photography.

Six months later, Nhem En was sent back to Phnom Penh. He was assigned to Unit 870 of the Ministry of National Defense under Pol Pot and posted at S-21 prison to photograph inmates. I asked for his first impression of the place. "What made me really scared was when I saw the trucks loaded with people and they pushed the people off the trucks, and they hit the ground. I was still young and this scared me. Those people were blindfolded and their hands tied up." According to En, it didn't take long for the horror to become routine: "When I was first at Tuol Sleng I was scared, but after seeing the same thing every day, I got used to it. It became normal, like feeling numb."

At S-21 En had a small studio where he worked with several other photographers: "My assistants were Ry, Sam, Nith, Song, and Srieng. We set up the numbers every 24 hours. For example, if we had ten prisoners today we would start from one to ten, and tomorrow if we had 1,500 prisoners we would start with one and go up to 1,500. The period was from 7 a.m. until midnight." Nhem En received his orders directly from Khmer Rouge Interior Minister Son Sen and prison commandant Brother Duch. "These two guys were giving me assignments on a daily basis. I met with them nearby at the Planning Ministry, near the Hungarian embassy." En was told to remain "clean-minded" because he was one of the "representatives of the Angkar." I asked if Son Sen or anyone else ever told him why he was taking photographs of the inmates. "He [Son Sen] told me to keep track of the photos, because they might want to use them for conducting investigations on issues about the CIA spies, KGB, Vietnamese." Nhem En insisted that he never laid a hand on a prisoner. "My only job was to photograph them, and it was someone else who tortured and killed those people. As a photographer I had no right to beat, torture, or kill the prisoners. I could not touch them."

I asked En what happened if he made a mistake. He said it was rare and only happened a handful of times. Once when he developed some photographs of Khmer Rouge and Chinese leaders, the negatives were spotted beyond recognition. En feared for his life when he was sent to the work camp at Pray Sar and ordered to pick water spinach. He stayed there for a month and a half, but when the rest of the film came back with spotted negatives, proving that the flaws weren't his fault, he was returned to his old job at S-21. I asked if he had seen the top Khmer Rouge leaders inside the prison. "I met them all, but outside Tuol Sleng, in conferences or meetings. Sometimes they had meetings nearby the Independence Monument." "Did any of the top brass go *inside* Tuol Sleng?" I asked again. En paused for a moment. "Only Son Sen came to visit." Nhem En claimed that all of the photos and documents were reviewed by the Khmer Rouge leaders. "All the documents made at S-21 were sent to Ta Duch, who gave them to Son Sen, who gave them to Nuon Chea and to Pol Pot. I knew this because sometimes when Ta Duch was very busy, I had to take the documents to them myself. No one else knew about where they were being sent besides Ta Duch and myself."

I asked En if he had any idea why he had been singled out and chosen for leadership positions over and over during the Khmer Rouge years. To him, the answer was obvious: "I'm proud because I was chosen a leader. I have been a hard worker, honest, capable, and garner respect, this is why they chose me." Then, most unexpectedly, this twenty-seven-year Khmer Rouge veteran began to extol the virtues of the free market and democracy: "To make people love you, you must first promote democracy, freedoms, take good care of the farmers, let the farmers work by themselves without any pressure or interference from the government officials. If a leader can do all of these then he can be a good leader." I was astonished and asked En where he had learned about democracy. He explained that he had kept a portable radio at low volume in his room. "I listened to American and Chinese radio and began to learn about democracy." No one was allowed to listen to those broadcasts. "If people didn't obey this rule, they would be killed."

Nhem En said that in the last Khmer Rouge stronghold, Anlong Veng, "there are still some leaders who want to promote democracy. But they can't make it happen. I myself could talk about democracy in Anlong Veng, because people liked me and all of my colleagues." Wasn't it dangerous to preach democracy under the nose of Ta Mok? I wondered aloud. Realizing that the people in Anlong Veng wanted greater freedoms like the Khmer Rouge cadres under Ieng Sary in Pailin and Phnom Malai, Nhem En started his secret, pro-democracy group. "I knew they liked what I said. I didn't worry, because at that time I established a small party to work against Pol Pot and Ta Mok. This party was called *Eysey Sar* [the mythical name of Brahmins searching for Nirvana]. I was the president of this party."

En said that he lost faith in the Khmer Rouge after witnessing so much violence inside S-21. "From my point of view, only five percent of the population were guilty, and 95 percent were innocent. I knew what they were doing in Tuol Sleng was a big mistake. And I knew this from the start, after I was there only one or two days." By 1978, he said, he had begun to feel "shocked and desperate" because of the "dictatorial, cruel, summary justice. . . . A big or small mistake was enough to be arrested. Even if they had not betrayed the country, they were still accused and arrested. Nothing was done in a democratic way." Looking at entire families facing death, he was "very sad, very sorrowful, but there was nothing I could do about it." His most difficult day came in 1977 when his cousin Chorn, a prison guard, was arrested and brought before En's camera. They did not talk; En feared that "if they knew he was my cousin I might also be arrested." The cousins "just looked at each other," too scared to speak. "During those three years that day was the worst. But it was not the only bad day; there were many other days I felt bad. All of my cousin's family members were also killed. My heart burned until the day I left Anlong Veng," En said.

The photographer recounted a survival strategy that reflected S-21's unique culture of extreme—and justifiable—paranoia. "It was sad to see all my colleagues, and I had to just act normally. I knew them, but their business was their own business, and I just cared about my own business." I asked if any of them had tried to speak to him. "They were all handcuffed, and when they saw me they didn't talk to me either. Their faces looked sad, they didn't ask for help." How did you feel photographing people you knew would die? "I knew when the photograph was taken they would be killed, but as I mentioned before, I felt numb because I saw this every day and there was nothing I could do." When I asked En if he ever feared these photos would later be used as evidence against the Khmer Rouge, he fell back on the Nuremberg defense: "I never had a thought what would happen to the photographs. I made them because I was ordered to. I never thought anything would happen to them."

We told Nhem En that we had spoken to S-21 survivor Van Nath and that Nath had remembered him. En searched his memory for a moment. "Oh yeah, I remember now. But it wasn't only to Van Nath. I spoke to many other colleagues who worked at the prison, some were artists, cleaners, cooks, and I told them how to organize and prepare themselves to fit into the Khmer Rouge ideology and to follow the rules and be cool." He said that Nath taught him how to draw pictures and carve wood. "I was fifteen or sixteen years old at the time. He must be very old now." I pulled out the photograph of American S-21 captive Mike Deeds that Van Nath had lent us and asked En if he remembered the American prisoners. He took the photo and studied it. "Those white guys were captured from Kompong Som, and they were also tortured exactly like the other prisoners. I took their photographs." He remembered that "the white guys" at Tuol Sleng "tried to act normal. But I noticed they did not act normally. They communicated with one another visually."

When I asked Nhem En about the Khmer Rouge retreat from the Vietnamese onslaught, the photographer smiled and laughed. He joked that fully describing "the bad experiences from that time" might take a week. He left Phnom Penh on January 7, 1979 and first clashed with the Vietnamese at Tbaing Kpos: "There were too many Vietnamese troops in this battle. I remember many of them were wounded and killed. I wasn't scared of the Vietnamese, but because our forces broke up, we tried to pull the forces together and then we had a problem."

En retreated and fought the Vietnamese again at Kompong Speu. At Tropeang Kroloeng, he commanded 100 soldiers until he was shot in the right leg and carried to a hospital in Kirirom. The Vietnamese attacked the hospital a few weeks later and burned it to the ground. According to En, the 52 patients who could not run away were burned alive. His own wound was almost healed, so he was able to escape and spent the next two months being carried by Khmer Rouge troops through the jungle, toward Phnom Krovaing. They survived on tree leaves and roots, and did not eat a single grain of rice for five months. En's claim that he had stayed with the Khmer Rouge due to his fear of Vietnamese reprisals sounded half-hearted and unconvincing compared to his clear and energetic description of the regime's glory days. He said that he did not return home after 1979 because "the Vietnamese might slit my throat."

I asked Nhem En how he felt about the fact that his Tuol Sleng photographs had drawn international attention. "I feel both pride and regret because all of the photographs were sad photographs and were from a painful experience. From now on I won't change my name, even though people suggested I should. I don't want to change my name because I want to show the world about the tricks of the Khmer Rouge leaders!" According to En, Pol Pot was alive and lived in Kbal An Song, twenty kilometers from Anlong Veng, conveniently located right on the Thai border in Sisaket province. "I wrote a letter to Hun Sen telling him not to believe it [that Brother Number One was dead], that Pol Pot is still alive. The last time I met him was in 1978, but before I left Anlong Veng in September 1995, I saw him at Kbal An Song."

Nhem En claimed that he no longer supported the Khmer Rouge because "all they think about is fighting and they don't allow people to have rights." He said that Ta Mok, now the most powerful Khmer Rouge leader, "handles everything, civilian and military affairs"; Ta Mok's philosophy "is to fight with Hun Sen and the Cambodian government until he's dead." When I asked En about a group of Cambodian hostages held by the Khmer Rouge in Anlong Veng, he said they must be dead. If they survived, "Ta Mok could be Thevadda Number 2. What this means is that if Ta Mok lets them survive then Ta Mok changed his mind, and *if* he changed his mind then he is no longer Ta Mok."

En ended the interview with a forceful plea: "I have 5,000 supporters right now, but I have no money to support them. A person like me, when I was in the Khmer Rouge, there were a lot of people who love me. That is why I just wrote a letter to [U.S. President] Clinton to ask for his financial support. The reason why I am asking Clinton for the money is that I want to promote democracy and peace in Cambodia and I trust myself, I can do it." En was aggressive: within two hours of meeting me, he was squeezing me for cash and introductions. He made it clear that he wanted to oust Pol Pot once and for all. While I was fascinated by En, I absolutely did not trust him.

We thanked Nhem En and left the guesthouse. I was moved by both his story and his impassioned delivery, but I had an uneasy feeling. The eloquence of En's well-practiced denials reminded me of a C-grade Ieng Sary. Above all, he seemed pretty secure, even smug, for someone who had been at the heart of horror, taking passport photos for the afterlife. As we talked about our impressions of the interview, Niven and I did our best to justify our interest in the charismatic Nhem En, the dreaded photographer of death.

iii

The next afternoon the phone rang at around four; it was Sok Sin, calling on his cell phone from the car. "I think this afternoon good for interview with Huy. You very lucky, ox cart still broken, he need to go back [to the country] tomorrow to fix for rice harvest. I come get you at five, we do interview at special place, make Huy comfortable." Nervously, I began to write up questions. I hadn't expected to be able to talk with Him Huy so soon. Sok Sin had quietly set this up on his own. Many S-21 survivors and even former staff members said that Huy was the worst of the worst. Rumored to have driven the prisoners to the killing fields at Choeung Ek, some claimed that he executed thousands with single blows to the backs of their necks with an ox cart axle. It was much easier to try to put a good face on Nhem En. He had been a teenager when he began working at S-21, and although I thought that he was more complicit than he had let on to be, En did not have blood on his hands. Doug Niven had asked Nhem En if he remembered Huy. "I knew he was very mean because he was one among the killers." En said that Huy was small but "knew judo and captured people easily." I asked if En had ever witnessed him killing a prisoner. "Among the killers Huy was the worst, he was the cruelest. Even I was scared of Huy."

Because Huy had been interviewed so many times before I got to him, I decided to try a different approach. Sok Sin and I drove away from the river and turned near the French embassy's giant white wall. We drove down a dirt road and pulled into a garage. Sok Sin jumped from the car and yelled "Huy" to a woman who ran upstairs, and immediately, an impish little man dressed in crude brown polyester pants and a blue dress shirt with a huge collar came down. He smiled at me broadly, and limply shook my hand. So here he was, the man whose name appears at the top of the execution lists at S-21. There was a sort of feral innocence to Huy's demeanor that took me by surprise, but his eyes were hard—not so much mean as dull and lifeless.

We walked up the stairs of an incomplete apartment building. Two floors were finished, but the other two were just crude forms and concrete slabs. We continued up another rickety staircase to the top floor, which overlooked Boeng Kak Lake, and sat cross-legged on the concrete. I opened my duffel bag and offered a variety of fruits and drinks, the standard party favors I brought along to all my interviews, to Huy. He went for the Tiger beer and Marlboro cigarettes. Sok Sin and I also had a beer. Then the former guard began his autobiography. Born in Kbal Chroy village in 1954, Huy was from an ordinary peasant family. "Recruited" in 1973 when the Khmer Rouge came to his village, he was sent to an army camp at Krang Yov and given basic military training and political indoctrination, and taught not to miss his parents. Unlike En, Huy claimed that he was a reluctant warrior: "I told people to tell my parents to come and ask for me to come back home. But when they came, they didn't allow me to return home. So I continued to follow the others." When Huy's father came a second time, Huy had to appear upset because his commanding officer was watching the reunion. Huy asked his father, "Why did you come? It's such a long way here. I know it's difficult for you." "Why do you say that?" his father replied. In fact, Huy missed his family very much. "I said this so the team chief wouldn't blame me for contacting my parents."[15]

Huy was not a fastidious hard worker, just a homesick teenager. Finally, when he could bear it no more, he told his commanders that if he could visit his parents, "I would be satisfied even if I die." When this request was rejected, Huy tried to sneak home and was caught. He was selected to fight in the leading wave of forces against the Lon Nol army at Prek Krasar and Kleong Meoung. In his first battle, Huy was badly wounded: "The bullet hit me in the head. They told me that I would die, so I did not fear any longer. I

HIM HUY (FOURTH FROM RIGHT) AND TUOL SLENG GUARDS, 1977
TUOL SLENG MUSEUM OF GENOCIDE

stood up, firing back, and was hit in the leg, arm, and buttocks." Huy rolled up his pant leg and pointed to a grayish lump in his ankle, then parted his hair and showed me another scar. I touched the ankle; it felt like there were ball bearings under his skin. I instinctively grabbed my crotch and Huy laughed and shook his head. "No, not the family jewels," Sok Sin artfully translated.

Huy recovered from these wounds in time for the invasion of Phnom Penh in April 1975. Just outside the city, he spotted a Lon Nol soldier dressed in a black Khmer Rouge uniform just as he threw a grenade that landed nearby and peppered Huy's body with shrapnel. "I crawled up to a high house to get away from the soldiers. There were no physicians, they were all gone. I could not walk." In the morning, Huy continued to crawl and hide, more worried about being found by one of Lon Nol's soldiers than about dying of his wounds. In Huy's style of war there were no Hague and Geneva agreements, there was only the thought of your adversary cutting out your liver and eating it in front of you—if you lived that long. Huy crawled from house to house, finding them all deserted. At dawn he was rescued by Khmer Rouge soldiers and taken by tank to a hospital where he would spend the next two months recovering.

Huy believed that after the Khmer Rouge victory, life would return to normal. Farmers would go back to their fields and workers back to the factories. He returned to his unit, farming land. One afternoon, the leader of his group told Huy that he had been chosen to go into a new unit. That night, the leader rode Huy on his bicycle to S-21 prison. Along the way he asked, "Comrade, do you know what you are guilty of?" Huy also feared that he might wind up a prisoner. He was not designated a guard immediately, so for the first few days, he just ate and slept and tried not to draw attention to himself. "I was afraid. I was thinking that I had the same fate as the other prisoners." Huy was then asked to serve as an interrogator, but he refused because his "head was broken [wounded]." He was made a guard instead.

Huy said the prison stank badly, but was quiet because the prisoners were forbidden to speak to one another. I asked about the cries of those being tortured and he said that the victims "were not allowed to scream out. They just groaned." He admitted being present: "I did see the torture. It was at the interrogation place. I didn't dare approach them." As the months went by, life at S-21 grew increasingly perilous for Huy as his superiors were arrested and killed one by one. "I pitied them, we used to live together with each other and never had any problems with each other. We were all the same; why were they imprisoned?" When another guard Him Huy knew was accused, Huy was ordered to take him to his cell. When he quietly asked the guard what had happened, "I have been accused by someone" was the only reply.

The former Tuol Sleng guard said that the strain of S-21 was too much for another guard named Chek to bear. Before he could be accused and put through a procedure he knew all too well, he chose another way out. Chek told Huy, "Brother, I'm going out to cut bindweed for the rabbits." "Okay, hurry back for lunch! If you don't come at lunch, they will eat all the food!" Huy replied. A few hours later, Huy noticed that his friend had not returned and began to search for him. When he found Chek dead, hanging by the neck, he rushed to tell the head guard, Phe Phai Pheap, known as Hor. "It's your business, I don't know. You're responsible for him. Now you go and report it yourself to Duch," Hor said. Huy had often considered killing himself too. "At Tuol Sleng, I was about to shoot myself several times, because I'd been told off too often." One day, when he was on guard duty, Hor cursed at him. "I sat crying alone. I wanted to shoot myself then." However, thoughts of his family kept Huy from committing suicide. "My parents would have been jailed. They would have been accused."

I asked Huy to describe his typical day at Tuol Sleng, but a combination of Sok Sin's bad translation and the Tiger beer got him off on a completely different track. He began to tell me about taking prisoners from S-21 to their final destination, the killing fields at Choeung Ek. He said that about twice a month, two or three trucks under Hor's command drove prisoners to the killing fields. When I asked if it was hard to watch people being driven to their deaths, he chuckled. "Hard. I was thinking that one day, I would be taken there, too." He described the mechanics of the process. "They told us to drive two or three trucks in the entrance. Peng [the head guard] went around and collected those who had already been interrogated. They walked the prisoners up to the trucks." About thirty handcuffed and blindfolded prisoners were dispatched each time.

Sometimes, Huy went with Hor and, "if they were high-ranking people, Duch also went with us to check." Huy said that by the time the prisoners reached Choeung Ek, they were "frightened and pale" and "knew that they would die." They were herded out of the trucks and made to write their names on a list. Once the paperwork was complete, Huy said, he "waited until the executioners said they had collected their strength." I asked how the victims were killed: "They were ordered to kneel down on the edge of the hole. Their hands were cuffed behind them, then they were beaten on their nape with an ox cart axle—an iron tube." According to Huy, Hor inspected the killing and he wrote down the names. "I just wrote the names down, and made it clear. We took the names back to Thy [the officer in charge of prison records], who would verify them himself. They could not have any missing names." Here Huy's story began to get murky. Many S-21 survivors and former staff members claimed that he was one of the executioners, but he insisted that there was an execution squad based at Choeung Ek.

After two top guards were killed in early 1978, Huy was promoted to head guard. "Finally, there were no men left except a few of us who were the oldest. Then, we got pushed up." Did Huy worry that he would be promoted and then killed? "I was also thinking about this. I was worried that I would face the same thing soon, because the big men had been promoted and then jailed." When Huy's superior, "Big Huy" (Hor) was arrested, "Little Huy" began to worry. "When will it be my turn?" he wondered. I asked if he felt any regrets about the thousands killed at S-21. "I feel regret that I shouldn't have been [working] there." Was it a kill-or-be-killed situation? Huy laughed, seeming uncomfortable. "I don't know what to say. If they told us to do and we didn't do it, they would kill us. It was just death either way." I asked how he felt about the women and children killed. Huy's demeanor changed. "Don't mention that," he replied with new seriousness, looking me dead in the eye.

In late 1978, Khmer Rouge Minister of Defense Son Sen called a meeting of S-21 staff at Brother Duch's house and described the battlefield situation and the Vietnamese invasion. When Son Sen turned to Huy and asked, "Do you, Comrade Huy, dare to fight the *yuon* [Vietnamese]?" Huy sensed an opportunity to make a graceful exit from S-21 and seized it. "I said: 'I dare. Now I'd like to ask Uncle to go back to army." His request was denied. When the S-21 staff heard the approaching gunfire of the advancing Vietnamese army, they evacuated the prison and organized the guards into battle groups. When I asked Huy who won, he laughed and rolled his eyes. "How could we win over the Vietnamese? There were so many Vietnamese." After a clash near the train station, the S-21 staffers retreated into the mountains outside Phnom Penh. Old tensions among them reemerged in these hours of strife: "After climbing up the mountain, Hor had a dispute with Duch." Huy tried to convince Hor not to go with Duch but to return to their home village. Hor refused, and Huy and others escaped in the middle of the night. "After I had left, they killed him and they ordered a group to follow and kill us," he recalled. When Huy reached his village, he did not know his starving parents and disabled brother: "When I arrived home I couldn't recognize my parents. My parents were all sick, there was no rice to eat. I cried when I arrived there, I saw my parents so thin I cried." Since then, Huy had struggled to survive as a farmer. His greatest concern was filling the rice pot.

Like many Cambodians with a past, Huy claimed to be apathetic about Ieng Sary's recent amnesty. "I don't know, it's up to the government." I told him that I wanted to know his opinion. "The main [person] is Pol Pot, Pol Pot is the biggest leader. He should be punished according to the laws. He was the person who made the others to become bad."

By the time we finished the interview, the sun had set; lightning touched down on the other side of the lake. Sok Sin and I thanked Huy and said good-bye. The next day, Doug Niven and I were at the Agence France Presse office. A group of Cambodians across the street were carrying political banners and creating a ruckus. I asked Niven if he knew what it was all about. "Sam Rainsy's having a demonstration. We want to be the fuck out of here for that. This place could explode."

HIM HUY, 1995
CHRIS RILEY

7

"AM I A SAVAGE PERSON?"

i

At 8:30 a.m. on March 30, 1997, Sam Rainsy's Khmer Nation Party had just begun a political rally in a Phnom Penh park when four grenades landed in the middle of the gathering of 150. Rainsy was shielded from the blast by bodyguards, one of whom was killed instantly by the explosions, along with dozens of other demonstrators. Two of the grenades were thrown from behind the crowd and one or two more were tossed from a passing car or motorcycle. When the crowd began to pursue the attackers on foot, they were stopped at gunpoint by soldiers loyal to Hun Sen, who had been in the park since the beginning of the rally. Some of the injured staggered to the nearby Kantha Bopha Children's Hospital, only to be turned away by hospital workers afraid to get involved in political strife.[1]

The Khmer Nation Party leader, Sam Rainsy, was the former Minister of Finance. After slamming the Hun Sen government for corruption and all-around abuse of power, he was expelled from the National Assembly in June 1995.[2] After the 1997 attack, Sam Rainsy declared: "Hun Sen is behind this. He is a bloody man. He will be arrested and sentenced one day." He called for an international intervention: "I think the time has come to set up a genocide tribunal like in Rwanda to stop the killing hands of CPP, of Hun Sen."[3] While

Hun Sen in his official response deemed the grenade attack a tragedy, he also threatened to "drag the demonstration's mastermind by the neck to court."[4] Prince Ranariddh called for a UN investigation of the bombing because he said that he did not trust the Cambodian government.[5]

Once again, exiled King Norodom Sihanouk could not remain silent. He said that it was his "duty to ring the alarm bell" and warn about the "dark" Cambodian future. Sihanouk believed that Hun Sen's pardon of Ieng Sary and the negotiations with the Khmer Rouge lent "respectability" and "legitimacy" to the "Polpotist Revolution." The king ran down the laundry list of Cambodian ills: "Permanent deforestation, trafficking of all kinds, wild capitalism, the systematic destruction of our natural resources, the irreversible 'de facto' partition of the State, the decline of moral values at the heart of our society, the irreversible advance of AIDS and other vices of Sodom and Gomorrah."[6] Prince Ranariddh and forty other members of the Cambodian parliament appealed to UN Secretary-General Kofi Annan in April, warning that the country was sliding toward dictatorship. The MPs argued that reforming Cambodia would be impossible as long as "the biggest human rights abuser is the most powerful man in the country." Since the Hun Sen–led coalition had taken power in 1993, nine Cambodian journalists, including Thun Bun Ly, had been attacked and four killed for writing articles critical of the government.[7]

In mid-June, the situation grew even more volatile after unconfirmed reports said Pol Pot was on the run, having ordered the execution of his longtime ally, Son Sen, the Khmer Rouge official most closely associated with S-21. Son Sen, his wife Yun Yat, and nine others were killed and their bodies run over by a dump truck on June 9, 1997.[8] Other than Pol Pot, Son Sen would have been one of the most likely suspects for a war crimes tribunal.

Co-Prime Ministers Prince Ranariddh and Hun Sen continued to compete for the favor of Anlong Veng's defecting Khmer Rouge soldiers. Although Hun Sen had gained an advantage by negotiating the surrender of Ieng Sary, Ranariddh was now in the lead. Khmer Rouge documents recovered later would show that the leaders were planning to use the prince as a Trojan horse: "Ranariddh's boat is sinking in the sea but our boat is not. We have to help him but the way we help them is to offer him a stick—not a hand, not an embrace, not to let him cling to our boat—or we all die. We have to play a trick."[9]

Khmer Rouge radio announced on June 19 that Pol Pot had been captured alive and was being held by Khmer Rouge forces in Anlong Veng. The two prime ministers put their differences aside and called a joint press conference the next day. Hun Sen stood by impassively as Prince Ranariddh announced that they would ask the United Nations to set up an international tribunal for Brother Number One. "Pol Pot is a criminal, a criminal against humanity," Hun Sen declared. The official request was sent to Secretary-General Annan on June 21; it asked for help to bring "to justice those persons responsible for the genocide and crimes against humanity during the rule of the Khmer Rouge."[10] Even U.S. Secretary of State Madeleine Albright acknowledged the significance of Pol Pot's capture, announcing on ABC's *This Week* that the United States would "make sure that there is international justice carried out against this major war criminal."[11]

However, Albright and the Americans received a significant setback on June 25, when China, the Khmer Rouge's greatest patron, announced that it would not support the creation of a UN war crimes tribunal for Cambodia. This move should have been anticipated, given China's historical relationship with the Khmer Rouge. Cui Tiankai, the spokesman for the Chinese foreign ministry, framed the issue in terms of national sovereignty and maintained that "it should be decided by Cambodians themselves without foreign interference."[12] The news of Pol Pot's capture turned Phnom Penh into a media circus. The Foreign Correspondents Club in Bangkok was forced to postpone their annual ball because most of their members were in Cambodia.

At dawn on July 5, Hun Sen's troops launched a full-scale attack on Prince Ranariddh's headquarters in Phnom Penh. Hun Sen would later charge the prince with a "policy of provocation." While the two sides exchanged rocket, mortar, and small arms fire, Hun Sen's forces blocked the roads out of town and established strategic strong points throughout the capital. The radio station controlled by Prince Ranariddh's royalist FUNCINPEC Party was off the air by July 6 and the prince fled to France. Hun Sen's coup appeared to be a smashing success, at least militarily.[13] The United States issued a cool diplomatic response the next day. State Department spokesman Nicholas Burns described the fighting in Cambodia as "sufficiently murky so that we don't want to shoot arrows at one side or another today." He asked for time "to try to make better sense of the political alignment of forces in Phnom Penh and throughout the country" before releasing an official statement.[14]

Hun Sen blamed four senior FUNCINPEC officials for the trouble. Later, in a nationally televised address, he would accuse Ranariddh of "illegally" negotiating with the Khmer Rouge leaders in Anlong Veng. The prince was also charged with bringing weapons into the country and moving Khmer Rouge defectors into Phnom Penh.[15] Hun Sen's troops swept the city, blatantly searching for Ranariddh's top officials. One of the four, Ho Sok, a Cambodian

Ministry of the Interior official and a critic of Hun Sen, was arrested and found dead in jail from a gunshot wound a day later. Hun Sen's advisor, Khieu Sopheak, announced that Ho Sok had been involved in "sabotage and plots," and "was shot down by people who were angry with him."[16] The next day, Prince Ranariddh's senior security official Chau Sambath, another of the four, was shot dead under "mysterious circumstances." Prince Ranariddh's residence and the headquarters of Sam Rainsy's Khmer Nation Party were openly ransacked, and Hun Sen's troops even looted Pochentong Airport. Human Rights Watch and UN human rights officials confirmed "a wave of arrests."[17] When the Clinton administration remained reluctant to call Cambodia's fourth of July extravaganza a coup, Mike Jendrzejczyk of Human Rights Watch said the American nonresponse was "outrageous."[18]

Hun Sen warned western leaders, "You should not want to threaten Hun Sen, you can threaten anybody else, that's all right, but not Hun Sen." The prime minister produced two documents intended to prove that Ranariddh had been attempting to forge an alliance with the Khmer Rouge hardliners in Anlong Veng. This was not an unlikely proposition, but it was a strange charge coming from Hun Sen, the one who'd pushed amnesty for Ieng Sary.[19]

The purges in Cambodia continued. At least twenty-five FUNCINPEC officials were dead within a couple of weeks. According to a government official, another four hundred were alive but undergoing "reeducation." David Hawk, head of the UN Center for Human Rights in Phnom Penh, confirmed these accounts: "Our immediate concern is the physical safety and well-being of those government officials associated with the ousted first prime minister. They have been disarmed and arrested and neutralized. Opposition party headquarters and residences have been seized and trashed."[20] A UN official confirmed that Hun Sen's purges had been more widespread than initially thought. Speaking on the condition of anonymity, he claimed that at least forty people had been killed and hundreds of others arrested. Some had been shot while surrendering; others were found dead and mutilated. High-ranking generals Krouch Yoeum and Sam Norin, the two surviving Ranariddh officials, were shot when they tried to surrender.[21] King Sihanouk continued to speak out, calling for an end to the killings.

Cambodia's prime minister considered himself unfairly maligned, like boxer Evander Holyfield: "Ranariddh employed the tactics of Mike Tyson, by biting the ear. If your president or prime minister did the illegal thing, like importing weapons, would you accept it?"[22] Hun Sen replaced Prince Ranariddh as first prime minister on July 16 with Ung Huot, a fifty-two-year-old Australian-trained bureaucrat. There were pockets of resistance to Hun Sen, but overall, his brief and bloody Summer Coup was a smashing success. Not only had he split the Khmer Rouge and gained the loyalty of Ieng Sary's breakaway faction in Pailin, he had simultaneously disposed of his most important domestic political rival. Although Hun Sen was now isolated on an international political level, on the home front, his consolidation of power was near complete.[23]

ii

I received a call from Doug Niven in Bangkok in late July, informing me that journalist Nate Thayer and cameraman David McKaige were on their way to Anlong Veng to film the "trial" of Pol Pot. I was happy for Thayer and a bit jealous. It was nice to see that a parachute journalist from New York City wasn't going to steal the show from a reporter who'd paid his dues in Southeast Asia. Several were trying, but nobody was getting into Anlong Veng without an invitation from Ta Mok, who was orchestrating the judicial assault on his former boss. A few nights later, Thayer's interview footage appeared on Ted Koppel's *Nightline*. After two decades of intrigue and mystery, the elderly Pol Pot was finally revealed on international television. He sat in a plastic chair, looking old and pathetic, like the Wizard of Oz pulled rudely from behind his curtain. Brother Number One and three of his aides faced about one hundred of his most fanatical former supporters. Now they pumped their fists and chanted in robotic, rehearsed unison: "Crush! Crush! Crush! Pol Pot and his clique!"[24] One Khmer Rouge veteran sounded a common theme: they had sacrificed so much and had nothing to show for it. "Our parents and all of us are children of peasants and farmers, we have sacrificed everything for the sake of the movement, but at the end we kill each other."[25]

Pol Pot's "crimes" were read over a loudspeaker and one by one, former cadres went to the podium to denounce him. "We want to put an end to the leadership that has betrayed our organization and the people!" shrieked a former follower.[26] There was no defense in this "trial." Pol Pot sat quietly and took abuse from soldiers, women, farmers, and others for about two hours. Clearly, the spectacle had been staged for the western journalists and was intended to demonstrate that the Khmer Rouge had purged the evil *one* responsible for the entire genocidal regime. Few examples, even in the checkered history of political justice, could match this ridiculously choreographed show. Finally, Pol Pot was sentenced to life under house arrest: "These are the criminal acts—the betrayal by Pol Pot and his clique—against the people, armed forces, and our cadre. In conclusion, we all decide to condemn and sentence this clique to life imprisonment."[27]

Compared to Pol Pot's 1997 Anlong Veng trial, his 1979 *in absentia* trial by the Vietnamese looked as legitimate as Nuremberg's International Military Tribunal after World War II. Above all, the 1997 trial served to illustrate just how deluded the remaining Khmer Rouge hardliners had become after so many years of war, isolation, and indoctrination.[28] Anlong Veng governor Ta Neou announced that "the international community should understand that we are no longer Khmer Rouge and not Pol Potists!"[29] The crowd, eager to demonstrate their new political sensibility, chanted, "Long live the new strategy!" When the show was over, Pol Pot was shuffled into the back of an old Toyota Land Cruiser (one of the UN artifacts) and driven away. Khmer Rouge leader Tep Kunnal announced that he would not surrender the prisoner to an international tribunal: "Before there were two dangers for Cambodia: Pol Pot and the Vietnamese puppet Hun Sen. Now there is only one." While in Anlong Veng, Nate Thayer confirmed that both Hun Sen and Prince Ranariddh had been aggressively courting the Khmer Rouge faction before the Summer Coup, and that the prince had reached an agreement on July 4, the day before.[30]

Hun Sen began to shore up his losses on the international front with a new policy that would play nicely in the West: Khmer Rouge war crimes trials, just the thing to provide a welcome diversion from the coup and its bloody aftermath. Hun Sen announced "the trial of the century" and told the UN he hoped to apprehend and "hand over those notorious criminals, including Pol Pot, to your proposed international criminal tribunal."[31] He added that Prince Ranariddh should also be tried for "colluding" with the Khmer Rouge. While professing to support a war crimes tribunal for the Khmer Rouge leaders, Hun Sen seemed more intent on putting Prince Ranariddh on trial.[32]

Pol Pot had disappeared after his trial, and several brand-name reporters were trying to get interviews. Once again, Nate Thayer was ahead of the pack; he spoke to Pol Pot, still under arrest in Anlong Veng, on October 16. When Thayer reminded the aging leader of this historic opportunity to set the record straight, Pol Pot said that his "conscience is clear." When Thayer continued to press him, he denied everything: "First, I would like to tell you that I came to carry out a struggle, not to kill people. Even now, and you can look at me, am I a savage person?" When asked if he felt any remorse for the "very serious mistakes you made while you were in power," Pol Pot continued to avoid Thayer's questions and said only that the Khmer Rouge had prevented the Vietnamese from swallowing Cambodia.[33]

When Thayer asked about Tuol Sleng prison, he hit a nerve. "I was at the top. I made only big decisions on big issues," Pol Pot insisted before calling the museum "a Vietnamese exhibition." He even attempted to cast a shadow of doubt over the authenticity of the photos: "People talk about Tuol Sleng, Tuol Sleng, Tuol Sleng, but when we look at the pictures, the pictures are the same. When I first heard about Tuol Sleng, it was on Voice of America. I listened twice." Pol Pot said that this was not until 1979. "No, I never heard of it. And those two researchers, they said that those skeletons, they were more than ten years old."[34]

When Thayer asked Ta Mok, Anlong Veng's new Brother Number One, if he planned to hand Pol Pot over to an international tribunal, the one-legged general made a counteroffer to be communicated to the West: "I will turn Pol Pot over, no problem, if you bring Hun Sen and they go together."[35] Now that Pol Pot had been purged and the movement shattered, many former Khmer Rouge sought some explanation. "All of us—our parents, our children—are poor peasants. And we have agreed to abandon everything for many years to join the struggle—and, ultimately, in order to kill each other. How can that be?" General Khem Nuon asked, as if he were waking from a twenty-year bad dream.[36] Under Ta Mok's leadership, the remnants of the Khmer Rouge would try to implement a new political strategy, and because they had engineered Pol Pot's trial, they considered themselves redeemed. Thayer reported that Anlong Veng was now decorated with freshly painted slogans like DEFEAT FOR THE TRAITOR POL POT WHOSE HANDS ARE STAINED WITH BLOOD and CAMBODIANS DON'T KILL CAMBODIANS. The new Khmer Rouge leader believed that a show trial and a few new slogans constituted political rehabilitation. "Reports reach me each day saying that the new policy that 'Cambodians Don't Kill Cambodians' is a magic slogan indeed," Mok explained to Thayer. Unfortunately, there would be no grand extradition or international trial: Pol Pot died under appropriately mysterious circumstances less than a year later.[37]

Hun Sen continued to consolidate power, seemingly immune from reprisals despite irrefutable evidence of his violent tactics. When a spokesman for the prime minister claimed that some of the royalists who'd been killed died while fighting, an Amnesty International official commented, "People don't die in armed conflict with their hands tied behind their backs."[38] The Cambodian office of the UN Center for Human Rights issued a scathing report on August 21 entitled, "Evidence of Summary Executions, Torture, and Missing Persons Since 2–7 July 1997." There had been 41 to 60 "politically-motivated extrajudicial executions" since the coup and more than 600 people remained in government custody.[39] UN officials in Cambodia believed that Hun Sen's forces were targeting "senior officers and their key associates and subordinates." Most of the victims' bodies had been cremated before autopsies could be performed, and when the officials tried to get more information, they were "intimidated and insulted."[40] The badly mutilated bodies of Ranariddh's key military officers Ho Sok and General Chau Sambath were recovered, however. "Their hands and ankles were tied. They had broken necks. Their eyes were gouged out. Their heads, chests and stomachs were cut open."[41]

By December 1997, a major split had developed between western and ASEAN nations over Cambodia. While countries like the United States pushed for ceremonial economic sanctions, Japan put regional harmony before human rights, and most of Cambodia's other neighbors did not appear keen to meddle in internal affairs.[42] Japan put forward the "Four Pillars Initiative" to end the Cambodian civil war, and pledged $3 million in aid for the Cambodian elections, to be held in July 1998. The initiative called for a military truce between Hun Sen's and Prince Ranariddh's troops, still fighting on the Thai border, and for the prince to break all ties with the Khmer Rouge.[43] The third and fourth pillars, by far the strangest part of the plan, allowed Hun Sen to try Prince Ranariddh *in absentia*. King Norodom Sihanouk would then grant Ranariddh amnesty. Although farcical to western eyes, this setup allowed both sides to save face and Prince Ranariddh to return to Cambodia and run in the election. Amnesty International called the Japanese plan "a neat diplomatic formula," but warned that it was a "tacit endorsement" of Hun Sen's coup.[44]

A courtroom was hastily constructed at the Ministry of Defense in Phnom Penh, and nine witnesses testified that they had discovered a two-ton cache of weapons bound for the prince. Within hours, on March 17, 1998, Ranariddh was found guilty of "plotting a coup with Khmer Rouge leaders," sentenced to 35 years in prison, and fined $54 million. After the verdict was announced, Hun Sen called for a royal pardon: "The door is always open for Ranariddh to return home to participate in the election."[45] This abrupt conciliatory statement made sense: Hun Sen needed "credible elections" to avoid alienating his western financial supporters. But the week before the election, Amnesty International charged that Hun Sen's security forces were still intimidating and harassing his political opponents and described the political climate in Cambodia as "institutionalized impunity."[46]

Cambodians took to the polls on July 25, 1998, in a "show election" no more legitimate than Prince Ranariddh's March show trial.[47] The losers, FUNCINPEC Party members, immediately complained of election fraud, but the United States minimized these charges and accepted Hun Sen's victory. State Department spokesman Jamie Rubin announced on July 30, "Highly respected Cambodian nongovernmental organizations indicated these complaints are not widespread and should not fundamentally alter the outcome of the election."[48] After opposition demonstrators were beaten by pro–Hun Sen goon squads in street clashes in Phnom Penh, the government warned of sterner measures to curb this "worrying anarchy."[49]

Cambodia was fast emerging as the world's best example of what Fareed Zakaria described as "illiberal democracy."[50] Much to her credit, Pulitzer Prize–winning journalist Tina Rosenberg, who only two years earlier had written about the dawn of a new era of international law, pointed to an emerging and unpleasant truth that many in the West were happy to ignore: "The speed and enthusiasm of the world's embrace raises troubling questions about whether it is democracy or merely its appearance that the world demands, and whether the international rules are any less cynical today than during the cold war."[51] In fact, the rules were significantly more cynical, as the renewed debate over Khmer Rouge war crimes trials would soon demonstrate.

iii

The death of Pol Pot, the defection of top Khmer Rouge leaders Ieng Sary, Nuon Chea, and Khieu Samphan, and the violence following the July 1998 election pushed the war crimes trials issue to center stage in 1999. However, the motives were mixed. Prime Minister Hun Sen hired a Washington, D.C. public relations firm for an image makeover. Porter, Wright, Morris, and Arthur recommended that "Hun Sen should immediately begin leading the charge to bring the Khmer Rouge to trial before an international tribunal." It appeared that in exchange for joining forces with the prime minister, the three highest ranking Khmer Rouge had been granted *de facto* amnesties; by defecting, they neatly avoided any blame for the atrocities. From start to finish, the Cambodia–UN debate over war crimes trials would prove to be a *Rashomon*.

Hun Sen said that he felt a "mixture of emotions." Although happy about ending his nation's thirty-year civil war, he admitted "unpleasantness" continued because the Khmer Rouge leaders had been "responsible for the deaths of millions."[52] The prime minister had approvingly cited an *Asiaweek* article that described him as "the grand master" for his Khmer Rouge strategy. The survivor of battlefields and decades of Cambodian political intrigue, he faced a hard truth that many in the West ignored or glossed over: in order to end the war, a sacrifice had to be made. Justice and reconciliation did not necessarily go hand in hand: "To destroy 70 percent of the KR forces, we needed to pay a price too—that was the amnesty provided to Ieng Sary."[53] Hun Sen said that his goal had not been to capture Ieng Sary, but "to checkmate Brother Number one, Pol Pot. . . . Without peace, justice cannot be found." He offered a telling metaphor: "I have said in the past, we should not talk about how to cook the fish while it is still in the water—first you need to catch the fish."[54] Now that Hun Sen was catching fish, chefs from around the world descended on Phnom Penh and attempted to storm his kitchen with exotic, foreign judicial recipes.

Hun Sen mocked the UN and the United States for their newfound interest in Khmer Rouge war crimes and never tired of reminding both of their twenty years of cynicism and moral cowardice: "I still remember with pain that in 1990–1991, at the discussions [toward] the Paris Agreements, I alone insisted on the word 'genocide.'" For this, he had been attacked as "a person with no goodwill to end the war."[55] The prime minister recalled with disgust a recent conversation with an American diplomat. In 1990, the same diplomat had urged him to forget the past and negotiate with the Khmer Rouge. Eight years later, he was demanding Hun Sen's support for a Khmer Rouge war crimes trial:

> It is political hypocrisy. A certain person came to see me the other day—this person was responsible for providing weapons to coalitions on the border. They recalled the situation when they pressed me to include the KR in the Paris peace agreements, saying that if we did not do so, China would veto it. That same person is now asking me to lobby China not to use its veto in the Security Council against the establishment of the court. Before the US and China were colluding in supporting the Khmer Rouge. The US now wants to use Hun Sen against China. I do not like to be the pawn of any foreign country.[56]

Hun Sen would never forget the roles played by the United States, China, Thailand, and the UN during the 1980s and would never stop reminding westerners that "when the Khmer Rouge came to an end in 1979, if everyone had accepted the fact and they had not been supported, there would have been no war."[57]

Although it was clear by early 1999 that Hun Sen would not buckle under American or UN pressure on the subject of war crimes, his response to recommendations made by UN experts spelled it out for even the dimmest to see. The UN sent three war crimes "experts" (Steven Ratner, Ninian Stephen, and Rajsoomer Lallah) to spend a week in Cambodia meeting with politicians and reviewing the evidence in March 1999.[58] The experts recommended trying the former Khmer Rouge leaders in an *ad hoc* international court under charges of crimes against humanity and genocide. These were very ambitious plans, calling for an independent prosecutor appointed by the UN, a tribunal with two chambers, and judges also appointed by the UN. The trio not only recommended moving the trial out of the country but also sought to limit the role of Cambodia's judiciary. That might ensure a fair trial, but it was a slap to the face of Hun Sen. He had, after all, created the conditions that allowed these unprecedented discussions to take place. Moreover, it was not as if the UN had moral authority; it had not captured war criminals during its tenure in Cambodia.[59]

Once again, Hun Sen trumped his critics with action: while the UN experts were delivering legal pronouncements, he was capturing war crimes suspects. One picture tells the whole story—the prime minister sitting in front of a bank of reporters' microphones, with a grin that he cannot conceal. On a television screen in front of him is a grainy video image of his latest prize: the infamous one-legged general Ta Mok.[60] Hun Sen savored this final domestic political triumph. With China and Thailand's backing, he began to take a harder line with the UN. The trial of the Khmer Rouge would be a Cambodian affair and if necessary, would be conducted by the same Cambodian judiciary that had tried Prince Ranariddh. One thing was crystal clear: the "recommendations" of the UN "experts" would not provide the basis for war crimes trials in Cambodia. Hun Sen was holding all the cards and if the UN wanted to play, it would be by his rules.[61]

When asked about the experts' criticism that a national tribunal could be vulnerable to political maneuvering, Hun Sen replied, "I think this is the talk of a lawyer. A lawyer is a lawyer. I respect what a lawyer argues. A lawyer is not a politician." Unlike many during the 1990s, the prime minister had a very firm grasp of the difference between politics and law and never tired of pointing it out: "During the UNTAC era, they never talked about trying the KR, [but] they talked about recognizing the KR to participate in a political solution." He did not bother to veil his contempt for the recent UN visit and shrugged off the seminar room legalism of this most recent crop of international advisors: "if the lawyers have evolved and changed both in morals and in politics I think that they should end their careers as lawyers and work in politics."[62]

Just as the UN and NGOs were said to suffer from "Cambodia fatigue," perhaps Hun Sen was suffering a similar exhaustion: "I would like to tell you that the Cambodian people have found justice by themselves, not through foreigners. It was through their contribution that the KR organization, both political and military collapsed."[63] Furthermore, Cambodians of all walks of life supported the "idea" of a trial. In January 1999, the Institute Français de la Statistique, de Sondage d'Opinion et de Research sur le Cambodge had asked 616 urban and 887 rural Cambodians, "Do you want Khmer Rouge leaders under the Pol Pot regime to be prosecuted?" Eighty-one percent responded, "Yes."[64] But what expectations had been raised! Could the trial of a handful of old men bring a resolution and transform their nation?

Meanwhile, one of the strangest episodes in the Khmer Rouge breakup was the emergence of S-21 prison commandant Brother Duch. The former teacher who had overseen the systematic torture and executions of at least 14,000 people was living in Battambang and had become an evangelical Christian. Baptized by American Pacific College missionaries in 1996, Duch now worked for an NGO called the American Refugee Committee.[65] British journalist Nic Dunlop had been fascinated by Duch as I had been fascinated with En, and for many years had carried Duch's picture whenever he traveled to Cambodia. When Dunlop saw a familiar-looking buck-toothed, rabbit-eared man in a village near Samlot in 1999, he was almost certain it was the former Tuol Sleng commandant. Duch introduced himself to Dunlop in English and said that he was a former schoolteacher from Phnom Penh named Hang Pin. The Englishman returned to Bangkok and traveled back to Samlot a week later with American journalist Nate Thayer to help him verify the man's identity.[66]

The reporters found "Hang Pin" in the same village, and when he began to preach the gospel of Jesus Christ, Thayer cut the sermon short: "I believe that you also worked with the security services during the Khmer Rouge period?" At first, "Hang Pin" tried to deny the charge, but he soon broke down: "It's God's will that you are here. Now my future is in God's hands." Unlike Pol Pot and the rest of the former Khmer Rouge leaders, Brother Duch admitted his guilt. "My unique fault is that I did not serve God, I served men, I served communism. I feel very sorry about the killings and the past. I wanted to be a good communist." When the journalists presented Duch with a memo he'd written, authorizing an interrogator to torture a prisoner to death, he apologized: "I am sorry. The people who died were good people ... there were many who were innocent." The former S-21 commandant admitted, "Whoever was arrested must die. It was the rule of the party." Duch said that he had had "great difficulty in my life, thinking that the people who died did nothing wrong."[67]

One American Refugee Committee official was flabbergasted when Duch's identity was revealed to him before Dunlop and Thayer reported it in their respective newspapers in April 1999. "We are in a state of shock frankly. He was our best worker, highly respected in the community, clearly very intelligent and dedicated to helping the refugees." Duch accepted his fate, admitted his guilt, and took responsibility for his actions: "I have done bad things before in my life. Now it is time for *les reprisals.*" Duch's pastor, Christopher LaPel, remarked, "Duch is so brave to say 'I did wrong, I accept punishment.' The Christian spirit has filled him to his heart. Now, he is free from fear. He is free—not like Khieu Samphan or Nuon Chea, or other top leaders." Many Cambodians were confused by this western religion that appeared to allow for such easy absolution of horrible transgressions. A Cambodian working for another Christian NGO, fired for crashing a company car, observed, "That wall [into which I crashed] was fixed in one week. I was broke and they fired me. But Duch, he killed thousands and they forgive him. I don't get it."[68]

Another UN delegation headed to Phnom Penh in the final week of August 1999 to reach an agreement with the Cambodian government on an international war crimes trial. The UN "draft proposal" was a compromise that gave up many of the positions of its experts. Anette Marcher of the *Phnom Penh Post* best summarized the response: "The United Nations draft proposal for a trial ... for the former leaders of the Khmer Rouge has achieved a unity rarely seen in Cambodia: everyone hates it."[69] When Hun Sen addressed the UN General Assembly on September 20, 1999, he described his nation as a "fully integrated country without rebels" and even bragged about his recent victory in a "free and fair" election. When it came to the war crimes trial, though, he hedged and said that although justice was important, so was the "need for continued national reconciliation and the safeguard of the hard-gained peace as well as national independence and sovereignty, which we value the most."[70] Hun Sen's point man on the question, Sok An, was the senior minister in Cambodia's Council of Ministers. They met with Kofi Annan at UN headquarters in New York City and gave the UN three choices, none of which was in keeping with the recommendations of the experts: the UN could have only a minority of judges and prosecutors in a trial in a Cambodian court; the UN could simply provide legal advice; or the UN could not participate in the trial. The only thing that was certain was that mutual distrust had been firmly reestablished.[71]

Senior Khmer Rouge leaders Nuon Chea and Khieu Samphan had not seemed too worried about impending war crimes prosecutions when they faced reporters at the luxurious Hotel Le Royal in Phnom Penh earlier in the year. "Yes sorry. I'm very sorry," said Samphan when asked about the killings under his former regime. However, he stuck to the old party line of national reconciliation.[72] The more complicit Nuon Chea was less convincing and jokingly offered, "Sorry as well for the lives of animals endangered during the war." Khmer Rouge spokesman Long Norin did not believe that a trial would "benefit the nation" and made it clear that the Khmer Rouge had a few cards of their own to play: "This will also involve the 200 days and nights of [U.S.] bombing. It may also drag in China. This is a complicated issue. If they push for [an international tribunal] we will dig up the past and present our own case."[73]

Many human rights groups had already condemned the UN's "draft proposal" because it was such a marked departure from the recommendations of the war crimes specialists. Human Rights Watch director Kenneth Roth declared the Cambodian judiciary incapable of conducting "trials of this sensitivity and complexity." He seemed to believe that the protective mantle of sovereignty had been pierced by "universal jurisdiction" and argued that "the international community has a legitimate interest to intervene when fair trials cannot be assured or when justice will be incomplete."[74] Roth and many other human rights advocates acted as if their power extended beyond the op/ed page of The New York Times, but had "universal jurisdiction" put Pol Pot or indicted Serb general Ratko Mlladic behind bars?

Cambodian social reformer Chea Vannath was especially bothered "that nobody has ever seriously and objectively asked the Cambodians themselves how they feel about this."[75] With so many people speaking on their behalf, I was curious to find out what Cambodians themselves thought. Above all, I still did not believe that legitimate war crimes trials were within the realm of the possible. The dispute over control of any court involved fundamental questions that could not be papered over, particularly in the confusing case of Cambodia. During the fall of 1999, as the war crimes court proposal was stalling in the Cambodian parliament, I remained unconvinced that trials, legitimate or illegitimate, would be forthcoming.

8

"SHE IS NICE GIRL, BUT SHE IS SICK."

i

When I arrived in Cambodia in November 1999, Sok Sin picked me up at the airport. He was already anticipating a business boom and acting as if the war crimes tribunal was a *fait accompli*. Although I had no objections to seeing Ieng Sary and Nuon Chea in a defendant's dock, I still doubted the Cambodian prime minister's political will. Sok Sin drove to the Foreign Correspondents Club and we went upstairs. Three middle-aged American women sat in the shade of the third-story veranda, each fawning over her recently adopted or purchased Cambodian baby. Looking down at the park across the street, I watched two Mormon missionaries in bike helmets trying to recruit a Cambodian teen. Not far from them, a pedophile was trying to close the deal with a shoeshine boy. Farther on, Africans were selling counterfeit U.S. dollars. I was beginning to wonder if Cambodia's social fabric had been torn beyond repair. What had the billions of dollars in aid money and hundreds of NGOs actually achieved? Some have accused me of having a perverse eye for the grotesque, but to ignore all of this was to blind myself in one eye. Cambodian Touch Bunnil shared my suspicions: "Whether it is a Frenchman molesting children in his care, or a Christian hospital forcing an alien religion on the dying . . . Cambodians should feel uneasy and must question whether Cambodia needs over 300 NGOs."[1]

Many everyday Cambodians were growing increasingly frustrated with the two-tiered system of justice maintained by Hun Sen's Cambodian People's Party government and the impunity it afforded the rich and well connected. Although there were fewer weapons in Phnom Penh in 1999, there were disturbing new trends in street justice. Many Cambodians were losing faith in the police and judiciary, and civilians formed impromptu tribunals, handing down and carrying out death sentences with shocking regularity. Get caught stealing a motorcycle, get lynched or stoned to death. That was now "customary law." Cambodian Police Chief Cham Sitha believed that a daylight lynching in his district was bad because he had to pay (112,000 *riels*, less than $40) for the victim's cremation. However, things could have been much worse: "If either of those two [Mormon] missionaries had gotten killed, I'd have lost my job."[2] The Cambodians understood the double standard and accepted it.

Some of the powerful wives of Cambodia's rulers were getting revenge their own way: disfiguring their husbands' mistresses, or "second wives," with acid attacks. The question of impunity became impossible to ignore after Cambodia's most famous actress, Piseth Pelika, was gunned down execution style while shopping with her niece at Phnom Penh's Russian Market. In the coming months, the French magazine *L'Express* would publish extracts from her diary that revealed that she had been Hun Sen's mistress and suggested she had been killed on the orders of Hun Sen's wife, Bun Rany.[3] Karaoke singer Tat Marina was eating in the Olympic Market with her young niece when a woman grabbed her by the hair and dragged her to the ground. Five men beat her unconscious and poured several liters of nitric acid on her face. The singer's brother-in-law, chasing the perpetrators, saw a man rip smoking, acid-soaked pants off his body and a woman with vapors rising from her dress flee in a waiting car. They were later identified as the bodyguard and wife of Cambodian Under-Secretary of State Svay Sitha, with whom Tat Marina had been having an affair.[4] When asked if she would seek justice, Tat Marina said, "We are so poor, we have no power. We have no money and even if we complain to the court, we will lose."[5]

Even more ominous than the one-party state that had emerged in the wake of UNTAC, the war crimes impunity enjoyed by former Khmer Rouge now running the country, or the political corruption to rival the Lon Nol regime was AIDS. The fate of a dozen old Khmer Rouge leaders did not compare to the threat the disease posed to everyday Cambodians. It was well known that the virus was running rampant in the rabbit warren brothels of Tuol Kok and Kilometer 11, where drunken soldiers purchased sex in small wooden cubicles for a few dollars. While condoms were available, so were AIDS "prevention" creams and protective amulets.

There was one AIDS patient recorded in Cambodia in 1991.[6] The first official AIDS death was in 1995; while there were 1,000 official cases of HIV infection that year, the true number was much higher. The rate of blood donor HIV also rose dramatically: from .08 percent in 1991 to 4.3 percent in 1994 to a staggering 6.76 percent in 1995.[7] Ignorance about modern medicine and basic hygiene was illustrated by an article in *Chivit Kamsan*, a Cambodian magazine, claiming that women whose partners used condoms increased their risk of cancer: "This is because the women . . . cannot get the sperms from the men . . . therefore they lose the capacity to prevent breast cancer." According to Cambodian reporter Moeun Chhean Nariddh of the *Phnom Penh Post*, "Others claimed that AIDS was invented for condom manufacturers and that AIDS could be transmitted by mosquitoes. One newspaper had published advertisements for a 'cure' for AIDS offered by traditional healers."[8]

The outlandish stories and spurious cures were only the tip of the perverted iceberg. Western entrepreneurs like Dan Sandler saw Cambodia as a paradise where anything could be purchased; spreading AIDS wouldn't stand in the way of their erotic pleasure. A sadomasochistic pedophile brothel/club called Rape Camp offered discounts for patrons with HIV-negative test results; a positive result only meant a higher price.

> Welcome to the Rape Camp!
> Welcome to the year 2000
> Welcome to Kampuchea
> It's not just a live video chat
> It's an international experience.

Sandler, the Rape Camp Web site creator, described Cambodia as "the land of impunity. . . . No stalking laws here." Cambodia was a country where "a female must serve a man on request," he wrote. Virgin girls were also popular and cost US$300–700. Furthermore, many Cambodian men believed that sex with a virgin could cure AIDS.[9]

Most of the bars in Phnom Penh were staffed by attractive young Khmer women whom one expatriate discreetly labeled "the long-black-haired language instructors." Over the years, many of my western colleagues had fallen in love with these mysterious beauties, but rarely did things seem to work out. One night I was eating dinner at an outdoor restaurant attached to a bar and noticed a stunning Khmer girl of eighteen or twenty, with high cheekbones, long black hair, and a statuesque bearing, on the arm of a well-dressed Frenchman. He was in a navy blue, double-breasted blazer with shiny brass buttons; she wore a long silk skirt. They made a splendid couple, even if it was only for the night. A few days later at the same bistro, a Cambodian man rushed in, yelling and running toward the beautiful bar girl. When he grabbed her, she broke from his grip, covered her ears with both hands, and put our table between herself and her pursuer. I happened to be dining with a Thai boxer who easily restrained the man while the bar's owner walked the girl out to the street and sent her home on a mototaxi. It was clear that something very serious was going on; the beautiful girl's countenance had changed in a split second as a result of whatever the Cambodian man had said. Even as she was driving away on the back of the moto, she never removed her hands from her ears. When the restaurant owner came back inside, she sensed my curiosity and said in passing, "She is nice girl, but she is sick."[10]

A few days after my arrival, I read that Im Chan, the man who had jolted me from my academic complacency and humbled me in 1994, had died. Chan had forced me to face how irrelevant many of my questions about war crimes were to the actual victims. Did it really matter to Cambodians whether the Khmer Rouge atrocities were classified as "genocide" or "crimes against humanity"? Two million people had died in less than four years, most simply worked to death.

My moto driver zigzagged around the puddles of black water on the road that ran alongside Tuol Sleng Museum. We followed our ears to the apartment building where the funeral service was in progress. A man in a white shirt confirmed that this indeed was Im Chan's funeral and led me up a flight of stairs into a room full of mourners and chanting monks. Chan's widow and sons were easily identifiable by their freshly shorn heads. On an altar sat a picture of the Carver and some of his possessions surrounded by flowers. After the ceremony, I met the Carver's eldest, teenaged son and told him that his father had taught me a great deal. He seemed genuinely touched and invited me to join the funeral party for a lunch of noodle soup with baby birds. During the meal, Chan's artist colleagues described a very different man from the one I had interviewed. I was glad to learn that his art had brought him solace.[11] I owed a great debt to Chan: he had not only humbled me, he had also made me rethink my most basic assumptions.

ii

A few days later, Sok Sin called me from his car and said that he was "coming by with a friend from Anlong Veng." When the familiar white Toyota sedan pulled up to the Cathay Hotel, Tuol Sleng photographer Nhem En smiled at me from the passenger seat. En was back in Phnom Penh after helping to broker a deal between the breakaway faction of Khmer Rouge at Anlong Veng and Hun Sen. En showed me a laminated identification card with his photo and the insignia of the CPP. He had been made a member of the party, but once the deal had been cut En was unceremoniously cast aside. Now he had a new career: En stayed at Sok Sin's guesthouse while the master fixer pimped him for interviews.

Television crews from all nations were taxed equally for the smallest scraps of secondhand information. Sok Sin would somberly inform visiting foreign journalists that he was going to Anlong Veng to find En. It would take several days and be a very dangerous job, but for them, he would bring En back to Phnom Penh. Sok Sin would then lie low in Phnom Penh for a few days and let the suspense build. Just when the reporters were about to give up hope, he would appear with En. But that was the least of it. A natural-born scammer, En got wise to the western press quickly. Now that it was safe to return to Anlong Veng, he went on regular reconnaissance missions, searching for saleable Khmer Rouge historical artifacts.

There was only one problem with En's new interest in history: he was hawking photographs and film that belonged in Cambodian archives. By selling them to the highest bidder, En was scattering them to the winds. I knew that he had already sold film footage to Japanese TV and others. Craig Smith of *The Wall Street Journal* nailed En in an article entitled "Profiting from His Shots of Pol Pot's Terror." Smith described Nhem En as "a disturbingly dispassionate 37-year-old former Khmer Rouge guerilla, handsome and robust, interested now in making money on the notoriety, that . . . these photographs have brought him in the West."[12]

My old friends Chris Riley and Doug Niven had come under fire for a book of Tuol Sleng photographs they had edited, *The Killing Fields,* published in 1996. Although it won numerous awards and was widely and favorably reviewed, some bitterly criticized the book's format because they believed it trivialized the photographs. This was a perfectly reasonable aesthetic point, but the sad truth was that there was little interest in publishing the Tuol Sleng photos. Twin Palm Press agreed to publish the book with a historical essay by David Chandler, but while Niven, Riley, and their team of volunteers would get to select the actual images, the format and title of the book were out of their hands.

New York's Museum of Modern Art had displayed a handful of Tuol Sleng images in a small gallery in June 1997. In a review, "Killing Fields of Vision," published in *The Village Voice*, Guy Trebay charged Riley, Niven, and MOMA with cultivating "ignorance about Southeast Asia." I was floored by Trebay's error-studded opening paragraph: "The wounds of Pol Pot's spectacularly psychotic Maoist regime still afflict that ravaged country, where as many as 2 million people were systematically murdered over a four-year, CIA-supported civil war." Trebay believed that "The artifacts of the killing fields are put on display in glossy art books and museums. The Cambodian dead are held up for consideration in the cool light of formalist concerns."

After savaging MOMA for showing the photos, Trebay moved on to Niven and Riley and got more personal: "Although motivated initially by a desire to save the precious negatives from destruction, Riley's and Niven's ensuing decision to sell art-quality portfolios of 100 prints from the Tuol Sleng archive, and to obtain international copyright on them for their recently incorporated non-profit organization, raises serious questions." Niven and Riley had done an excellent job restoring and reprinting the original negatives, but nobody got rich in the process. In fact, when they finished their work in Phnom Penh in 1994, they were deeply in debt. What money was generated by sales and museum shows still did not cover their debts.[13]

Unlike many western journalists and historians, Youk Chhang, the director of the Documentation Center of Cambodia (DC Cam), and his team of Cambodian researchers adhered to a strict policy: no paid interviews, no bribery—squeaky clean. The center had been started by westerners in 1995 and taken over by Cambodians in 1997 when Youk Chhang succeeded Craig Etcheson. Their work was truly nonprofit. Chhang was baffled by Niven and Riley's decision to copyright the Tuol Sleng photographs. And the DC Cam director was definitely not a fan of Nhem En or Sok Sin. Chhang flatly refused to play En's games, and I didn't blame them. I, however, couldn't resist the lure.

Sok Sin drove me to his guesthouse and led me to En's room. The Tuol Sleng photographer handed me a stack of unfamiliar photos that were the Khmer Rouge equivalent of Hitler's *Berchtesgaden* photos. They were of the Khmer Rouge leaders at play: Nuon Chea smiling and holding Pol Pot's baby daughter; Pol Pot on the beach dressed like a Waikiki tourist; Ta Mok yukking it up with peasants; Pol Pot inspecting souvenirs in a Thai gift shop. Most were just innocuous snapshots that would have been banal had they not captured a human side of the leaders of one of the most brutal regimes of the twentieth century. Sok Sin was aggressively pushing me to buy the photos and I knew that he had quietly lined up buyers in case I balked. My feelings were mixed; I sensed a hustle and did not trust En. I made a counteroffer: no deal without the original negatives and exclusive publication rights. En hemmed and hawed, but I held firm.

When I interviewed En that day, I noticed that he had become a very practiced performer since I had first met him. Rarely did he break from his script; when I tried to press him, I got only metaphors. "If I look at the years 1977 and 1978, the situation now is quite different. It was like being a frog in a well that can only see the sky."

I began to wonder if En viewed the reign of the Khmer Rouge negatively at all. He certainly had not been punished for his role; if anything, we curious westerners were rewarding him. I tried to get him to answer my original question. "Now that you can see far and wide, how do you look back on working in Tuol Sleng and the reign of the Khmer Rouge? Do you see them as a model government? Something that should be tried again?"

En shook his head and compared the Khmer Rouge leaders unfavorably with Hun Sen, "who knows nothing but how to lead the country well. The Khmer Rouge leaders who were well educated led the country crazily."

En surprised me when he announced that he supported the UN's plan for an international trial for the surviving Khmer Rouge leaders. "As far as I know, the 1978 to 1995 Khmer Rouge leaders must be tried. The Khmer Rouge leadership has made me suffer." He was especially riled up by the fact that today, those people have money and security. "I do not like their leadership. In the end, we were all injured. Look!" En exclaimed and pointed to a bullet scar on his leg. "If the Khmer Rouge leaders are tried by the UN, I would be pleased to be a witness because I really know their activities."

"What would you testify to?" I asked.

"The evidence I will get from Tuol Sleng."

According to Nhem En, the political organization of the Khmer Rouge was very simple; the leadership consisted of Pol Pot, Ieng Sary, Son Sen, and Nuon Chea: "They all know everything. If there was no order from the top leaders, no one dared to kill. We could only kill ordinary people by ourselves, but for high-ranking people from the district level or Americans, or diplomats brought back from other countries—if they did not order us to kill them, they would not die."

I found En very sanctimonious for someone many would consider a war criminal and asked him, "How do you respond to those that say the branch of the tree should also be punished?"

POL POT AND FLOWER
DC CAM

"If they are tried by the UN, I think that the people below are like rubbish," he replied.

Sok Sin continued to insist that I buy all of the photographs, but I continued to hold out for the negatives and exclusive rights. Although I had mixed feelings about putting hundreds of dollars in En's pocket, too much from the Khmer Rouge archives had vanished into private hands, and this was a chance to salvage something for DC Cam. When I showed the photos to a couple of colleagues later, they agreed that albeit strange, the snapshots were historically significant.

Nhem En supposedly returned to Anlong Veng to find the negatives but was still not back on the day of my departure. Hours before I was to leave for the airport, Sok Sin found me having coffee with a friend and told me that En had returned. We went back to Sok Sin's guesthouse, and En handed me two plastic sleeves filled with negatives. I held them up to the light and was somewhat reassured to see that they were of the same photos, at least. Sok Sin asked me for my fountain pen and the contract that I had written on a piece of notebook paper. He made three small beads of red ink across the bottom. "I will make thumbprint, and En will take serious," Sok Sin said before barking at En, grabbing his thumb, and pressing it into the ink and then onto the paper. The deal was closed.

When I returned to the United States, Del and Wes, my photo technicians, told me that the Pol Pot snapshots Nhem En had sold me weren't originals—someone had very carefully taken photographs of photographs. "They did a good job," Wes added. En had simply rephotographed the prints and given me the new negatives to shut me up. Even better, the *Phnom Penh Post* published some of the same photographs within months. En had sold all of us the same pictures and exclusive rights![14] I sent my set of photos to Youk Chhang. DC Cam has since published many in their monthly magazine *Searching for the Truth*.

iii

One of the few encouraging developments resulting from the debate over Khmer Rouge accountability was the prominent role assumed by Cambodian institutions like Chea Vannath's Center for Social Development, established in 1995, and Youk Chhang's Documentation Center of Cambodia. Vannath held public forums in three different cities under the banner "National Reconciliation and the Khmer Rouge," and invited prominent former Khmer Rouge as well as ordinary citizens. She believed that trials were only a topical solution that did not address Cambodia's profound social problems: "We Cambodians need to sit down and talk about this issue, to exchange views and discuss openly. That also includes hearing the opinion of the minority—in this case, the KR." Vannath took a holistic view of the situation. "We Cambodians must know the truth … of the events that happened during the Khmer Rouge period. It is important for our grandchildren to know their history." At the first forum, in Battambang in February 2000, Khmer Rouge leaders like Long Norin continued to warn that war crimes trials might reignite the civil war: "If there is a trial against those who defected, it seems that the lesson we pass on to our children is not to integrate, but to keep fighting until we win."[15]

While Youk Chhang supported the efforts of Chea Vannath, he was wary of providing the Khmer Rouge with yet another outlet for their propaganda. Chhang was a hardliner. As a young teen, he had watched a Khmer Rouge soldier slit his sister's pregnant belly, believing she was carrying not a baby but stolen rice. Before that he had nearly been killed for picking watercress for the same starving sister. "This act was considered criminal under the Khmer Rouge regime, so they hit me with an ax, pushed me to the ground, tied me up with rope, and put me in jail for weeks." His mother did not cry when they

POL POT WITH NEIGHBOR CHILDREN
DC CAM

were torturing him because "crying was also a crime under the Khmer Rouge regime."[16] Youk Chhang believed the proper venue for a dialogue between former Khmer Rouge leaders and their victims was a courtroom, not a group therapy session. "We have already suffered so much and still granted them so much patience. Now only law can deal with the KR. Besides, what would a criminal say if you asked him whether he should stand trial? What would a criminal say if you asked him what his punishment should be?"[17]

Youk Chhang had taken over the controversy-plagued and State Department–funded Cambodian Genocide Project in 1997.[18] In 1994, the State Department had awarded Yale professor Ben Kiernan a $500,000 grant to investigate Cambodian war crimes. There was a conservative outcry and soon Kiernan was a favorite whipping boy of *The Wall Street Journal*. That spring, a group of conservative U.S. Senators led by Bob Dole, Trent Lott, and Jesse Helms wrote to U.S. Secretary of State Warren Christopher calling for Kiernan's removal as head of the project. Under the direction of Kiernan and Craig Etcheson, Yale's project did an excellent job, given the endless political attacks.[19] In 1997, Youk Chhang, who had not only survived the Khmer Rouge regime but also gone on to become the country's leading archivist of the Khmer Rouge regime, transformed the Documentation Center of Cambodia (DC Cam) into a truly Cambodian institution: an independent research institute, staffed by Cambodians and dedicated to documenting the history of Pol Pot's Democratic Kampuchea. Every member of the center's all-Cambodian staff began as a volunteer and "worked their way up from the bottom." DC Cam strongly advocated war crimes trials: "The punishment of the Khmer Rouge leaders is the most effective way in which Cambodia can begin to dismantle this culture of impunity and build a new Cambodia on the basis of law." Chhang believed that Cambodians could not forgive one another "until they know who to forgive, and for what," and stated that DC Cam's "focus on memory and justice seeks to assist Cambodians in discovering the truths upon which a genuine national reconciliation depends."[20]

DC Cam, funded by grants and gifts, went far beyond sponsoring lectures and issuing utopian sermons about international law, the specialties of all too many western academic organizations. Their team of Cambodian researchers was busy recovering documents and photographs, conducting remarkable oral history interviews, and mapping killing fields using ArcInfo Geographic Information System (GIS) GPS technology to record their exact latitude and longitude. DC Cam researcher Kosal Phat reported that "On the average, the Khmer Rouge killed 5,200 people every week for a period of 3 years, 8 months, and twenty days. Another million people died due to the general serious mistreatment and neglect of the Democratic Kampuchea government, from such causes as starvation, disease, lack of medicine and forced labor."[21] Since 1995, the mapping team has located over 400 genocide sites. If anything, it appears the tally of Cambodians killed between 1975 and 1979 will be closer to two million than one. Many of DC Cam's findings have been published in the monthly magazine *Searching for the Truth*. Khmer-language copies are distributed free throughout Cambodia with the intention of offsetting decades of propaganda.[22] In addition to ongoing genocide research, legal analysis, and a family-tracing page, *Searching for the Truth* publishes editorials by Chhang that often spark public debates within Cambodia. He believes that the memories "are hard to take, but too precious to remain untold."[23]

When the issue of war crimes trials first began to be discussed, the DC Cam director was outraged by the Khmer Rouge rhetoric of national reconciliation: "The gall of such talk from the same people who wreaked havoc on Cambodia defies comprehension. How can you reconcile with the people who killed your own family?" He pointed out a sad truth that many observers far from Cambodia were happy to ignore: "sufficient laws and evidence are not lacking, but political will is in the case to prosecute the Khmer Rouge leaders."[24] Pushing the debate, Chhang had taken some very compelling stands. For example, he argued that for the sake of historical clarity it was better to grant Ieng Sary "a clear amnesty from war crimes prosecution" along with a lifetime ban from "participation in Cambodian politics on political grounds, rather than to pretend that he will not be tried because evidence and law are lacking." To accept Ieng Sary's claim that he knew and saw nothing was to begin the "process of historical revisionism."[25]

I had been impressed by Youk Chhang's strong position when China attempted to undermine the planned war crimes court. "China seems to act as if they're the only country that can interfere in Cambodia's affairs. Who do they think they are?" He found it ridiculous that China was now invoking the principle of "noninterference" given their historical relations with Cambodia. Chhang pointed to an unpleasant truth, China was the only nation to back the Khmer Rouge from beginning to end through thick and thin: "Their interference cost almost two million lives."[26]

iv

Doug Niven wrote me early in 2000 that according to test results, Nhem En either was HIV positive or had full-blown AIDS. Even though En had hoodwinked me on the Pol Pot photos, I was still fascinated by this character. I wanted to show him the East German documentaries and ask him for more information. I also naïvely wondered if facing his own mortality might change En's view of the past. Coincidentally, the Chinese leader was making the first state visit to Cambodia since the reign of the Khmer Rouge on November 13 and 14, 2000. I decided to return and see how Cambodians would receive the Chinese leader.

Sok Sin was grinning from ear to ear when he met me at Pochentong Airport. As we walked through the parking lot, he told me that he had completed his guesthouse. He stopped suddenly and the brake lights of a smart, silver mini Toyota Land Cruiser flashed as its alarm chirped. Sok Sin pointed to the Toyota. He finally had done it: just hours before, he had taken delivery of his first "high-profile" vehicle. According to Sok Sin, this would help us in many ways: "They don't stop high-caliber car. Poor car they stop. High-caliber car, they think they are colonel, general, or something like that. Police do not stop high-profile car. Get many interviews now." He was certain that he would be able to get us onto the tarmac for the Chinese president's arrival. Sok Sin solemnly informed me that the time had come for me to leave the research behind and become a "high-profile journalist." I would need to stay in "high-profile" hotels, wear safari suits, trade my boots for loafers, and swear off taking mototaxis.

After getting settled at my guesthouse, I went to the office of the *Phnom Penh Post* and spoke to the paper's cofounder, Kathleen O'Keefe, who confirmed that Nhem En had tested HIV positive. Sok Sin called a few days later to tell me that En was at his house. When we met again shortly thereafter, the Tuol Sleng photographer looked much the same. I asked him how long he had known he was HIV positive. "When I frequently came to see you, I was already infected." En appeared more emotional than during our previous interviews. He said, "Every day, I try to control my feelings. I tell you the truth, I've controlled my feeling for two years." I wondered if this terminal disease had changed En's view of the past, and asked if he found it strange that he had survived decades of war only to contract a lethal virus. "I joined the revolution when I was ten years old. I had come across hundreds of kilometers of minefields, but I never had any accidents. I am very sorry now that I have bad honor and won't have a future." He paused and added, "I wanted to tell you [about having AIDS] before, but didn't dare to do so."[27]

En continued to insist that he wholeheartedly supported war crimes trials for the Khmer Rouge leaders and was ready to testify. Above all, he claimed that he wanted some clarity, some explanation: why had the regime he'd supported gone so horribly wrong? Like so many former Khmer Rouge,

En acted as if he too were a victim, not one of the elite. While he readily acknowledged that the period 1975–1979 was bad for most Cambodians, he maintained that his own life did not change until 1995. Nhem En said that many Khmer Rouge rank and file were now miserable too and wanted to see their former leaders "shot and killed or put in jail. The people badly want to know." I reminded En that Chinese President Jiang Zemin was arriving in Cambodia the next day, and asked what he thought about the reemerging Cambodia–China alliance and the recent Chinese denial of any responsibility for the Khmer Rouge. "China was the reason why the Khmers had this disaster," En insisted. "If the West had been involved, there wouldn't be so many Khmers dead and the Khmers would not be miserable like this."

In that day's *Phnom Penh Post*, Ieng Sary's assistant Suong Sikeoun was quoted as saying that China bore no responsibility for Khmer Rouge atrocities. I asked En for his opinion; he shook his head and rolled his eyes. "During the three years period [1975–1978], Chinese institutions were all over Phnom Penh—in factories, agriculture, industry, commerce, and public works. Naval techniques, military techniques, machinery, and planes were all brought from China. So why did he say China hadn't interfered? It was interfering. Now, put the period from '75 to '79 aside. From '79 to '80 and the Paris Agreement on Cambodia, who were not interfering? The Khmer Rouge only had its penis! All the shorts, clothes, boots, caps and everything were [provided] by China. Everything was from China. So who was helping? It was China!" Did the UN's deferential relationship to China and overcautiousness about Cambodia during the 1980s bother him? "The UN shouldn't have been afraid of China. It controlled more than 180 countries, so they shouldn't have allowed the Chinese to interfere." Was there a lot of Chinese aid to the Khmer Rouge at the border camps? "From what I saw with my own eyes, the aid was mostly from China. Everything was from China."

I told En that I would show him the East German documentary films on Tuol Sleng after the Chinese state visit. En explained that he was in Phnom Penh looking for a Cambodian doctor who could "cure" his AIDS. When I tried to explain that although there was no cure, with the proper medications, one could live with the virus for many years, he remained unconvinced. When he began to complain about his poverty, I asked him what he had done with the money from the photographs he had sold. He said that he had already spent it on "cures."

As Sok Sin drove me back to my guesthouse, we compared western and Cambodian views on health. The fixer was a man of the twentieth century, but he also adhered to some quite shocking traditional medical practices. He told me that he, too, was currently getting "vitamin shots" from an herbal doctor. I wondered if he was undergoing a midlife crisis—if Cambodians had such things. Maybe it was all this talk of health with En, but I had never re-membered Sok Sin worrying about his health.

Sok Sin peppered me with another endless stream of questions about health care, diet, medicine, and sex the next morning as we drove to a *Bangskol*, a Buddhist memorial ceremony for the victims of the Pol Pot regime at Choeung Ek. The weather was soggy and gray, and we were among the first arrivals. A large Plexiglas *stupa*, or monument, was filled with skulls and bones that had been found and dug up a few dozen yards away. An old Buddhist monk stood at the top, staring intently into the eye sockets of the skull he was cradling with both hands. Sok Sin pointed out a member of the Cambodian parliament. I approached him and asked if the ceremony had been timed to coincide with the arrival of the Chinese delegation. He admit-ted that the timing was intended to "show Jiang, not to demonstrate against, but to quietly remember. We want to celebrate the day and inform the Chinese that they participated in killing." Did he believe that war crimes trials were a possibility? While he supported the idea, he did not believe his government was interested in holding trials: "Still too many communists!"[28]

Sok Sin approached a group of women with shaved heads who were standing next to us at the top of the stupa and asked if they were willing to be interviewed. An older peasant woman, maybe fifty, with reddish-black, betel nut–stained teeth spoke first. "I am here to participate in a religious ceremony for those who died," she said. "I always want to come to celebrate, everyone suffered before they died." The crowd began to grow around us, and as the first woman continued to speak, another began to sob. The older woman consoled her and explained to me, "She lost her husband and child." More and more women were gathering, all of them speaking at once, pour-ing out their stories in torrents of tears, words, wails—a psychic dam had broken. Sok Sin could not keep up with the translations, but his shorthand was all too familiar: "Starving, work, overworked, overworked and killed, no period, cannot be sick impossible, herbal medicine was rabbit shit." Up to this point, I really had only seen Sok Sin's tough side, but now I watched him ap-proach the women with tenderness and respect. In an instant, they trusted him. As reporter Seth Mydans had so aptly put it, Sok Sin was "burdened with a tender heart."[29]

Finally, Sam Rainsy's wife, Tioulong Saumara, arrived. I approached and asked her about the purpose of the ceremony. "The students stirred some debate [about the Chinese visit] so some of us decided to pray, to meditate—to remember."[30] Sok Sin and I had to rush to the airport for the Chinese president's arrival. We walked toward the car as the crowd of a hundred, with thirty Buddhist monks, gathered under the tarps to begin their ritual. A misty rain suited the occasion and their sad, buzzing chants hung in the air.

As we neared the airport, it became clear that Phnom Penh's schoolchildren had been given the day off. Close to 100,000 of them lined the streets for miles, listless in the broiling late morning sun. Their placards bore not very flattering portraits of Mr. and Mrs. Zemin. Sok Sin said that his children had also been issued signs and were curbside: "They are not happy, my children all must stand in the sun with no water! Even the little ones! They do not like!" We were stopped by soldiers, but Sok Sin knew the commanding officer and sure enough, our "high-profile" vehicle was allowed to drive all the way to the airport as if it were the lead car in a diplomatic procession. "See! See! High-profile car! We get many interviews now," Sok Sin chortled with glee. By the time we got to the tarmac, there was a rumor circulating that an anti-Chinese protest at the university had been quickly quashed by "counter-demonstrators" and police. Jiang would be in Phnom Penh for less than twenty-four hours, and his only scheduled interaction with the press was a twenty-minute press conference to be conducted by Zhu Bangzoa, first spokesman for the People's Republic of China, at the Hotel Le Royal.[31]

There was a huge turnout at Pochentong. Even King Sihanouk had come to greet the Chinese leader. First to arrive was a plane full of Chinese media and security personnel. The Chinese press crashed the media area like an Australian rugby team at last call, easily elbowing their western "colleagues" out of the way. Chinese security goons in dark suits, carrying rifles in what looked like nylon guitar cases, fanned out across the red carpet. Finally the Chinese leader's plane landed. After the ceremonial greetings, the Chinese delegation was whisked off to a series of private meetings with King Sihanouk, Prince Ranariddh, and Hun Sen.

That evening at Hotel Le Royal, the Chinese spokesman read a prepared statement that described the visit as a "major event of great importance" and the friendly reception by 200,000 Cambodians as evidence of the strength of Cambodian–Chinese friendship. Zhu Bangzoa reported that after an "in-depth exchange of views" among Jiang, King Sihanouk, Hun Sen, and Prince Ranariddh, they had reached a "complete consensus." The Chinese spokesman was heartened by Cambodia's rejection of Taiwan's independence and its "adherence to a one China policy." When the floor was opened for questions, one reporter asked if there had been any discussion of the proposed Khmer Rouge trial. "I can tell you explicitly that question was not covered," Zhu Bangzoa replied sharply; he then dismissed the trial question as a "Cambodian internal affair." Phelim Kyne from the *Phnom Penh Post* asked why the UN Secretary-General's Special Representative for human rights in Cambodia, Thomas Hammerberg, had publicly pointed to Chinese pressure as a key factor undermining international support for a war crimes trial. Zhu Bangzoa vehemently denied the charge. "China always followed one principle—noninterference in internal affairs."[32]

When a Cambodian reporter asked for a comment on the Cambodian students' demand for an official Chinese apology, the spokesman reminded him that "Democratic Kampuchea was actually recognized by the international community." He then abdicated responsibility for any Khmer Rouge deviations from the script that China had authored in 1979: China "did not support the wrong policies made by the Khmer Rouge leadership." After precisely twenty minutes, Zhu Bangzoa declared the press conference over; when a reporter tried to ask one last question, he snapped, "No!"[33]

V

I resumed my interview with Nhem En after the Chinese delegation left Phnom Penh. Above all, I wanted to know how his life had changed since his years working at S-21. "I think of a hundred things. I think of the past when I passed through the storm of the war," En said, visibly distraught. Not only was he poor, but soon his children would be orphans. If he grew too sick, he said, he would "commit suicide without the knowledge of my wife and children. I can now walk, but I won't cause any difficulties to my wife if I become too sick."[34]

I played him the videotape of the East German film on S-21, *Kampuchea: Death and Rebirth*. The first image was especially ghastly: two men whose throats had been cut so deeply that they were decapitated, with their stomachs cut from belly button to sternum. I asked En why these people had been so brutally butchered. "This was to show to Pol Pot lest he didn't believe the man was killed," he replied. I fast-forwarded to an image of two more dead men, throats similarly slashed and stomachs split open and pulled apart like lapels. What was it like to take these gruesome photos? "I took photos of six people. But there was another expert [photographer] named Sry," En said dismissively.

I fast-forwarded to an image of a Cambodian woman who had returned from France. She was dead and had rope burns on her neck. "Did you take this photo?" I asked.

"There were five or ten people who had a rope burned on their necks," En replied.

Was she from France? "There were so many of them coming, but I didn't take notice of them," En replied.

So after taking the photos, you just forgot them? "There were too many." He shrugged.

Who received the photographs after the prisoners had been killed? "Those who saw them were none other than Duch, Chan, and Hor." En also made an interesting admission further implicating Him Huy: "Huy also knew this, but I don't think he dares to speak. Huy knew best, but he is afraid [to talk]. That's why I told him the other day that: 'Don't be afraid. Just talk, you wouldn't be taken to be killed.' But he was afraid and didn't dare to talk about the truth. But I don't hide the truth."

Nhem En said that he still did not fear a trial. "Let them do so. I was a pho-tographer, nobody would have known this if I hadn't taken photographs. And if I didn't do it, I would also die!" En taunted me: "So, if they also take me to the trial, those who are thirty years old and older must be taken to the trial as long as they are in Cambodia. Now, the population of Cambodia is twelve million. So, twelve million minus six million [and] the six million must be taken to trial, because we don't know." En believed that if the Khmer Rouge leaders were not tried, it would "be a bad influence on the world."

I cued the video to the section on the S-21 employees. Photos of prisoners and guards flashed onto the screen and En began to narrate. Chan, one of the top Tuol Sleng guards who has remained underground, came on. "Chan is now living at Phnom Malay." Can you find him? "If there is money, I will go and find him. But I've heard that they are trying to hide him." En continued, "This guy's name is Soeun. He came from Kompong Chhnang, he's a guard, he's still alive. I met him once in Kompong Chhnang." Suddenly En's eyes bugged. He stood up and rushed toward the television: "Yes! This is Chorn!" he exclaimed. En turned to me and asked with genuine amazement, "How could they get this photo? He is my relative! He is my distant cousin! This guy was killed. He lived in my village!" Like many, Chorn began as a guard at S-21 and wound up a prisoner. En said that when Chorn was accused he didn't dare to ask why, and after he took this photograph, he simply walked away.

Two photos of Chorn were on the screen, side by side. In the first he was a guard and in the second, he was a prisoner. En shook his head and made a clucking sound as he moved close to the television and began to read the document on the screen. "It's very clear—Trangil village, Trangil commune, Kompong Leng district, Kompong Chhnang province. This photograph was to be attached to the biography. I'll go and tell his relatives. His relatives named Ran and Reth didn't believe [he was killed]." I asked if anyone had defended Chorn. En looked at me as if I were crazy. "No. Definitely, nobody dared to say anything. If they dared to say anything, they would also be arrested. They had their slogan that 'Whose hair it is belongs to whose head it is.'"

I next showed En the interview with Ieng Sary and his claim that Vietnamese agents were responsible for the Cambodian genocide. En shook his head in dismay. "There might be some Vietnamese agents. But in fact, it was Nuon Chea, Ieng Sary, Son Sen, and Pol Pot who gave the orders!" What did he make of Sary's 1980 claim that he was a supporter of Ronald Reagan? "His mind was communist, totally following the Chinese. It's normal. As I've said, when it had come to this stage, he just said things upside down according to his will." Did it bother En that Ieng Sary was flying around the world first class, wearing nice suits, and drinking expensive wine, while En was fighting the Vietnamese? "In fact, it was not only me, but all the former Khmer Rouge were angry with him. He, his partisans and relatives had traveled and enjoyed themselves in Thailand, China, Korea, and America. After he came back from the pleasure trips, he tightened up on his own Khmer Rouge guys." Did En consider the young cadres at S-21 perpetrators or victims? En said only that he believed those who worked at S-21 were considered the best people of Angkar, "the number one people of Cambodia."

I commented that En seemed to still have a soft spot for the old ways of the Khmer Rouge. "Yes," he agreed, "because I was an ignorant and uneducated person in the countryside. But then I could come to Phnom Penh and go to study in China, I even knew how to shoot a film, video, and to make a map. This is something that should be considered."

"What is so great about that?" I wondered aloud.

"It was wonderful, because I was a child of farmers in the countryside and I could come to study and I learned something. And I had a sort of knowledge that I shouldn't have had. That's one thing. Another thing is that there were enough food to eat and clothes to wear. Nothing was hard." Maybe nothing was hard for Nhem En, the prince of the Khmer Rouge, but what about the millions of "New People" who perished between 1975 and 1979? En expressed no remorse: "Looking back to the past, talking about regret, I don't regret. But life is different between now and then. First, we had equality at that time. But the difference now is that the poor remain poor and the rich remain rich."

I asked if Hun Sen's Cambodia seemed worse than the reign of the Khmer Rouge to him. Nhem En was "pessimistic" because he considered himself a "lower [less important] person in this present society." According to him, communism, not the Khmer Rouge, was the culprit because communist regimes kill in the same instinctive way that birds fly and fish swim: "In general, all the communist countries in the world killed people. A communist country needed to abolish the capitalists, the feudal, the intellectuals [and the high-ranking] personalities."

It was hard for me to understand En's continued admiration for Pol Pot. I told him that today, most historians agree that the Khmer Rouge was one of the worst regimes of the twentieth century. They killed millions and people still starved! En begged to differ. He said that today, rural Cambodians, "ordinary people praise Pol Pot." He believed that life was better under Pol Pot, "it was very easy [and] there were no rich or poor people. It was equal."

It wasn't very equal if you were educated or urbane, I countered. "The two million who died were mostly the New People. As I said at the beginning, the communist regime needed to abolish the rich, the capitalist, the feudal, the intellectuals, the teachers, and the students." Why did they kill these people? "If they didn't kill, people would oppose them," En said. Then he recited a poem from the Khmer Rouge era: "'If you did something wrong, you were an enemy, and if you did something right, you were an enemy.'"

I asked what was his worst memory of the Khmer Rouge years. "The worst memory was the very unjust torture." I asked for an example of a good person who was caught and tortured. "One of them was a person named Srun and another named Chorn, they were pure children of farmers from the [home] district, they were very good people. But they were accused of being enemies when they let prisoners escape [and] didn't cook rice well. This was excessive and unjust."

What did you think then? "It was horrible. Though I had the idea to protest and support them, but I didn't dare to do so—'Whose hair it is belongs to whose head it is.'"

I persisted: "If you knew that they were brutal and nobody was really in control, why did you stay with Pol Pot until 1995?" En argued that the Vietnamese were "taking our land" and filling it with Vietnamese illegal immigrants.

Nhem En said that he "had pity on the victims, but I didn't dare to say. Whether it was my brother or someone else's, I had my own mercy. As I told you, 'Whose hair it is belongs to whose head it is.' If you tried to find out someone else's affairs, you would also be jailed." Did you think that the revolution was eating its own? "Yes, I knew. It's an ancient saying that, 'Those who learned to become a witch would cast evil on themselves if they couldn't do it on others.'"

En repeated that before he died, he wanted to testify in a trial. "I am not afraid of death. If they think that I am a traitor, they can kill me. It's up to them."

Now came the part that I had been dreading for three days. En had re-turned to Phnom Penh with an assortment of prints to sell. He handed me the stack of images and I quickly flipped through them, setting aside four black-and-white pictures of the Khmer Rouge leaders meeting in the jungle in 1979. Then I opened my briefcase and took out a recent issue of the *Phnom Penh Post*. I showed En the photos he had sold me last time and asked how the *Post* could publish the same ones if I had purchased the exclusive rights and he had given me the original negatives.

Sok Sin cringed as he translated my question. En looked down as Sok Sin spoke, then suddenly got up and rushed out of the room. I was a bit nervous. Why had he bolted so suddenly? Sok Sin went after him and I walked out onto the balcony, wondering if I could jump if En came back for revenge. Our interaction had been building to this for several days, making me more and more uncomfortable. However, En hadn't played straight, so I was prepared to accept the consequences.

A few minutes later, they returned. Seeming to pretend as if the previous scene hadn't happened, En was begging me to buy more photographs, but I took only a handful of the new black-and-whites. He was still pleading with me for money when we said good-bye. I had gotten my interviews and on some level, had gotten even with Nhem En, but I did not feel good about it. En was a dying man and we all knew it.

9

"I AM NO LONGER HIV POSITIVE."

i

The Cambodian war crimes debate dragged on into the new millennium with basic questions still unresolved and both parties trading blame for the stalemate. UN Secretary-General Kofi Annan wrote Prime Minister Hun Sen a threatening letter in February 2000 blaming Cambodia's CPP government for the lack of progress. Neither side was willing to cede control. Furthermore, this was only a subsidiary of a larger conflict: "universal jurisdiction" versus national sovereignty.[1]

U.S. Senator John Kerry traveled to Phnom Penh again in April, attempting to restart negotiations between the United Nations and the Cambodian government. Led by Ambassador to Cambodia Kent Wiedemann and Ambassador-at-Large for War Crimes David Schaffer, the United States was beginning to play an increasingly important role as mediator and advocated a "mixed tribunal" composed of both Cambodians and UN appointees. While Wiedemann admitted that the "mixed tribunal" demanded by Cambodians was a compromise at best, he urged human rights advocates not to forego the opportunity for trials and to make "the perfect . . . the enemy of the good."[2]

Anette Marcher of the *Phnom Penh Post* asked the ambassador if he was downplaying a rumored split between the United States and the UN. "I would say that the US is not undermining the UN or any principle. We have made it clear from the beginning that we support the UN," he replied. But he admitted, "Certainly, we have offered views that do not comport with some particular lawyers within the UN and we have argued with them. But is this US pressure? Or is that the right of a member state to express his view? . . . I'm sure some human rights groups would prefer to refer to that as the US pressuring the UN to surrender its absolutely correct, maybe even sacred, legal principles." Above all, the American ambassador was amazed that human rights advocates, so eager to see justice done, were now the harshest critics of the "mixed tribunal."[3]

By June, it looked as if the UN had compromised on all the points of contention. Although the proposed court had two conspicuously complicated chambers, there was a Cambodian majority at every level. But once again, the United States and the UN were working double time to jump-start the trial discussions, and the Cambodian National Assembly had not approved the draft law. UN representative Hans Corell returned to Cambodia in early July for more meetings with the government. Corell was losing patience after the endless delays and years of fruitless debate, and suggested that unless the Hun Sen government took action, "the secretary-general would probably draw the conclusion that would be the end of the story; we cannot continue indefinitely."[4]

When Hun Sen traveled to the UN's millennial summit in New York City in September 2000, he could honestly claim that the National Assembly had begun to review the draft law, even if it had taken them seven months. Anette Marcher best described the prime minister's strategy as "One small step forward, a long pause, international pressure to continue the process, then another hesitant step, another delay and more pressure from the outside."[5]

When former Khmer Rouge commander Chhouk Rin was acquitted by a Cambodian court in late 2000 for the 1994 murder of the three western backpackers, a new wild card was tossed into the game. Although Rin had admitted attacking the train from which the tourists had been kidnapped, he got off on a legal technicality enacted after the murders: he had defected to the government under a 1994 amnesty law. Could this same law and logic be applied to surviving Khmer Rouge leaders like Ieng Sary, Khieu Samphan, and Nuon Chea in the proposed mixed tribunal, which would be Cambodian controlled? Many considered Chhouk Rin's acquittal a signal from Hun Sen to reassure former Khmer Rouge leaders that if they found themselves in a courtroom anytime soon, there was a way out.[6]

ii

The four-year debate over war crimes trials became even harder to take seriously after I received the news that Sok Sin had tested HIV positive in April 2001. He had been feeling so sick that he got a passport and traveled to Thailand for the first time in his life. Doug Niven had taken him to the best hospital in Bangkok for a series of tests and was sitting next to Sok Sin when the doctor delivered the news. "Turns out the poor guy is HIV positive, fucking harshest thing you could imagine,"[7] Niven wrote me.

There was an immune-boosting program available in Bangkok, so Niven contacted many of the reporters Sok Sin had worked with over the years and took up a collection to pay for it. Jason Barber of the *Bangkok Post* offered to put Sok Sin up during his treatment. Documentary filmmaker Lisa Miller was left with the most unenviable task: she had to break the news to Sok Sin's wives back in Phnom Penh and get them tested for HIV. Because Sok Sin's condition was not very advanced, his most immediate problem was an intestinal disorder that had plagued him for a year and left him unable to eat even his favorite Chinese noodles.[8]

While all of us westerners agreed on Sok Sin's course of action, there was only one problem—Sok Sin. He wanted to go home and deal with this, or not deal with it, his way. Niven pointed out the sad truth: "I agree about the treatment and your suggestions about lifestyle, etc., but that sounds like a strange Western fantasy to these poor guys. The stigma [of AIDS] is just too heavy in Cambodge. I had already suggested the same today and it just went right by the poor guy." Doug reminded me, "The concepts just don't exist."[9]

All in all, the trip to Bangkok had been a crushing experience for Sok Sin. Besides the diagnosis, Bangkok's efficiency, prosperity, and abundance, such a contrast to Cambodia, depressed him. While he was touched by our collective concern, he wanted no part of the treatment program. After he returned home to Phnom Penh, he turned off his mobile phone and went in search of the traditional, herbal HIV "cure" that Nhem En claimed to have found. Sok Sin was supposed to go back to Bangkok for treatment in the coming weeks, but never did. In addition to the prevailing superstitions and abundance of spurious "cures," the fact that much of Cambodian society did not see AIDS sufferers as victims further reinforced his decision to handle the problem his own way. Some compassion might have been expected from the likes of Samdech Tep Vong, one of Cambodia's top Buddhist monks. Instead, he chose denial and challenged the HIV figures, arguing that they were inflated to embarrass Cambodia. As for those already infected, "it is the mistake of the people who get AIDS. They do not have good morals."[10]

I knew that Sok Sin trusted me when it came to health and nutrition. He seemed to believe that, as Lon Nol's "magic shirts" protected his soldiers from bullets, my imported Power Bars endowed me with special strength. He had listened to my 1999 lecture to En about living with AIDS with great interest and spent the next week asking me follow-up questions. I should have guessed the reason.

An especially troubling e-mail came from reporter Seth Mydans in July. Sok Sin thought the world of Mydans and was proud of his affiliation with *The New York Times*. Over the years the pair had tracked down numerous Tuol Sleng prison alumni. Still, it seemed that not even Seth Mydans could convince Sok Sin that he was sick: "He says the Thai doctors were wrong; an herbal doctor told him he's not infected. In another month he'll be, as he says, 'fleshy' again. He's still having trouble eating but he's certain that will be better soon." Mydans confirmed my worst fear: Sok Sin had turned to Nhem En for medical advice.

En had convinced the fixer that traditional doctors had "cured" his AIDS: "As Sok Sin said many times, Nhem Ein is looking very buff—totally cured by herbal drugs and no longer HIV positive." Sok Sin, too, was now taking a traditional AIDS "cure," getting shots every day, and ingesting a pharmacological fruit salad of pills. He continued to suffer weight loss and discomfort from the intestinal virus that his collapsed immune system couldn't overcome. Seth Mydans said that Sok Sin was afraid to return to Thailand because treatment—in which he had little faith to begin with—was so expensive: "What can he do to prolong his health, given financial constraints? It's not a happy picture."[11]

Having been unable to reach Sok Sin on his mobile phone for months, I really had no idea how badly he was doing until I returned to Cambodia in August 2001. Ostensibly I was there to complete the research for my book, but really, I had to satisfy my sick curiosity about Sok Sin's fate. Besides, I still believed that I could talk some sense to him. It felt strange not to have him pick me up at Pochentong Airport and brief me on what we would be doing. I grabbed someone else's cab, stowed my gear at the Foreign Correspondents Club, and took a moto to Sok Sin's guesthouse, feeling trepidation as my driver cruised down the dirt road next to the French embassy's giant wall. I recognized Sok Sin's "high-profile" Toyota SUV gathering dust in his guesthouse parking lot.

The five-story apartment building with discreet indoor parking had a suspiciously large number of single young women inhabiting the first three floors. When I later asked Sok Sin if he was running a whorehouse, he explained that it was "a hotel that rented rooms by the hour." It was not quite a brothel, more of a "no-tell motel." At the foot of the stairs, Sok Sin's niece sat in a chair behind a glass case filled with cases of condoms. With a massive key ring around one forearm and a walkie-talkie in her hand, she was a chip off the old block. When I asked for Sok Sin, she barked into the walkie-talkie, then vacated her chair and told me to sit. As she practiced her English on me, I heard a familiar voice: "Welcome to Cambodia, I am sorry that I was not there to pick you up at the airport." I looked toward the stairs and at first did not recognize my friend. I tried to hide my shock. Skin and bones, Sok Sin could not have weighed 100 pounds, and he was covered with sores.

It took considerable effort on his part to lead me up the three flights of stairs to his room. I slowed my pace and as I walked behind him, noticed that his knees were now the widest part of his legs. What hair he had left was cropped down to the scalp. His two sons, aged seven and fourteen, and two daughters, aged nine and four, scrambled to get chairs for us on the balcony overlooking Calmette Hospital. The two boys were from a previous marriage and the two girls were from his present wife. I gave the kids one of the Power Bars I had brought for their father and they devoured it. Sok Sin pointed to his youngest daughter, Srey Pich, "diamond girl." Her face was smeared with chocolate, and she sucked at the bits still stuck to the wrapper. "See very smart, boss already! She got the most chocolate," he said proudly.

Sok Sin told me confidently, "I am no longer HIV positive. Asian HIV was different, herbal doctors cure." He pointed to the alleyway behind Calmette Hospital and showed me young women, obviously in various phases of AIDS, buying "cures" from slick salesmen who did a brisk business. His most immediate problem was diarrhea, so I gave him special antidiarrhea pills that a friend with AIDS in New York City had sent. When I returned to his guesthouse the next day, Sok Sin seemed more like his old self. He said that the pills had helped. Just as I was beginning to feel a hint of optimism, he showed me the herbal "cure" that he was using to chase my medicine. The dirty Johnny Walker bottle held a concoction that looked like muddy river water. When I asked what it was, I regretted it: "Pangolin blood with water and herbs." Sok Sin also showed me a mishmash of pills of every shape, size, and expiration date. His regimen of any and every "medicine" available, his frailty, and his pessimistic demeanor made it clear: he was slipping away. Never one to mince words, Sok Sin told me that he felt "lonely and isolated at home." It seemed he had made a decision—as though in Bangkok, something had broken inside of the "excellent survivor." He was checking out.

It was very difficult for me to work without my collaborator. Cambodia felt very stark and sad without his manic energy feeding off of mine and vice versa. When I left the guesthouse that afternoon, I left my hope for Sok Sin behind. He was going, and I finally accepted it. But Cambodia was not a country where one had to look far to find sadness and misery. One day I noticed my moto driver was unusually subdued. When I asked him how he was doing, "Sad. Wife die with baby thirty-five days ago, no money, hospital would not take," he said matter-of-factly.

Sok Sin's recovery was short-lived; over the next three weeks, he continued to fade. Many times I went to the guesthouse and found him asleep or unable to get out of bed. It was very difficult to see him wasting away as his four bright and healthy kids played nearby. For me, these miseries, particularly Sok Sin's decline, cast a harsh light on the four-year debate over war crimes trials. While I fully supported trials if Cambodians wanted them, I knew they were no panacea for larger problems like corruption, disease, and poverty. While Ieng Sary and his family had grown rich from the timber and gem trade, the average Cambodian family subsisted on less than $400 per year. What little infrastructure existed outside the main cities was crumbling.

The trials in Cambodia and, more significantly, the very nature of the post–Cold War world political order were laid bare on September 11, 2001. I was having a late dinner at the bar of the FCC when Agence France Presse's Luke Hunt came bounding up the staircase shouting, "World War III's started! World War III's started! Turn on CNN!" A plane had just flown into one of the World Trade Center towers, and Hunt claimed that it was part of a larger first strike against the United States. Huddled with the other patrons around the television set, I wrote it off in my mind as an accident and did my best to downplay the event. I had already decided that this was a limited attack when a second plane slid into the frame and disappeared into a ball of flames. It took a minute to comprehend that this wasn't a replay. In real time, we had just watched a second jet fly into the World Trade Center. Mobile phones started ringing nonstop. Luke and I, along with South African journalist Rob Carmichael, moved to my room to watch the unfolding drama in privacy. When the first building began to burn, I insisted that it would not collapse. A few minutes later, it imploded in a fiery avalanche and a mushroom cloud of concrete dust rose over Lower Manhattan. The second tower collapsed soon afterward. Carmichael was on the phone and couldn't figure out why the TV screen had turned gray. "They pancaked," I said. It was my only correct interpretation of the night.

My wife, Annabelle, was in New York City. I had tried to reach her on Luke

Hunt's phone, but it was impossible to connect. The three of us continued to drink as we struggled to come to grips with the event we had just witnessed. Hunt had just spent a year as AFP's correspondent in Afghanistan and immediately grasped the significance of the attack. Now CNN was flashing to images of the Pentagon burning. Like Pearl Harbor, this was a remarkable first strike that demonstrated how vulnerable the United States was to a surprise attack aimed at civilian targets. We all went to bed dazed. The next morning I received an e-mail from my wife. She was fine but New York City was not. The collapse of the World Trade Center had punctuated the end of the "human rights era" (inaugurated in 1989 by the fall of the Berlin Wall) with an exclamation point. The post–9/11 world looked like the "neo–just war" era I had described in my dissertation in 1993. War crimes trials would soon become "so September 10th," as the saying went.

I arrived for my final visit with Sok Sin on September 15, the day before I was to return home. His youngest daughter, "diamond girl," was playing downstairs. She smiled when she saw me and led me by the hand up the stairs to her father's bedside. Sok Sin was asleep, but she woke him. When he said that he would get up "to say good-bye," I swallowed hard and was relieved when his sons asked me to play badminton in the hallway. They were both quite good and his older son was beating me soundly when Sok Sin came out of the bedroom. His daughters placed our plastic chairs by the balcony's steel rail and brought us water. I was sweaty from the badminton, and Srey Pich came over and began to comb the hair on my arms like I was the unkempt family dog.

Sok Sin, like many Cambodian friends, was very kind to me in the wake of September 11. They knew that my wife and home were in New York City and apologized for the attack. Almost all of the mototaxi drivers at the FCC asked about my wife and expressed their condolences. It was very moving, now that the shoe was on the other foot. I suspected that most Cambodians hadn't experienced such sympathy from Americans and other foreigners in the past. Sok Sin was no exception. He told me not to worry about him and that it was time for me to return to the United States. "You stay with your wife now," he said several times.

Sok Sin took out a box full of old photographs of him with different reporters taken all over Cambodia over the previous two decades: "If I have guest, anywhere I go. Any battle, I go. And so I always advise to my children, 'The property that we have here is from my risking.'" Sok Sin talked about the many reporters he had enjoyed working with over the years: Jason Barber, Seth Mydans, Nic Dunlop, Phil Shenon, David Lamb, Vernon Loeb, and many others. He regaled me with tales of journalistic malfeasance and then hassled me for the final time about becoming a "high-profile" journalist. I had to stop riding motorcycles and staying in guesthouses. I was married now and needed to make money for my family; I needed to eat my meals at hotel buffets and drive around in the back of a European sedan. In other words, I needed to enter the self-contained, air-conditioned westerners' bubble in order to "succeed." At one point, Sok Sin slipped while describing one journalist and said, "Very, very low class, even lower class than you." I laughed. He never minced words and it was, after all, Sok Sin's brutal honesty that gave so many of us a window into a society and culture so different from our own. Then he began to rail against his detractors, those who "rubbish Sok Sin."

Finally, I changed the subject to the matter of his children's futures. Sok Sin wanted to get one of his sons out of the country for school. I knew that he had at least two wives and four kids. He carefully wrote down all of their names and birth dates on a piece of paper and handed it to me. The finality of it was very sad. Sok Sin was certainly no saint, but he had taught me a great deal, and both of us knew that we would never see each other again. Stoic to the end, Sok Sin shook my hand, looked me dead in the eye, and said good-bye.

I left Cambodia trying to get my head around Sok Sin's fatalism and the long-term impact of the events of September 11. The four-year-old negotiations over a war crimes trial thirty years after the fact seemed irrelevant, a mere distraction compared to the impact that AIDS was having on hundreds of thousands of Cambodian families.

Sok Sin's condition deteriorated quickly. My friend Lisa Miller kept me informed when he entered Calmette Hospital in October. Doctors believed that he was suffering from meningitis and inflammation of the cerebral cortex. He no longer tried to get out of bed and slept most of the time. "I spent an hour and a half with him today. He cried a lot. He talked about how his parents were killed in Pol Pot time and there was no one to look out for his family," Lisa wrote to me in an e-mail. When she tried to console him and told him that he should be proud of his many accomplishments, Sok Sin, like En, worried that his children were about to become orphans. Lisa told him that we had been in touch and asked if he had a message to pass along. He said, "I don't want anyone scared for me."[12] Sok Sin was heartened by visits from Seth Mydans, Jason Barber, Nic Dunlop, and many other journalists who came to pay their final respects.

When Regis Martin, a French doctor with *Médecins du Monde,* took over his case, he noticed Sok Sin had been taking tuberculosis medicine on top of everything else. The hospital quickly filled with Sok Sin's relatives and family. "Good ol' Sok Sin, 4 wives and 7 children is my latest count. I wouldn't be surprised if a few more came out of the woodwork," Lisa Miller e-mailed. One of the doctors looked at the crowd assembled around Sok Sin's bed and asked who this guy was. His wife Sarin "casually informed him that he worked for *The New York Times*."[13] Once again, Lisa had the task of explaining the HIV virus and the need to get tested. "As late as last night I was having to explain about AIDS. The level of denial has compounded the problem immeasurably."

Sok Sin died on the afternoon of Wednesday, November 7, 2001, in the intensive care ward at Calmette Hospital. The funeral would be a traditional Buddhist ceremony; Sok Sin was taking no chances when it came to his afterlife. A very suave Khmer man in his forties, equal parts priest and wedding planner, was hired to oversee the entire week-long event. Overnight, Sok Sin's guesthouse garage was transformed into a Buddhist temple. The following morning a dozen monks filed in to begin the rituals, and the crowd of mourners spilled out onto the street. Seth Mydans, Chris Decherd, Lisa Miller, Jason Barber, and close to a hundred others attended various stages of the funeral. Unable to return to Cambodia, I watched much of the ceremony on the videotape Lisa sent me afterward.[14]

As the monks offered a blessing for his soul, Sok Sin's emaciated corpse, dressed in his favorite clothes, lay on a mattress with his briefcase and car keys next to it. Behind him was a giant altar with two huge, Kentucky Derby–size wreaths and dozens of other flower arrangements. Both flashing disco and Christmas lights surrounded a picture of Sok Sin in the center. In front of the shrine, his children burned fake money in clay pots. For the next seven days, his body was mourned with chants, prayers, and final good-byes. The emotional pitch seemed to ebb and flow. At one point his wife took Sok Sin's face in her hands and wailed inconsolably as Srey Pich tried to comfort her. Finally, his body was placed in his $1,000 hand-carved wooden coffin, which was lifted by six uniformed men and placed inside a truck painted to resemble a giant green and red dragon. Six monks rode inside with the coffin and everyone else made their way to the cremation temple on fool.

The funeral procession was led by Sok Sin's son, the one who had beaten me so easily in badminton. With his shaved head and the weight of the world on his young shoulders, he looked much older than his fourteen years. When they arrived at the temple, the six handlers lifted the coffin out of the dragon truck and placed it on a gurney that ran on steel tracks while the family hastily reconstructed the shrine in front of the mouth of the crematorium. His eldest son lit the fire and pushed the coffin down the rails into the flames. The family launched into one final chorus of grief, and it was over. Sok Sin was gone.

Jason Barber had kindly sent me an e-mail telling me the time of the cremation. That day was blustery on Oahu's north shore, but I walked down to a bend in the reef and threw a lei in the Pacific Ocean for Sok Sin. He was gone, but I would not forget him.

10

"I AM NOT DEAD. I AM ALIVE."

i

By 2003, war crimes trials were still nowhere in sight. UN Secretary-General Kofi Annan called Hun Sen's bluff in February 2002 by withdrawing from the trial discussion. Annan accused the Cambodians of negotiating in bad faith, and stated that he believed they were neither interested in nor capable of conducting fair trials. But although the UN had officially pulled the plug, there were back-channel efforts to jump-start the negotiations. It seemed that Hun Sen might simply be using the trial issue as a public relations distraction, like he had in 1998.

I returned to Cambodia in January to complete the research for this book, this time with my wife Annabelle along. Security was tight when we arrived in the capital. The Association of South East Asian Nations tourism conference was under way and Prime Minister Hun Sen was making sure that nothing would shatter the veneer of Cambodian stability and prosperity while the foreign dignitaries were in town. The brothels in Kilometer 11 were temporarily shut down and mototaxis were barred from the grounds of four-star hotels like Hotel Le Royal. Phnom Penh seemed to be putting its best foot forward for Annabelle's first visit. The main drag, Sothearos Boulevard, was blocked by city police in light blue shirts and military police in green fatigues, all armed with AK-47s. Expensive sedans sporting a variety of national flags made their way around Phnom Penh with police escorts and sirens blaring. The bodyguards were easy to spot due to the long, shiny antennae on their radios.

We made our way to Hotel Le Royal on the final evening of the ASEAN conference, just to watch the scene. Overdressed delegates from around the world began to file into the Elephant Bar, and by 5 p.m. it was a hive of activity. Asian delegates dominated the pool table while the Europeans drank convivially at the tables. As the evening wore on, military officers in stunning dress whites arrived for the formal banquet. We ate dinner in the hotel's Café Monivong, and noticed an American woman holding her Cambodian "take away" child on her lap. The hotel's vast buffet must have been quite a sight for this child raised on rice and the occasional bit of fish or pork: gooey French cheeses; steam trays brimming with curry, chicken, and shrimp; gorgeous knots of perfectly cooked lamb glowing in the warm red light of a heat lamp; lettuce that looked as if each leaf had been hand scrubbed; and for dessert, a sweaty silver tub of vanilla ice cream sitting next to a gravy boat filled with hot fudge. For such Cambodian children, this was, quite literally, their first taste of a new life of plenty.[1]

Americans were adopting, some said buying, Cambodian children at an ever-growing rate. The State Department had just lifted a ban on American citizens adopting Cambodian children. Even with the ban, it was nothing that could not be "fixed" with a few well-placed bribes. Globalism in Cambodia meant that by 2003, the U.S. dollar could buy anything: a young girl's virginity; a human organ; rocks of 100 percent pure heroin; an original bas-relief carving from the temples of Angkor Wat; maybe even a war crimes amnesty—you only had to name it and meet the terms of the deal.[2]

ii

My first morning in Phnom Penh, I read a story in *The Cambodia Daily* claiming that a Tuol Sleng survivor long counted among the dead had resurfaced and presented himself at the Documentation Center of Cambodia. Extremely curious, I hailed a moto and rode to the DC Cam offices. I banged on the steel gate until finally an older woman opened a peephole and looked at me suspiciously. I handed her my driver's license and she disappeared for a few minutes. Then the latch slid and slammed as the gate creaked open. We exchanged "*Soksabai,*" greetings, and I walked up the narrow stairs. When I opened the glass door to the DC Cam offices, I beheld an astounding sight.

A tiny Cambodian man dressed in a striped dress shirt and gray pants sat cross-legged on a pillow. He was painting a canvas that rested on two wooden U.S. 82-mm. ammunition crates. The work in progress was of five emaciated Buddhist monks lining up for rice gruel at a Khmer Rouge compulsory commune. I looked to my left and saw Youk Chhang, who greeted me warmly; he was beaming. A survivor had risen from the dead. Many of the DC Cam staff were filing in and out of the room to watch him paint, but nobody interrupted his quiet reverie. Although he was now much older, I remembered this artist, Bou Meng, from the photo taken by the East German documentary film crew in 1979. The seven survivors stand with their arms draped around one another in front of the prison's barbed-wire gate. The jaunty little man, a foot shorter than everyone else, head held high, was Bou Meng. Like fellow survivor Van Nath, Bou Meng had painted murals of Marx, Lenin, and Pol Pot in order to survive. Unlike Van Nath, who wrote a book and has been interviewed often enough to be overexposed, Bou Meng returned to work as an obscure commercial artist in the provinces. We had all assumed that he was dead because he had kept such a low profile over the years.

Only when a copy of DC Cam's magazine arrived in Bou Meng's village and he saw his photograph inside did he learn that he had been presumed dead. The S-21 survivor had shown up at the gate of DC Cam in January 2003 and asked to see Youk Chhang. When they first met, Bou Meng pulled out a plastic bag containing a few tattered pages from an old issue of *Searching for the Truth*. He pointed to his picture and told Chhang simply, "I am not dead. I am alive. I want to show to the national and international media that I am alive. It was just a rumor."

Bou Meng believed that a war crimes trial was imminent. He had traveled to Phnom Penh "to be allowed to join in the trial against the Khmer Rouge because the media said they have arrested them already." This was "important for me as well as for Cambodian people who were tortured cruelly by the Pol Pot's group through many methods."[3] While careful not to expose him to a media feeding frenzy, Youk Chhang also knew that he could not hide Bou Meng. His first encounter with the press was at Tuol Sleng Museum, where he spoke forcefully about the need for a trial, the cruelty of S-21 commandant Brother Duch, and his willingness to testify. Youk Chhang noticed that Bou Meng seemed shaken by the experience, so they drove to the Russian Market and bought painting supplies. Bou Meng returned to the DC Cam offices and spent much of the night painting.

Now Chhang and I watched as the painting took shape. In addition to the Buddhist monks, this very somber, black, white, and gray portrait now included a mean-faced Khmer Rouge leader at the head of the table, doling out the gruel. I had been watching and talking quietly, but really, we were just basking in Bou Meng's aura. The staff at DC Cam had an often grim and thankless job, and this was one of the few moments of instant gratification. As a result of their magazine and nothing else, another Tuol Sleng survivor had come in from the cold. Questions raced through my mind, but I could not ask Bou Meng anything now; I did not want to break his trance. His painting, his spirit, and his focus were all worth tens of thousands of my hollow words. Brother Duch, Tuol Sleng, torture—none of it had broken him, and words simply could not do him justice at this moment. About an hour later, Bou Meng stopped painting and stood up. The top of his head did not reach my armpit. We shook hands, but I could not bring myself to ask him a single question.

DC Cam's magazine *Searching for the Truth* was beginning to play a leading role in both the debate over Khmer Rouge accountability and the burgeoning public discussions of a painful history. Because the magazine was written in Khmer for a Cambodian audience (with a simultaneous English edition offered), Cambodians now had a forum. Each month, amazing letters arrived at the DC Cam office. Many Cambodians learned the fate of their loved ones after more than twenty years of uncertainty from *Searching for the Truth.* Meas Sarin read the facts of her cousin's death and shared the news with the rest of her family: "Afterwards, the whole family sat down and sobbed. I want to know who were the leaders of the country. They must have been foreigners, understand? If they were Khmer, how could they kill their own people?"

Searching for the Truth was forcing Cambodians to confront their history in terms they could understand. "Who are they? Why did they kill people?" continued Meas Sarin before expressing her support for an international trial. DC Cam Director of Finance Sohka Irene thanked the center for introducing her to her missing uncle through his December 1978 Tuol Sleng confession, preserved in the DC Cam archive and reproduced in the magazine. She added, "My uncle's innocent soul is still wandering, asking for justice." Simple expressions of gratitude, like this one from Kratie province, were common: "Beloved Director of DC-Cam. . . . I am a victim, the Khmer Rouge killed: father, wife, three children, and in laws, all were accused of being KGB agents. Thanks."4 Some correspondents were looking for long-lost parents and siblings. Chany was five in 1979 when she was separated from her family and had not seen them since. Vanarith was the son of Touch Khamdoeun, the former Cambodian ambassador to Cuba and China. When his family returned to Cambodia in 1975, his parents were sent to S-21, and Vanarith was the only survivor. Youk Chhang responded to his request for any information on his family, "The Documentation Center of Cambodia holds a document concerning your father. I would like to express my regret and share my condolences with your family. At your convenience, please come and pick up the document."[5]

DC Cam was also winning the trust of former Khmer Rouge cadres and even former Tuol Sleng prison workers. Later in the week, I returned to interview two of the center's leading researchers, Meng Try Ea and Sorya Sim. Born in 1973, Meng Try was too young to remember much about the Khmer Rouge years but believed that working at DC Cam was more than just a job because "Cambodian people, they want to know about the Khmer Rouge history."[6] He wanted a trial for the Khmer Rouge leaders so that Cambodians could reconcile with the past and each other, and get on with their lives: "Not only to provide justice for the survivors and for the former victims, it has to build a rule of law for Cambodians."

Meng Try felt that this would be difficult to achieve: "If you need reconciliation, then you will have to lose some degree of justice." I asked if he believed it was possible to divorce a legal problem from its political and religious context. It seemed to me there couldn't be one set of standards; things had to shift and flex on a case-by-case basis. And on a larger scale, there could never be a truly united international community, only groups with particular interests that come together in certain circumstances. "You are right," he said, and made an important point that westerners, so often full of advice but ultimately risking so little, tend to overlook: "Whenever you want to have security you cannot have full justice."

Meng Try and the rest of the staff at DC Cam were worried about the fate of the tribunal, but they continued their work. DC Cam had just published Meng Try and Sorya Sim's short book, *Victims and Perpetrators*. This remarkable oral history of eighteen former Tuol Sleng guards and staff argues that the young Khmer Rouge prison employees were both.[7] I wondered how it was possible to be a victim and perpetrator at the same time—where is the ethical point of no return? *Is* there an ethical point of no return? The subjects interviewed were low-level Khmer Rouge cadres who were fourteen to sixteen years old at the time. "You would cry talking to them and understanding their situations. Leaving the village, taken from place to place, hungry, suffering punishment, not enough food. When they return home they don't see their parents, they were taken away and killed by the Angkar," Meng Try said. Because many of the Khmer Rouge rank and file "are still blamed for the slaughter, they want to clear their names." I asked him how he regarded the men he interviewed: "I feel pity, they were ignored as children and they are poor people because the KR made them poor."

Maybe Meng Try and Youk Chhang were growing tired of all the sagacious western advice when it came to their people's pain. Chhang had written in a recent issue of *Searching for the Truth*: "I am a bit troubled by the terms 'truth commission,' 'reconciliation' and 'healing'—with that language. Maybe I am a non-academic person, so I am not up to that terminology." He maintained that Cambodians were coping with this trauma "by practicing their own version of a truth commission." The DC Cam director believed in "People writing their story . . . invisibly, a truth commission is already being practiced in Cambodia." Even former Khmer Rouge were reading and responding to *Searching for the Truth*. Khmer Rouge leader and prime war crimes trial candidate Khieu Samphan wrote to the magazine "to express my deepest respect to the souls of our innocent countrymen, who were the victims of the killing and heinous acts during the Democratic Kampuchea regime." While Samphan still pled ignorance, he offered an apology: "To those who lost their loved ones to the regime, I am sorry. It was my fault to be foolish, and failed to keep up with the real situations. I tried my best for the sake of our nation's survival, so that we might enjoy development and prosperity like other nations."[8]

iii

When I left DC Cam, I hailed a moto and headed toward my hotel. We were soon slowed by a pack of twenty or thirty students, riding three abreast, each motorcycle carrying two to four passengers. All of them were honking their horns and waving pieces of paper over their heads. I thought that they were students celebrating the end of final exams, but my moto driver told me otherwise. He said the Cambodian youths were protesting the alleged statements of Thai soap opera star Suwanan "Kob" Kongying, printed in a Cambodian newspaper. Associated Press reporter Chris Decherd later told me a much stranger story. The beautiful and demure-looking Thai actress was said to have claimed that Cambodians had stolen the temples of Angkor Wat from Thailand. Although she publicly denied making any such statements and even apologized, Prime Minister Hun Sen and the Cambodian press continued to fan the flames.[9]

Hun Sen entered the fray on Monday, January 27. He gave an inflammatory speech from Kompong Cham that was broadcast on Cambodian radio. The prime minister said that the life of the Thai movie star "is not equal to a few bushes of grass near Angkor Wat" and called for a boycott of all things Thai. Papers like *Rasmei Angkor* and *Koh Santepheap*, and Beehive Radio continued to spread the story far and wide. Hun Sen warned the Thai television station in Cambodia, TV5, to stop broadcasting "Kob" Kongying's films "because I am afraid people will go to destroy the television station."[10]

Rumors about the cause of the unrest multiplied. Some believed that Hun Sen was encouraging disorder to create a pretext to clamp down on his opposition in anticipation of the 2003 election, to be held in August. Others believed that it was a severe outbreak of chip-on-the-shoulder nationalism. Some blamed Sam Rainsy or Prince Ranariddh; still others thought it was a feud between Thai oil magnates jockeying for an offshore lease.[11] I did not take these protests very seriously. The gangs of students on motorcycles had no small arms or radios. I was more irritated than afraid as these Khmer youths drove with the recklessness that only sixteen-year-olds worldwide can muster.

I stopped by the AP office on the afternoon of Wednesday, January 29, to tell Chris Decherd I had lined up an interview with Bou Meng the next morning. As we talked on the street outside, we watched a much larger, more vocal pack of students than I'd yet encountered zoom by, four abreast, honking their high-pitched horns. The motos in front carried Cambodian flags on long, relatively thick wooden staffs that I realized would double nicely as bats.

One of Cambodia's best homegrown reporters, AP's Ker Munthit, came out and watched too as the noisy mob passed, honking horns and chanting something in Khmer. He seemed to be taking this seriously; I registered some concern on his face. Whatever it was, it was completely lost on me. Bou Meng was the only thing on my mind, since I was planning to leave for Bangkok after the interview. I bade farewell to Chris, then made the rounds to say good-bye to Youk Chhang and the rest of the DC Cam staff. As I was speaking with Chhang, there was a deafening roar from the street and the sound of hundreds of beeping motorcycle horns.

A mob of motos was swarming around the Independence Monument roundabout, a major downtown intersection just outside. At one point it looked as if half the traffic circle was filled with protestors. There were now at least a hundred motorcycles, many with riders waving Cambodian flags. "The pride of Cambodia!" the DC Cam director joked, but I could hear nervousness in his voice. Youk Chhang is a brave man; he had never backed down from the Khmer Rouge. I respect him like few others, so I should have picked up on his tension, but the uproar still seemed trivial.

By 6 p.m., a student demonstration at the Thai embassy had gotten out of control. Protestors were ransacking the place. Parts of the building were on fire, and Ambassador Chatchawed Chartsuwan and his staff were running for their lives. After climbing a fence, they escaped by boat on the river be-hind the building. Young Cambodians stole computer scanners and other high-tech gear, but used desks and pillows to stoke the growing fires. When riot police arrived, almost an hour after the attack began, they just watched the embassy burn. The Cambodian government's response—or lack there-of—stood in stark contrast to the methods I had seen Hun Sen and his Chief of Police Hok Lundy employ against their opposition in the past.[12]

Failing to provide adequate security for the Thai embassy was a violation of the 1961 Vienna Convention on Diplomatic Relations: embassy security is the responsibility of the host nation. This was now an international incident. Thai Prime Minister Thaksin Sinawatra called the mob violence "barbaric" and ordered C-130 airplanes and Thai commandos to evacuate his nationals first thing next morning. It would be a long night for the Thai population of Phnom Penh.[13]

Whatever point Hun Sen was trying to make by inciting student national-ism had been eclipsed, and this was fast turning into an international loss of face. Had the self-proclaimed "chess master" of international politics finally overplayed his hand? I had given Hun Sen the benefit of the doubt for years. Just as many human rights advocates' visions had been blurred by their dis-trust of the de facto dictator, mine was distorted by the opposite attitude. My disdain for the sanctimony of the UN and human rights advocates had begun to color my vision of the Cambodian leader.

Around 7 p.m. I headed back to the hotel. By now the sun had set, and the moto mob was building to a furious climax. My mototaxi driver informed me that the Thais had burned down the Cambodian embassy in Bangkok and killed the Cambodian ambassador. When I told him I had just come from the offices of the Associated Press and the *Phnom Penh Post* and knew these ru-mors were false, he refused to believe me. Other Cambodians said that even if the stories were not true, the Thais had been dishonoring and dominating Khmers for too long and had it coming. *The Cambodia Daily* best summed up the stories, highlighting the irrelevance of the facts: "Two people had been killed, the rumor went. Then 20. Then the Cambodian ambassador. None of it was true."[14]

The moto mob next attacked the Shinawatra building, an upscale Thai-owned office complex, and by 8 p.m. had moved on to the Thai-owned Royal Phnom Penh Hotel. The violence was spreading throughout Phnom Penh. Cambodian security guards bolted when the students began to pelt them with rocks. Tourists' dinners were interrupted when a bat-swinging youth came flying through the front window and the mob right behind him demolished the dining room. Within an hour, much of the hotel was on fire and the rooms were being looted; some Cambodian hotel employees were joining in. The mob moved on to attack, loot, and destroy the offices of the Thai phone company, Samart; the Thai-owned Julianna and Regent Park hotels; and other Thai-owned businesses.[15] Slow to respond, the Cambodian police were nowhere to be found on the riverfront where Sisowath Quay and Sotheros Boulevard, the two main arteries, converge, just beyond the Foreign Correspondents Club. My wife and I were sleeping comfortably in our second-story hotel room just above when we were awakened by the drone of more than a hundred two-stroke engines. It was a menacing sound, like an angry swarm of bees. As the beeping horns and chants grew louder, I jumped out of bed, pulled open the thick curtains, and saw the moto mob converging from all directions, slowly filling the large intersection beneath our balcony. By 10:30 p.m., they were hundreds strong and blocked most of the intersection, chanting slogans denouncing the "Thai thief." I called Chris Decherd, who lived a block away, over a Thai restaurant we frequented. He said that the scouts had already arrived, but the restaurant owners had locked their steel doors and were inside, bracing for an attack.

The moto mob moved from the hotel intersection toward the Thai restaurant. In their wake, I heard and then saw my friend Rob Carmichael zoom by on his big, four-cylinder Honda motocross bike, jacked to the gills on adrenaline. The sound of breaking glass and the low gonging of bats resounding against steel security doors were met with raucous cheers, but still no police. Suddenly the mob was at the southeast corner of our hotel, whose owner was married to a Thai woman. After some tense pushing and shoving, the hotel's private, unarmed security guards held firm and the swarm of motos buzzed off in search of a softer target.

The mob stopped again, by the FCC, at about 10:45; we watched from the balcony. Chris Decherd called and said that the mob had launched a full-scale assault on the Thai restaurant, but had been unable to penetrate its steel façade. In the end, they only destroyed the sign and a few planters, but the Thai family would never be the same. Again I heard the timpani of breaking glass and the roar of the crowd and once again, *dunk, dunk, dunk*—the now-familiar sound of steel doors being battered by clubs. The mob then tore down the Thai flag on the riverfront and replaced it with the Cambodian flag.

The cavalry finally arrived at 11 p.m., heralded by loudspeakers broadcasting ominous warnings. The first and only truckload of military police I saw stopped and dispersed what was left of the mob down by the FCC. Next the

Moto mob, Phnom Penh, January 29, 2003
Annabelle Lee

truck pulled up in front of our hotel and four military policemen with AK-47s got out and conferred with the private security guards. The police had a plan and fanned out across the intersection. We could now hear long bursts of gunfire and see glowing tracer rounds, bullets making lazy arcs in the sky. They were coming from the direction of Wat Phnom, to the north; it seemed that the military had finally stepped in there as well and had the moto mob on the run. There were more long bursts of gunfire, and then the menacing chorus of horns and the sea of headlights approached down the narrow side street to the right of our balcony, where the police stood in a well-spaced line and shouldered their rifles. The commander was a hard-looking older man who handled his old Kalashnikov rifle with the dexterity of a battlefield veteran. The moto mob halted, and the young leader and the old commander stood toe to toe. When the kid began to mouth off, the old commander said nothing; he simply turned, took a few steps back toward his soldiers, and said something declarative to his men. Next came the sound of rifles chambering rounds. The commander wheeled and let loose the first volley of fire over the students' heads. No single warning shots or bursts in the air, but a full thirty-round magazine.

One or two of the other military policemen also emptied their rifles above the heads of the mob. The roar of the AK-47s was deafening as flames leaped from their muzzles and lit the intersection for a few seconds. Watching from the window, we expected the moto mob to return fire or at least throw one of the gas bombs I had seen earlier in the evening. However, the students' fear became visible, even palpable. They retreated in panic, some even running into each other in their haste to turn their bikes around. It looked like something right out of a Three Stooges comedy. The rest of the night was quiet, but we didn't sleep much. I jumped out of bed several times, imagining that I heard the evil buzz, only to rip open the curtains and see the darkened, empty streets of Phnom Penh.

At a press conference in Bangkok the next morning, shaken Thai Ambassador Chatchawed Chartsuwan said that he had called everyone he knew in Cambodia for help but when it came, it was very little, very late. When the Thai prime minister called Hun Sen afterward for some explanation, he was told that the Cambodian prime minister was "not available." The anti-Thai riots made me wonder about the young Cambodians who had ruled the streets that night. I could only compare this violent and explosive reaction to the alleged comments of a soap opera star to their quiet tolerance of the genocidists in their midst. It seemed that Cambodia's unique culture of impunity and denial had profoundly affected the generation born after 1979.[16]

Even in 2003, the history of the Khmer Rouge years was only superficially glossed over in Cambodian high school textbooks. Youk Chhang believes that Cambodia's present rulers still cannot differentiate between history and propaganda. According to DC Cam researcher Eng Kok Thay, the center receives letters from Cambodian high school students telling them that the number of people killed during the regime was 3 million. The outdated Vietnamese overestimate of Cambodian dead is one of "the few things their school textbooks tell them, even though there is no scientific justification for that 'fact.'" Even Pen Samitthy, the editor of *Rasmei Kampuchea*, Cambodia's largest daily newspaper, admits that although his son knows about the Khmer Rouge and Pol Pot, "he doesn't believe that it happened."[17] The information regarding the Khmer Rouge is incomplete, conflicting, and undermined by both selective memories and denial. Today in Phnom Penh, the sons of the rich and powerful often use their daddies' bodyguards to settle barroom scores. One rich young Cambodian summed up their attitude: "Cambodia is a good place. In the USA, we can't drink in front of the home or break things at a drink shop. The police will arrest us. Here it is okay. If you have a lot of money, you can do anything."[18]

iv

That morning of January 30, I was scheduled to interview Bou Meng, so I called a Khmer friend to drive me over to the Tuol Sleng Museum, where he was staying. One of Cambodia's greatest fighters, Sitha works in private security. He arrived in his familiar white Toyota with radio; a gun belt crammed with ammunition was draped around the top of his seat and the dashboard was covered with important military identification, safely laminated in plastic. "All police must use AK-47s," Sitha translated radio dispatches as we drove across town. The moto mob's rampage had been very selective and very thorough: everywhere, Thai Samart ad signs were destroyed; Thai businesses large and small were damaged, and some had been burned to the ground.

Tuol Sleng Museum director Sopheara Chey, who had agreed to act as interpreter, greeted me at the museum entrance. Bou Meng came into the office, smiled, and shook my hand. Today he wore a brown leather bomber jacket with a fur collar, and he looked as tired as we all felt. Since he was staying not far from the worst of the mob action, I guessed he hadn't slept very well either.

Bou Meng was a thirty-four-year-old industrial painter when the Khmer

THE AUTHOR AND BOU MENG, JANUARY 30, 2003
ANNABELLE LEE

Rouge took power in 1975. He had been sent to Tuol Sleng to be photographed, tortured, and interrogated. When told to admit that he was a CIA agent, he was at a loss for words. He told me, "I still don't know what to say." He stood, lifted his shirt, and showed me the horizontal scars crisscrossing his back. His moment of truth came when prison authorities asked if anyone could draw Pol Pot's picture and Bou Meng volunteered: "They said, 'If you can draw good picture of Pol Pot, you would be temporarily kept for use. If you cannot draw well you would be killed.'" The commandant, Brother Duch, was impressed enough by his sketch to let Bou Meng live.

When I asked Bou Meng what he would say to Brother Duch if he faced him in a court of law, the artist began to fish through the contents of his breast pocket and pulled out a 3" x 5" black-and-white Tuol Sleng picture of a young woman. Sopheara Chey interjected and began to explain: "Yesterday, he did not find his photograph [in the museum], but he found his wife's." Bou Meng looked at the photo and as he showed it to me, tears welled up in his eyes. There was his dead wife, twenty-something forever and composed under duress I could never imagine. "She was tortured and killed," he said. Answering my question about what he would say to Brother Duch, he replied only, "I would demand for the return of my wife and my child."[19]

Bangkok Airways and Thai Air had suspended all service from Cambodia to Thailand, our scheduled route home, so I spent most of the rest of that day scrambling around Phnom Penh, trying to find a flight to Thailand via Malaysia. The next morning, my wife and I boarded a Malaysia Air flight from Phnom Penh to Kuala Lumpur.

I picked up a complimentary *Time* magazine on the airplane, opened it, and there was a photo of Bou Meng, sitting on the floor of DC Cam, painting. The author of the accompanying article seemed to take seriously the notion that Bou Meng "could provide key testimony against his former jailers if long-planned tribunals for the perpetrators of Cambodia's killing fields go forward." I had seen that painting during my visit. The article claimed that "he once painted his nightmare; now he paints his dream." It had looked like a nightmare to me.[20]

CONCLUSION:
WAR CRIMES TRIALS AS A
WELCOME DISTRACTION

After five years and eleven rounds of talks, Cambodian representative Sok An and UN representative Hans Corell initialed a provisional war crimes tribunal agreement on March 17, 2003. The Cambodian prime minister ceded very little. Under the unwieldy "mixed" tribunal plan, the Cambodians would have a 3–2 majority on the war crimes court and a 4–3 majority on the appeals court. All binding decisions would require a majority-plus-one vote. This so-called "supermajority" was meant to counter the possibility of the Cambodians voting as a bloc and ruling by majority. The co-prosecutors, one UN and one Cambodian, would prepare indictments against roughly a dozen of the surviving senior leaders of the Khmer Rouge. The charges combined categories of both domestic and international law: homicide, torture, religious persecution, destruction of cultural property, genocide, crimes against humanity, war crimes, and crimes against internationally protected persons.

The only remaining hurdles were the approvals of the Cambodian National Assembly and the UN General Assembly. For the first time there appeared to be a consensus: potentially bad trials were better than no trials at all.[1] The draft law was better than some and worse than others, but at least the categories of criminality were consistent with those applied in UN political justice elsewhere. The biggest remaining question was the political will of Cambodian Prime Minister Hun Sen. Very soon, he would have to decide whether or not to deliver the eminently indictable senior leadership of the Khmer Rouge—Ieng Sary, Nuon Chea, Khieu Samphan, Ta Mok, Brother Duch, Ieng Thirith, and others—to trial.

Since the passage of the agreement, former Khmer Rouge leaders Nuon Chea and Khieu Samphan have been testing their respective defenses in the court of public opinion. Both portray themselves as patriots who prevented Vietnam from swallowing Cambodia. Nuon Chea only admits that his regime made undefined "mistakes." When it comes to the massacres in the killing fields and interrogations ending in death at Tuol Sleng prison, he continues to blame the Vietnamese. Brother Number Two asserts that his trial should take only a day, as he has no plans to appeal what he assumes will be a guilty verdict. Striking a bold pre-trial pose, Nuon Chea claims that he looks forward to living out his life in prison because it is "the home of the patriot." In a February 2004 interview, he continued to challenge the authenticity of S-21: "The bad people faked it. They controlled us for many years so they can invent this." The former Khmer Rouge leader remains convinced that his revolution saved Cambodia from absorption by Vietnam, and certain that "when I die my ideals will survive so my death will keep [those ideals] for the new generation." [2]

Khieu Samphan served as the president and frontman for Pol Pot's Democratic Kampuchea from the 1970s until the late 1990s. In April 2004, he published his defense in a book entitled *The Recent History of Cambodia and My Successive Positions*. This prime war crimes trial candidate has retained French criminal defense attorney Jacques Verges, who defended Nazi Klaus Barbie in Lyon, France in 1987. Today, Samphan freely admits that his "movement committed more violence than any revolutionary movement the world has ever known, leading to many deaths and unprecedented sufferings." Shrouded in his apology is an astounding claim that evokes memories of Nazi mea culpas of the 1950s: "To be frank, until recently I did not know that this regime utilized only such violence." Samphan's most absurd contention is that he did not know of Tuol Sleng until 2001: "I confess that I have just known the systematic widespread arrest recently, particularly when I watched a documentary of Mr. Rithy Panh entitled 'S-21: The KR's Killing Center' [*S21: The Khmer Rouge Killing Machine*]." [3]

Today, many Cambodians over the age of forty—old enough to retain vivid memories of the Khmer Rouge regime—continue to live in fear and simply want some form of historical clarity. Survivors like filmmaker Rithy

Panh gave up on punishment and reparations long ago. Today they simply seek acknowledgment. Born in 1964, Panh appears wise beyond his forty years. Perhaps it is the gray in his hair or the intensity of his gaze. Panh has engaged the issues of accountability, truth, and reconciliation like few others of his generation, motivated by the memories of those who died so that he might live: "I survived because many people helped me, and these people are dead. I take their place or they left me their place, I don't know. Just to tell that they are innocent, it is very simple."

Rithy Panh's most recent, award-winning film, *S21: The Khmer Rouge Killing Machine*, was reported to have brought the always glitzy Cannes Film Festival "back down to earth with a thud."[4] *S21* stars many of the same Tuol Sleng alumni who appear in this book. Survivors Van Nath and Chum Mey confront S-21 head guard Him Huy, photographer Nhem En, interrogator Prâk Khân, head clerk Sous Thi, and other former prison staff. Panh shot the film with a digital camera and used an all-Khmer production team. During our interview in September 2003, Panh made a point that I now well understood: "It is not the same relationship when you go to see En or Nath with white guys from the States or Europe. You can't help it. That is why we begin to educate people. All-Khmer team understands the language; we were there. Everybody was there, so when Huy tells something not true, we can tell [him], 'Not true. We were here, try again please.'"

The real star of *S21* is Van Nath, who presides over the meeting of victims and perpetrators with great dignity. Panh says that the "former jailers could not lie in front of Nath. Even when silent, he acted as a 'developer,' revealing the secrets of their souls." Nath rejects the idea that victims can and should simply "draw a veil over the past in the interest of reconciliation." Instead, he believes that Cambodians need some questions answered. Rithy Panh points to Nath as an example. He "has never known for which crime he was arrested, nor why he survived rather than someone else. He is haunted by these questions. But how can he tell his children that he is innocent? That he is not the forgotten remnant of a massacre?"[5]

Panh compared genocide to "nuclear contamination" because "you get it for the rest of your life." He hoped his film would help "to stop the transmission of this painful thing to the next generation." The Thai riots were only a warning about "What happens when a country does not do the work of history; what happens when young people do not learn history." He wonders about the two generations of Cambodians born after the Khmer Rouge era: "They don't know anything or nearly anything. They know the Khmer Rouge kill two million people, but they don't know how, why, and what happened."

Some young Cambodians have told Panh that "they hear from the politicians that the Khmer Rouge are in fact the Vietnamese in the soul, just the body Cambodian but the soul is Vietnamese. They come to kill first to open the country for the Vietnamese to come here."[6]

However clear the historical facts and the questions of war crimes accountability may seem to western scholars and human rights advocates, they remain unclear to many Cambodians, and for good reason. Over the past three decades, Cambodians have been subjected to the contradictory ideological propaganda of the U.S.–backed Lon Nol regime (1970–1974), the Khmer Rouge (1975–1979), the Vietnamese-installed People's Republic of Kampuchea (1979–1991); and the United Nations Transitional Authority Cambodia (UNTAC) (1992–1993). Since 1994, Cambodian politics have been dominated by the iron-fisted Hun Sen and his Cambodian People's Party.

Even in the absence of a tribunal, Cambodians like Youk Chhang, director of DC Cam, and Rithy Panh are reclaiming their history and trying to make sense of it, then communicate it in terms their countrymen can understand. Khmer magazines like *Searching for the Truth* and films like *Bophana* and *S21* have started this process. Even if it takes decades, Panh believes that the time has come for Cambodians to assume responsibility for themselves. "Now when people come to help us, most of the time they look at us as a baby that the father wants to protect, it is not good for us. Some NGOs have been here for twenty years now, and they cannot transmit responsibility to local workers. How can we build this country if the people will not take responsibility?"[7]

Both the documentation center director and the filmmaker insist that any trials must take place in Cambodia, "not in The Hague, or Tokyo, or Paris or New York, here. We want to hear what they say." For Panh, trials could clarify some basic facts: "If they say, 'Now this man killed people, this man was a political leader who was responsible for this policy and must be condemned,' maybe for us it will be easier to mourn. Maybe people in my generation can talk to their children." When I asked why he couldn't talk to his children now, he exclaimed, "We don't know what happened! Why did they kill my father? He did nothing wrong. He stole nothing, he was a teacher, why was he killed? He was working in the ministry of education, not military. Why is he dead? I need these leaders to tell me, and maybe I will be able to explain to my children who is my father, who is their grandfather."

I asked the filmmaker why Khmer Rouge leaders lying about the past does not incite the same level of anger as the Thai soap opera actress whose supposed negative remark sparked the Thai riots. Ieng Sary, Nuon Chea, Khieu Samphan, and many others continue to live comfortably and even swan around like respectable public figures. Nuon Chea still denies everything and calls on Cambodians to "forget the past." Why, at least on the surface, does no one seem to mind? Panh believes that fear remains the biggest obstacle. "People stayed for a long time under the Khmer Rouge and they fear them still, and that is why the tribunal is very important, to get out the fear, this fear stops us in every action, every creation."

> When people fear something, fear is like a gun, you can use it. The guy who can get the gun can use the fear. But you cannot understand everything. Trying to do so has enabled me to start the process of mourning. But we must come to terms with our collective history. I do not want to leave this burden to our children. A time will come when they will be able to turn the page and be confident about the world around them. The ghosts will then stop haunting the living.[8]

By the summer of 2003, many everyday Cambodians seemed to back the idea of the "mixed tribunal." However, time was running out. Many of the senior leaders of the Khmer Rouge had already died. When Khieu Ponnary, Pol Pot's first wife, died in July, she was honored by her former comrades Ieng Sary, Khieu Samphan, and Nuon Chea. Journalist Moeun Chhean Nariddh, like many other Cambodians, was outraged by the Khmer Rouge nostalgiafest and best expressed their frustration: "Let me join my fellow Cambodians in expressing my sadness over the death of the 'mother of the Khmer Rouge,' Khieu Ponnary. Sad, not because she died, but because she could slip away from justice so easily like her ex-husband, the chief murderer Pol Pot. Maybe time and politics are robbing us of justice for the victims of the Khmer Rouge. Who will be the next Khmer Rouge leader to die peacefully? Presumably all of them will."[9]

When the UN had finally agreed to a joint tribunal in March 2003, it had drawn a great deal of criticism from human rights groups like Amnesty International and Human Rights Watch. They believed that the UN had entered into a Faustian pact with the Cambodian government by allowing Cambodia's notoriously corrupt judiciary a majority. These organizations had long criticized the Cambodian mixed tribunal concept on the ground that it was not up to "international standards." More significantly, Amnesty International argued that it marked "a significant retreat from current international law and standards," declaring the draft agreement so flawed that they "would oppose the United Nations signing the agreement without major revision." Human Rights Watch echoed these points on April 30, 2003. The organization's Washington director, Mike Jendrzejczyk, believed the

Cambodian mixed tribunal had "the lowest standards yet for a tribunal with UN participation." Sara Colm, a senior HRW researcher with vast experience in Cambodia, called the tribunal "a weak and substandard formulation." Like many human rights advocates, she saw it as "a dangerous precedent for international justice."

Long-time Cambodian war crimes trials advocate and lawyer Gregory Stanton broke with many of his colleagues and issued a powerful dissenting opinion that framed the Cambodian tribunal debate in especially sobering terms: "All-or-none standards are self-defeating. Perfection is the enemy of justice. The Cambodian people have waited twenty-four years for justice. AI's Report recommends yet more negotiations. The surviving Khmer Rouge leaders are old men, living in comfortable retirement." Stanton's opinion carried weight. He was especially respected both in Cambodia and in human rights circles because he had been working for a tribunal since 1981 and knew the issues better than almost anyone else. While he described Amnesty International and Human Rights Watch as "superb human rights organizations," he compared their approach to "saying that because all law-breakers cannot be captured and tried, none should be." Reporter Seth Mydans put it best: "So at its bluntest, the question now is whether a potentially flawed trial is better than no trial at all." Activist Chea Vannath pointed out that although the agreement was a good sign, "the political will to hold the trial is what is needed."[10]

Watching the renewed debate over the possibility and the specific details of war crimes trials, I shared Stanton's sentiments but had extremely low expectations. If Cambodians wanted to prosecute their former leaders in their own country, who were we westerners to object? While I respected the human rights advocates for their personal bravery, I thought that now they were wide of the mark. Slogans like "universal jurisdiction" were simply "saving ideas," and the notion that one set of international laws applied equally to all was demonstrably false after 9/11.

The gap between the theoretical and the actual that I confronted in 1994 now looks more like a canyon. David Rieff, who spent most of the 1990s staring into the same abyss where heart and mind part company, was brave enough to admit that by 2002, "the norms [of international justice] had outstripped the realities to a grotesque degree."[11] Perhaps the Cambodian tribunal is a first step in this direction, but even if trials actually take place, it will not be the result of draft agreements or technical points of law. It will depend on the political will of one man, Cambodian Prime Minister Hun Sen. The 1990s made one fact absolutely clear: international law, human rights, and international criminal courts are little more than sonorous fictions without political will.

Introduction

1. Susan Sontag, *Regarding the Pain of Others* (New York: Farrar, Straus & Giroux, 2003). David Rieff, *A Bed for the Night* (New York: Simon and Schuster, 2002) describes the modern human rights movement as a "secular religion" and is bitingly critical of Michael Ignatieff's "revolution of moral concern": "the confidence of human-rights activists like Ignatieff and of the UN officials from Secretary General Annan on down, constitute an offer of false hope to people who are desperately in need of rescue" (12). Rieff best described "glass-half-full" optimism as "the kind of rhetoric that gives hope a bad name. Every sunny statement … is open to question" (10).

2. Sontag, *Regarding the Pain of Others*, 60–61.

3. Peter Maguire, "Nuremberg: A Cold War Conflict of Interest," Ph.D. diss., Columbia University, 1993. Fredrick Fleitz Jr., *Peacekeeping Fiascoes of the 1990s* (Westport: Praeger, 2002), 11: "The UN peacekeeping mission in Cambodia (UNTAC), conducted from 1992 to 1993, was considered the prototype expanded peacekeeping mission. UNTAC avoided armed confrontations, took few casualties, and, most importantly, helped put an end to years of civil war. As a result of the loose prerequisites for expanded peacekeeping, the UN approved sending more than 182,000 troops to 34 peacekeeping missions, compared to 61,000 to 22 missions in the prior 44. A new international relations paradigm was born in 1992 with the unveiling of expanded peacekeeping missions. Unlike traditional peacekeeping, expanded peacekeeping operations were attempts at collective security." John Brown, "Interview with Gen. Sanderson," *Phnom Penh Post*, September 24–October 7, 1993; Damien Healy, LC, UNTAC HQ, "UNTAC Rebuts Critic," *Phnom Penh Post*, October 23, 1992.

4. Doug Niven and Chris Riley, eds., *The Killing Fields* (Santa Fe: Twin Palm Press, 1996); David Chandler, "Facing Death: Photographs from S-21," *Photographers International* (April 1995); David Chandler, *Voices from S-21: Terror and History in Pol Pot's Secret Prison* (Berkeley: University of California Press, 1999), 8, 13, 27–29.

5. Rieff, *A Bed for the Night*: "Paradoxically, the more influential the humanitarian ideal has grown, the more incoherent it has become" (272); see also Rieff, "Court of Dreams," *The New Republic*, September 7, 1998.

6. Bob Shacochis, "Soldiers of Great Misfortune," *Harper's*, December 1999. General Peter Schoomaker made this similar observation: "We have a fundamental problem in the well-resourced Western world dealing with warrior class cultures. Sometimes I wonder if anybody's been in a fistfight, deep down within that logic."

1. "So you've been to school for a year or two . . ."

1. Susan Sontag, *Regarding the Pain of Others* (New York: Farrar, Straus & Giroux, 2003), 60–61.

2. Craig Etcheson, *After the Killing Fields: Lessons from the Cambodian Genocide* (New York: Praeger, forthcoming), 13.

3. Robert Young Pelton and Coskun Aral, *Fielding's Most Dangerous Places* (n.p.: Fielding Worldwide, 1995), 207. Nate Thayer and Ker Munthit, "Govt. Soldiers Take Shaky Hold on Pailin," *Phnom Penh Post*, March 25–April 7, 1994.

4. The Dead Kennedys, "Holiday in Cambodia," on *Fresh Fruit, Rotting Vegetables* (Virgin Music Ltd., 1980).

5. Author's notes.

6. Philip Gourevitch, "Death in the Ruins," *Outside* (September 1995); Jon Ogden, "Foreigners Warned to Stay in Towns," *Phnom Penh Post*, April 22–May 5, 1994; Anugraha Palan, "Hopes Dashed for Release of Expat Hostages," *Phnom Penh Post*, June 17–30, 1994. "Appeal for Hostages," *Phnom Penh Post*, July 15–28, 1994.

7. Jon Ogden, "Newsmen Live on the Edge," *Phnom Penh Post*, April 8–21, 1994.

8. David Rieff, *A Bed for the Night* (New York: Simon and Schuster, 2002), 274, compares NGO workers to nineteenth-century colonials: "When one goes to a poor country where the humanitarian role is vital, the colonial atmosphere is unmistakable. Humanitarians live in houses previously occupied by cabinet ministers, or at least by the richest person in the village. Their user friendly democratic attitudes do nothing to disguise their power. Whether they are in sandals and old jeans or not, the reality is the same. And the youthquake clothing only makes them masters in mufti." For more on drugs and decadence in Cambodia, see Amit Gilboa, *Off the Rails in Phnom Penh* (Bangkok: Asia Books, 1998) and Robert Bingham, *Lighting on the Sun* (New York: Doubleday, 2000).

9. Evan Gottesman, *Cambodia After the Khmer Rouge* (New Haven: Yale University Press, 2002), 236–37; for more on the different types of mines, see *Landmines in Cambodia: The Cowards' War* (n.p.: Human Rights Watch and Physicians for Human Rights, 1998), 46–58; author's notes; David Chandler, *Voices from S-21: Terror and History in Pol Pot's Secret Prison* (Berkeley: University of California Press, 1999), 2; for contrasting views on Tuol Sleng Museum, see Lya Badgely, "Archives at Tuol Sleng Imperiled" and Serge Thion's response, "Meaning of a Museum," *Phnom Penh Post*, August 27–September 9, 1993.

10. "Declaration of James William Clark: Agent of the CIA of the USA," May 23, 1978, courtesy of Tuol Sleng Museum director Sopheara Chey. Chris Delance's confession is dated December 26, 1978.

11. Sopheara Chey, April 1, 1994, interview with author, Phnom Penh, Cambodia, tape recording.

12. Holly Burkhalter, "The Question of Genocide," *World Policy Journal* (Winter 1994/95):45. Rieff, *A Bed for the Night*, best described the decade as one in which form triumphed "over substance, legalism over reality, hope over experience" (54).

13. Im Chan, April 1994, interview with author, Phnom Penh, Cambodia, tape recording.

14. Ibid.

15. *The Teachings of Buddha* (Tokyo: Kosaido Printing Co., Ltd., 1966), 246. Marie Martin makes an important point about Cambodian Buddhism: "We must not suppose that Buddhism guides Khmers in their material lives. The official religion only superimposed itself on a deeply ingrained popular religion, the belief in supernatural

forces. After seven centuries of implantation, the Buddhism known as the Lesser Vehicle or Theravada has not succeeded in supplanting the spirits: like the other traditional traits, they impregnate the Khmers' whole life" (*Cambodia: A Shattered Society* [Berkeley: University of California Press, 1994], 18); see also the interview of Samdech Preah Udom Panha Daung Phang Nontiyo, head of the Prek Praing Pagoda, Kandal Province, by San Kalyann and Sayana Ser, *Searching for the Truth*, 2003.

16. Jon Ogden, "Western Trio Feared Dead After Finds," *Phnom Penh Post*, July 29–August 11, 1994; David Chappell, "A Letter to Cambodia," *Phnom Penh Post*, July 29–August 11, 1994.

17. Gourevitch, "Death in the Ruins"; Mang Channo and Gary Way, "Spies in City Aid KR's Train Ambush," *Phnom Penh Post*, August 12–25, 1994; Sue Downie, "Hostage Taking is Big Money Spinner for KR," *Phnom Penh Post*, August 12–25, 1994; Jon Ogden, "Embassies' New Advice," *Phnom Penh Post*, August 26–September 8, 1994; Jon Ogden, "King's Fax Clarified," *Phnom Penh Post*, August 27–September 8, 1994; Hurley Scroggins, "Do You Enjoy the Train in Cambodia," *Phnom Penh Post*, January 30–February 12, 1998; Lindsay Murdoch, "Australian Senators Wrap up Year-Long Hostage Probe," *Phnom Penh Post*, June 27, 1997.

18. Sou Sophornnare and Reuters, "Hopes of Captives' Release Decline," *Phnom Penh Post*, August 26–September 8, 1994; Heng Sok Chheng and Gary Way, "Kampot Closed to Hacks, Dips," *Phnom Penh Post*, August 26–September 8, 1994; "Tragic Find," *Phnom Penh Post*, August 26–September 8, 1994.

19. Gary Way, "Hostages Plead for End to Bombardment," *Phnom Penh Post*, September 9–22, 1994; Gary Way, "Officials Accused of Hostage Scams," *Phnom Penh Post*, August 27–September 8, 1994; Ros Sokhet, "Hostages Alive But Losing Weight," *Phnom Penh Post*, October 7–20, 1994.

20. Ker Munthit, "PM Laments Hostage Deaths," *Phnom Penh Post*, November 4–17, 1994; Mang Channo and Gary Way, "Spies in City Aid KR's Train Ambush," *Phnom Penh Post*, August 12–25, 1994; "Radio Transmission Points Finger at Paet," *Phnom Penh Post*, August 7–20, 1998; Mathiew Guerin and Samrath Sopha, "Daughter, Bodyguards, Say Paet Did Not Commit Murders," *Phnom Penh Post*, August 21–September 3, 1998.

2. "Do not kill any living creature, with the exception of the enemy."

1. Tim Bowden, *One Crowded Hour: Neil Davis Combat Cameraman 1934–1985* (n.p., Australia: HarperCollins, 1987), 265.

2. Elizabeth Becker is one of many who have made the very apt comparison between the Khmer Rouge youth and the wild boys in William Golding's *Lord of the Flies* (*When the War Was Over* [1986; reprint, New York: Public Affairs, 1998], 256). David Chandler, *Voices from S-21: Terror and History in Pol Pot's Secret Prison* (Berkeley: University of California Press, 1999) 32.

3. Becker, *When the War Was Over*, 24. "The first division was between the 'old people' and the 'new people.' The old people were those who had lived in the Khmer Rouge zones during the war and had contributed to the revolution. They were also called 'base people,' which refers both to their life in 'base areas' during the war and their origins in the basic classes—the worker and peasant classes in whose name the Khmer Rouge made the revolution" (226). "The old people were called '18 March people,' the date of the Lon Nol coup against Sihanouk which inaugurated the war. The new people were '17 April,' the date of the Khmer Rouge victory" (24); Heynowski & Scheumann

Film Studios, *Kampuchea: Death and Rebirth* (Berlin, 1979). The East German footage of Phnom Penh and Tuol Sleng Prison shot in early 1979 is the first of Cambodia after the fall of the Khmer Rouge.

4. Heynowski & Scheumann Film Studios, *Kampuchea: Death and Rebirth.*

5. "Phnom Penh Liberation," *Searching for the Truth* 4 (April 2000).

6. Heynowski & Scheumann Film Studios, *Kampuchea: Death and Rebirth.*

7. Jon Swain, "Sideshow: The War in Cambodia," in Horst Faas and Tim Page, eds., *Requiem* (New York: Random House, 1997), 226–27; see also Jon Swain, *River of Time* (London: Minerva Edition, 1996).

8. Roland Neveu, *Cambodia: The Years of Turmoil* (Bangkok: Asia Horizons, 2000), 11–12; "Phnom Penh Liberation," *Searching for the Truth* 4 (April 2000); see also DC Cam document D00710.

9. Aun Pheap, "Looking Back at the Fall of Phnom Penh," *Phnom Penh Post*, April 13–26, 2001; Sopheara Chey, April 1, 1994, interview with author, Phnom Penh, Cambodia, tape recording.

10. Swain, *River of Time*, 139. François Bizot described the invading soldiers as "genuine Khmer Rouge ... real country folk, free from all arrogance, but with slow witted expressions and incapable of overcoming the disgust that filled their hearts at the sight of an 'imperialist lackey'" (*The Gate,* trans. Euan Cameron [London: Harvill Press, 2003], 148–49, 153); "Some Last Messages From Encircled Capital," *The New York Times*, April 18, 1975. The full text of the cable was reprinted in Faas and Page, eds., *Requiem*, 298.

11. Swain, *River of Time*, 146.

12. Ibid. 147; François Ponchaud, *Cambodia: Year Zero*, trans. Nancy Amphoux (New York: Holt, Rinehart, and Winston, 1977), 6–9; Marie Martin, *Cambodia: A Shattered Society* (Berkeley: University of California Press, 1994), 171–72; see also Becker, *When the War Was Over*, 21.

13. Sopheara Chey, April 1, 1994, interview with author, Phnom Penh, Cambodia, tape recording.

14. Aun Pheap, "Looking Back at the Fall of Phnom Penh," *Phnom Penh Post*, April 13–26, 2001; Heynowski & Scheumann Film Studios, *Kampuchea: Death and Rebirth.*

15. Swain, *River of Time*, 142.

16. William Shawcross, *Sideshow: Kissinger, Nixon, and the Destruction of Cambodia* (New York: Simon and Schuster, 1979), 383. "Reds Said to Tell Civilians in Phnom Penh to Leave," *The New York Times*, April 19, 1975.

17. Shawcross, *Sideshow*, 362; Swain, *River of Time*, 133–34.

18. Bizot, *The Gate*, 168–71. "Sirik Matak looked straight at us. . . . 'I know what I have to do,' replied the prince decisively."

19. Becker, *When the War Was Over*, 160, 193: "The very top political figures were reportedly murdered at the Cercle Sportif athletic club, the French-built haunt of the elite near the city's Wat Phnom, beheaded on the tennis court"; the "traitors named by the Khmer Rouge were: Ung Bun Hor, president of National Assembly; Luong Nal, minister of heath; Princess Mam Monivann, Sihanouk's Laotian wife; Sirik Matak; General So Kham Koy; In Tam, former premier; Cheng Heng, president of parliament; and Son Ngoc Thanh."

20. "Cambodian Diplomat Is Bitter About 'Way the U.S. Used Us,'" *The New York Times*, April 17, 1975. Abdulgaffar Peang Meth was the press and information officer for the Cambodian embassy in Washington, D.C. from 1973 to 1975. He remained in Washington and did not return to Cambodia until 1979.

21. "Sihanouk Pledges 'Democratic' Rule," *The New York Times*, April 16, 1975; "Cambodian Communists in Paris Pledge a Policy of Nonalignment and Neutrality," *The New York Times*, April 18, 1975; "Peking Congratulates Sihanouk, Victorious Cambodian Forces," *The New York Times*, April 18, 1975; "Cambodians Designate Sihanouk as Chief for Life," April 25, 1975; "Sihanouk Is Willing to Pass Up Cambodian Rule," *The New York Times*, April 24, 1975.

22. Marvin and Susan Gettleman and Lawrence and Carol Kaplan, eds., *Conflict in Indo-China* (New York: Random House, 1970), 361. Henry Kamm, *Cambodia: Report from a Stricken Land* (New York: Arcade Publishing, 1998), 45, 195. David Ashley, *Pol Pot Peasants and Peace: Continuity and Change in Khmer Rouge Political Thinking 1985–1991* (Ford Foundation, 1991), 52; see also Henry Kissinger, *Ending the Vietnam War* (New York: Simon and Schuster, 2003), 126–27; Becker, *When the War Was Over*, 83: "Sihanouk was uncanny. As each situation had warranted, he had willingly collaborated with the Vichy French, the Japanese fascists, and then the French colonialists again."

23. Peter Scott, *Lost Crusade: America's Secret Cambodian Mercenaries* (Annapolis: Naval Institute Press, 1998), 35: "The army, under General Lon Nol … had crushed a communist-inspired uprising with remarkable fury and chased the communists into the hills. There were massive demonstrations in Phnom Penh against the presence of the hated you'ens in the sanctuaries inside Cambodia, the staging areas being used to wage the war against South Vietnam."

24. Prince Sihanouk, *Prince Sihanouk on Cambodia* (Hamburg: Mittelungen Des Instituts Für Asienkunde Hamburg, Nummer 110, 1980), 12. Sihanouk announced on March 23, 1970, the establishment of the National United Front of Cambodia (known as FUNK, its French acronym). After the Lon Nol coup, the Prince "sent a message to the Cambodian people through Radio Peking to say: 'You must join the Khmer Rouge.'"

25. There remains a debate over the U.S. role in the Lon Nol takeover. Elizabeth Becker argues that "The coup had the earmarks of American approval if not direct American support" (*When the War Was Over*, 139); Marie Martin is more skeptical in *Cambodia: A Shattered Society*, 122; see also Gettleman, Gettleman, Kaplan, and Kaplan, *Conflict in Indo-China*, 369; Milton Osborne, *Politics and Power in Cambodia* (Camberwell, Australia: Longman, 1973), 111–12. Gettleman, Gettleman, Kaplan, and Kaplan, *Conflict in Indo-China*, 382–83; Sihanouk replied to Nixon on May 2, 1970: "Today, I would like once more to draw the attention of all the peoples and governments throughout the world to the absolutely unjustifiable character of the invasion and occupation of my country, Cambodia, by more than 70,000 Yankee troops and south Vietnamese mercenaries . . . and to the ultra-criminal character of the intensive bombing by US B-52's of many of our provinces, especially Svay Rieng and Kompong Cham" (389–90).

26. John Ranelagh, *The Agency* (London: Weidenfeld and Nicholson, 1986), 543. Ranelagh believed that the Nixon Doctrine "involved giving others arms and material with which to fight, rather than having American troops do the fighting themselves. It was containment 'on the cheap,' because the other countries doing the fighting would buy their supplies from America. It also provided Nixon with a rationale for pulling out of Vietnam."

27. Pratt, *Vietnam Voices*, 94.

28. William Burr, ed., *The Kissinger Transcripts* (New York: The New Press, 1998), 126; James Miller, *Democracy Is in the Streets* (New York: Simon and Schuster, 1987), 310–11;

Gettleman, Gettleman, Kaplan, and Kaplan, *Conflict in Indochina*, 389; Becker, *When the War Was Over*, 119.

29. Becker, *When the War Was Over*: "Lon Nol made no secret of his dream of puri- fying the Khmer race, the Khmer culture, and Khmer Buddhism of the foreign pollu- tants he thought had sapped the country's energy and eaten away at its identity and territory" (123). See also Scott, *Lost Crusade*, 59.

30. John Clark Pratt, *Vietnam Voices* (New York: Viking, 1984), 494.

31. Becker, *When the War Was Over*, 124; Scott. *Lost Crusade*, 148.

32. Becker, *When the War Was Over*, 123, 131; see also Gettleman, Gettleman, Kaplan, and Kaplan, eds., *Conflict in Indo-China*, 368; Bowden, *One Crowded Hour*, 16.

33. Shawcross, *Sideshow*, 23–28; Hurley Skroggins, "New Details on U.S. Devastation, 1970–1975," *Phnom Penh Post*, April 14–27, 2000. Kissinger maintains that "Sihanouk had acquiesced in, if not encouraged, the bombing of these sanctuaries; we desisted from ground operations across the border; Hanoi continued to use the sanctuaries, if at a high- er cost" (*Ending the Vietnam War*, 128–29); Richard Wood, *Call Sign Rustic: The Secret Air War Over Cambodia 1970–1973* (Washington: Smithsonian Institution Press, 2002), 146–48.

34. David Chandler, *The Tragedy of Cambodian History* (New Haven: Yale University Press, 1991), 225; *The Vietnam Experience: Cambodia and Laos*, vol. 6 (Boston: WGBH Television, 1996); Kissinger, *Ending the Vietnam War*, 478–79.

35. Estimates of the number of Cambodians killed by American bombs range wide- ly. Some claim that as many as 500,000 were killed. But as historian David Chandler points out, "Casualties, although, certainly high, are impossible to estimate" (*The Tragedy of Cambodian History*, 225); see also Becker, *When the War Was Over*, 18.

36. Sam Adams, *War of Number* (South Royalton, VT: Steerforth Press, 1994), 202–3. "U.S. intelligence had neglected to inquire whether our enemies in Cambodia had raised an army" (193–95). Adams estimated Khmer Rouge forces numbered between 100,000 and 150,000 in June 1971. Loch Johnson, *America's Secret Power* (New York: Oxford University Press, 1989), 62–63.

37. Craig Etcheson, *After the Killing Fields: Lessons from the Cambodian Genocide* (New York: Praeger, forthcoming), 141; "The administration's appeals that the United States not desert an ally fell on deaf congressional ears" (Becker, *When the War Was Over*, 157); "Cambodia: Another Week of Survival," *Time*, March 31, 1975.

38. The WGBH documentary *The Vietnam Experience: Cambodia and Laos* features footage of Pol Pot and Sihanouk from the king's 1973 trip to the "liberated zones"; Chandler, *Voices from S-21*, 126–27.

39. David Chandler, *Brother Number One: A Political Biography of Pol Pot* (Boulder: Westview Press, 1992), 41, 131; Martin, *Cambodia: A Shattered Society*, 163.

40. Kamm, *Cambodia: Report from a Stricken Land*, 131; Prince Sihanouk, *Prince Sihanouk on Cambodia*, 28: "Khieu Ponnary and Khieu Thirith are sisters, very intelli- gent intellectuals, who speak French and English fluently, and who are really much more educated than their husbands Pol Pot and Ieng Sary. They form an oligarchy: four persons dominating the whole of Cambodia"; see also Becker, *When the War Was Over*, 171–73; Martin, *Cambodia: A Shattered Society*, 162–63.

41. Him Huy, March 14, 1997, interview with author, Phnom Penh, Cambodia, tape recording.

42. Rudy Abramson, "U.S. Aid Only Hope for Cambodia—Ford," *The Los Angeles Times*, March 7, 1975; "Ford Hints at Blame for Cambodia," *The Los Angeles Times*, March

9, 1975; see also Kissinger, *Ending the Vietnam War*, 169, 471. Between 1970 and the end of the war, the following restrictions on aid to Cambodia were passed into law: the Fullbright amendment, the Cooper-Church amendment, the Symington-Case amendment, the Second Supplemental Appropriations Act for Fiscal Year 1973, the Continuing Appropriations Act for Fiscal Year 1974, the Foreign Assistance Act of 1973. Kissinger argues that "Cambodia became a symbol and a surrogate for the whole controversy over Vietnam. To Nixon, it was 'the Nixon doctrine in its purest form,' meaning that our policy was to help it defend itself without American troops" [quoting Nixon to press, November 12, 1971].

43. Kissinger, *Ending the Vietnam War*, 478–79.

44. Ambassador John Dean to Secretary of State Henry Kissinger, February 6, 1975, www.ford.utexas.edu/library/exhibits/vietnam.htm; Becker, *When the War Was Over*, 157. New U.S. Ambassador John Gunther Dean arrived in spring 1974. See also Kissinger, *Ending the Vietnam War*, 519.

45. Frank Snepp, *Decent Interval* (Lawrence: University of Kansas Press, 1977), 97.

46. Kissinger to State Department, February 18, 1975, www.ford.utexas.edu/library/exhibits/vietnam.htm. Henry Kissinger has written extensively about his experiences during the American pullout and offered long-winded rebuttals to critics like William Shawcross, author of *Sideshow*. Yet Kissinger, under special arrangement with the Library of Congress, has not released the bulk of his papers.

47. Snepp, *Decent Interval*: "Kissinger detested Sihanouk and felt that withdrawal of U.S. backing for the Lon Nol regime would be seen in Peking and other foreign capitals as a sign of American weakness. . . . At long last, after stonewalling for over a year, Kissinger had decided to pursue the political compromise long advocated by Martin, Ambassador Dean and the French" (97, 279).

48. Johnson, *America's Secret Power*, 129. Former CIA official Ray S. Cline remembers that in 1966 American policy makers began to "lose interest in an objective description of the outside world and were beginning to scramble for evidence that they were going to win the war in Vietnam. By 1969, this pathology had reached disease proportions, lasting through 1974, when, Cline continues, 'there was almost total dissent from the real world around us.'"

49. "Jane Fonda Tells of Sihanouk Bid," *The Los Angeles Times*, March 14, 1975; "Chief of Communist Forces in Cambodia Hails Victory," *The New York Times*, April 23, 1975.

50. Bowden, *One Crowded Hour*, 303: "There always seemed to be some liver in the pot after a battle, and there weren't many animals about by then. . . . When I had eaten under those circumstances, there was one chance in five that I was having a bit of man soup or stew." Scott, *Lost Crusade*, 116; see also Martin, *Cambodia: A Shattered Society*, 15.

51. Kenneth Quinn, "The Khmer Krahom Program to Create a Communist Society in Southern Cambodia," February 19, 1974, DC Cam document D17476; see also Kenneth Quinn, *The Origins and Development of Radical Cambodian Communism* (Ann Arbor: University Microfilms, 1982).

52. Becker, *When the War Was Over*, 140–42, 144; see also Ith Sarin, *Regrets for the Khmer Soul* (self-published), 1973. See also Bizot, *The Gate*, 7.

53. Bizot, *The Gate*, 5.

54. National Security Council Minutes, April 9, 1975, www.ford.utexas.edu/library/exhibits/vietnam.htm.

55. Shawcross, *Sideshow*, 360; Bowden, *One Crowded Hour*, 314–15.

56. Becker, *When the War Was Over*, 26. Pol Pot said in a July 1975 speech to soldiers in Phnom Penh: "In the whole world, since the advent of the revolutionary war and since the birth of U.S. imperialism, no people and no army has been able to drive the imperialists out to the last man and to score total victory over them."

57. "Cambodia's Purification," *Newsweek*, May 19, 1975.

58. Denise Heywood, "Turning Over a New Page," *Phnom Penh Post*, October 22–November 4, 1993; Nayan Chanda, *Brother Enemy* (New York: Harcourt, Brace, Jovanovich, 1986), 197; Martin, *Cambodia: A Shattered Society*, 183.

59. Jack Anderson and Les Whitten, "Report Hints Blood Debt Being Paid," *Washington Post*, May 12, 1975; Arnaud de Borchgrave, "Bloodbath in Cambodia," *Newsweek*, May 12, 1975; for more on the Mayaquez Affair, see Ralph Wetterhahn's definitive account in *The Last Battle* (New York: Carroll and Graf, 2001).

60. "Cambodia's Purification," *Newsweek*, May 19, 1975; Henri Locard, *The Khmer Rouge Gulag* (Paris: author, 1995), 31.

61. Snepp, *Decent Interval*, 340.

62. "Life Inside Cambodia," www.ford.utexas.edu/library/exhibits/vietnam.htm.

63. Kalyanee Mam, "Evidence of Sexual Abuse during the rule of Democratic Kampuchea," *Searching for the Truth* 15 (March 2001).

64. Becker, *When the War Was Over*: "Family life had to be eliminated. The state had to usurp the authority of the family if it was to survive. . . . Any sex before marriage was punishable by death in many cooperatives and zones" (211, 224). Kep Kanithakim, "Clean-Cut Children: A Failure of the Revolution," *Searching for the Truth* 21 (September 2001).

65. Ibid.; Samondara Vuthi Ros, "My Life Under the Leadership of Pol Pot," *Searching for the Truth* 4 (April 2000).

66. Ibid.; Peter Sainsbury and Chea Sotheacheath, "Good Intentions Paved Road to Mass Drudgery," *Phnom Penh Post*, April 14–27, 2000.

67. Heynowski & Scheumann Film Studios, *The Angkar* (Berlin, 1979).

68. Murray Marder, "Kissinger: No Pangs of Conscience About Vietnam," *Washington Post*, July 1, 1976; Les Whitten and Jack Anderson, "UN Ignores Cambodian Death March," *Washington Post*, June 23, 1975; Shawcross, *Sideshow*, 395; Martin, *Cambodia: A Shattered Society*, 339–41.

69. Ben Kiernan, *The Journal of Contemporary Asia* 7 (44) (1977). This April 24, 1976 letter to the editor is one of many written by members of the Indochina Resource Center: "Most of these 'atrocity' stories are based on interviews with the same small circle of refugees in Thailand. . . . The sources of the stories are suspect, and their failure to convince those with the most at stake tells heavily against the credibility of the reports. It must also be suggested that, however unsuccessfully, the stories were placed in circulation with the aim of discouraging trained Cambodians from assisting in the reconstruction of their devastated country." GC Hildebrand Indochina Resource Center, DC Cam document D16286. Some of Chomsky's letters to influential literary power brokers like Robert Silvers of *The New York Review of Books* ran to twenty typed pages. The tone of the letters was much sharper than Chomsky's more public efforts. Amnesty International Report; DC Cam document D16147.

70. Hearing Before the Subcommittee on International Relations, "Human Rights in Cambodia," House of Representatives, May 3, 1977, 14.

71. Ibid, 19–20.

72. Ibid, 34–35.

73. Gareth Porter and John Hildebrand, *Cambodia: Starvation and Revolution* (New

York: Monthly Review Press, 1977); Noam Chomsky and Edward Herman, "Distortions at Fourth Hand," *The Nation*, June 25, 1977. Chomsky lumped the Khmer-speaking François Ponchaud with Barron and Paul of *Reader's Digest* and concluded: "Their scholarship collapses under the barest scrutiny. . . . Ponchaud's book lacks the documentation provided in Hildebrand and Porter and its veracity is therefore difficult to assess." Chomsky and Herman attacked Ponchaud for honest errors of scholarship: "But the serious reader will find much to make him somewhat wary. For one thing, Ponchaud plays fast and loose with quotes and numbers. . . . Most significant is Ponchaud's account of the evacuation of Phnom Penh in April 1975. . . . If indeed, postwar Cambodia is, as he believes, similar to Nazi Germany, then his comment is perhaps just, though we may add that he has produced no evidence to support this judgment. But if Cambodia is more similar to France after liberation, where many thousands of people were massacred within a few months under far less rigorous conditions than those left by the American war, then perhaps a rather different judgment is in order. That the latter conclusion may be more nearly correct is suggested by the analyses mentioned earlier." The Khmer-speaking Catholic priest did not back down under the assault by Chomsky and his followers: "I was compelled to conclude, against my will, that the Khmer revolution is irrefutably the bloodiest of our century. A year after publication of my book I can unfortunately find no reason to alter my judgment" (Ponchaud, *Cambodia: Year Zero*, xiii–iv); Jean Lacouture, "The Bloodiest Revolution," *The New York Review of Books*, March 31, 1977.

74. Ibid.; Chomsky and Herman, "Distortions at Fourth Hand."

75. Chomsky and Herman, "Distortions at Fourth Hand." Sophal Ear, "Romanticizing the Revolution," *Searching for the Truth* 16 (April 2001); William Shawcross, "The Third Indochina War," *The New York Review of Books*, April 6, 1978; see also letter to the editor from Gareth Porter. Shawcross, *The Quality of Mercy*, 55–63; Denise Heywood, "Turning Over a New Page," *Phnom Penh Post*, October 22–November 4, 1993; William Shawcross, "Cambodia Under Its New Rulers," *The New York Review of Books*, March 4, 1976.

76. DC Cam document D16565. David Hawk best summarized Chomsky's two-pronged strategy in a May 29, 1988, letter: "They minimize the Khmer Rouge human rights violations, yet insist that this was never their point or purpose. They deny that the Khmer Rouge policy was genocidal, but misleading misquote and misuse the title of the commercialized version of a report by a Finnish study group on Cambodia to talk of a 'decade of genocide'—the first 'phase' being that of the U.S. bombing, which caused the second 'phase' Pol Pot. This crude polemical device allows them to place the blame for it all on the Americans. . . . Chomsky and Herman further argue, most disingenuously, that they did not deny the Khmer Rouge atrocities at all, but only the misuse of Khmer Rouge atrocity stories by press and media functioning in the propaganda service of the U.S. imperialist forces." Ponchaud letter to Noam Chomsky, DC Cam document D17341; Noam Chomsky correspondence from the David Hawk papers, DC Cam Documents D17352–8.

77. The *New York Times* columnist denied the Ukrainian famine in 1933 (Anthony Lewis, ed., *Written Into History: Pulitzer Prize Reporting of the Twentieth Century from The New York Times* [New York: Times Books, 2001], xix, 89–90) and earned a Pulitzer Prize for his efforts.

78. DC Cam document D16565.

79. Jacques Bekaert, *Cambodian Diary: Tales of a Divided Nation 1983–1986* (Bangkok: White Lotus Press, 1997), 133–34.

80. "Tales of a Brave New Kampuchea," *Time,* November 21, 1977; Becker, *When the War Was Over*: "The film and magazine showed a happy, hardworking country of peasants and workers digging irrigation canals, planting rice, and reinvigorating small industry. The propaganda war to change Cambodia's image was under way. . . . Ieng Sary took his role in this mission seriously. He traveled to New York, where he addressed the United Nations. . . . He passed out the magazine, screened the film, and laughed at the stories of hardship told by refugees from Cambodia who had reached Thailand" (308).

81. Kamm, *Cambodia: Report from a Stricken Land*, 136–38; Becker, *When the War Was Over*, 139, 315–16.

82. "Nuon Chea 1978," *Searching for the Truth* 20 (August 2001); Chandler, *The Tragedy of Cambodian History*, 306; Becker, *When the War Was Over*, 322; Locard, *The Khmer Rouge Gulag*, 31.

83. Robert Brown and David Cline, *The New Face of Kampuchea* (Chicago: Liberator Press, 1979), 2; "US Leftist Editor Says Cambodians Are Thriving," *The New York Times*, May 12, 1978.

84. Chandler, *Voices from S-21*, 2–3.

85. Associated Press, December 15, 1979; Chandler, *Voices from S-21*, 136; John Bryson, "Cambodia Rakes the Ashes of Her Ruin," *Life* (March 1980); "Names of English Speaking Prisoners in 1979 Reported," *AFP*, January 12, 1980; Paul Vogle, "Cambodia Says Five Americans Slain by Khmer Rouge," *UPI*, October 2, 1982. The photograph of Clark was published in the *Life* article.

3. "The Angkar is more important to me than my father and mother."

1. David Chandler, *Voices from S-21: Terror and History in Pol Pot's Secret Prison* (Berkeley: University of California Press, 1999), viii, 2, 4, 17, 24, 78; some of the first images of S-21 prison appear in Heynowski & Scheumann Film Studios, *The Angkar* (Berlin, 1979).

2. Meng Try Ea and Sorya Sim, *Victims and Perpetrators? Testimony of Young Khmer Rouge Cadres* (Phnom Penh: Documentation Center of Cambodia, 2001), 7, 16; comparisons between parents and Angkar were common in self-criticisms found at S-21 in 1979; see Marie Martin, *Cambodia: A Shattered Society* (Berkeley: University of California Press, 1994), 182.

3. Chandler, *Voices from S-21*, 87; Him Huy, March 14, 1997, interview with author, Phnom Penh, Cambodia, tape recording.

4. Chandler, *Voices from S-21*, 152, 132, 108.

5. Youk Chhang, "Khieu Samphan," *Searching for the Truth* 7 (July 2000).

6. Tuol Sleng torture manual courtesy of Tuol Sleng Museum.

7. Steve Robinson, "For Four Americans, a Savage End to an Asian Caper," *Life* (March 1980). "Declaration of James William Clark: Agent of the CIA of the USA," May 23, 1978, courtesy of Tuol Sleng Director Sopheara Chey.

8. Chandler, *Voices from S-21*, 79, 92–93.

9. Ibid. 79, 110.

10. Meng Try Ea and Sorya Sim, *Victims and Perpetrators?*, 48.

11. Chandler, *Voices from S-21*, 25, 140.

12. Henry Kamm, "Vietnam Speeds Cambodia Drive, Pressing Capital," *The New York Times*, January 4, 1979; "Pol Pot's Lifeless Zombies," *Time*, December 3, 1979; Jacques

Bekaert, *Cambodian Diary: Tales of a Divided Nation 1983–1986* (Bangkok: White Lotus Press, 1997), 9.

13. "Cambodian Says Invasion Is a 'Life-or-Death Struggle,'" *The New York Times*, January 6, 1979; "Cambodia Appeals for U.N. Help Against Vietnam," *The New York Times*, January 3, 1979.

14. Graham Hovey, "U.S. Backs Cambodia at U.N.," *The New York Times*, January 4, 1979; "U.S. Is Not Committed on the Cambodia Issue," *The New York Times*, January 5, 1979; for an example of the new more moderate Khmer Rouge, see Henry Kamm, "Aide Says Pol Pot Regime Is Ready To Join Old Foes Against Vietnam," *The New York Times*, May 31, 1979.

15. "UN Urges Vietnam to Leave Cambodia," *The New York Times*, November 15, 1979; Bernard Gwertzman, "U.S. Officials See a Bright Future In New Relationship With Peking," *The New York Times*, January 2, 1979; Evan Gottesman, *Cambodia After the Khmer Rouge: Inside the Politics of Nation Building* (New Haven: Yale University Press, 2003), 36–38.

16. Heynowski and Scheumann made three films about Cambodia between 1979 and 1981.

17. Malcolm Browne, "Security Council to Meet Today on Crisis in Cambodia," *The New York Times*, January 11, 1979. Sihanouk claimed that the Khmer Rouge kept him alive between 1975 and 1979 "Because President Mao Tse Tung and Chou Enlai told . . . Pol Pot and Khieu Samphan in September of 1975, 'You will not kill Sihanouk, his wife and children'" Heynowski & Scheumann Film Studios, *Jungle War* (Berlin, 1981).

18. Fox Butterfield, "Sihanouk Requests Aid of U.S. and U.N.," *The New York Times*, January 9, 1979.

19. Kenton Clymer, "Jimmy Carter, Human Rights, and Cambodia," *Diplomatic History* (April 2003):245. Nayan Chanda, *Brother Enemy* (New York: Harcourt, Brace, Jovanovich, 1986), 377, 388–89. Gottesman, *Cambodia After the Khmer Rouge*, 31, 42–43; Elizabeth Becker, *When the War Was Over* (1986; reprint, New York: Public Affairs, 1998), 446; Bernard Gwertzman, "U.S. to Mute Voice in Cambodia Debate," *The New York Times*, January 10, 1979; Bernard Gwertzman, "U.S. Officials See a Bright Future In New Relationship With Peking," *The New York Times*, January 2, 1979.

20. "Cambodia Appeals for U.N. Help Against Vietnam," *The New York Times*, January 3, 1979.

21. Malcolm Browne, "Sihanouk Appeals to U.N. Council to Get Vietnam out of Cambodia," *The New York Times*, January 11, 1979.

22. Ibid.

23. "Reds Clash on Cambodia: Big Show at UN," *The New York Times*, January 13, 1979; "U.N. Council Talks on Cambodia Widen," *The New York Times*, January 13, 1979; "Third World and West Join to Assail Vietnam in U.N.," *The New York Times*, January 14, 1979; "Phnom Penh Falls Again," *The New York Times*, January 9, 1979; Malcolm Browne, "Third World and West Join to Assail Vietnam in UN," *The New York Times*, January 14, 1979.

24. Henry Kamm, "Cambodian, Peking-Bound, Vows War Will Go On," *The New York Times*, January 11, 1979; Henry Kamm, *Cambodia: Report from a Stricken Land* (New York: Arcade Publishing, 1998), 136, 154–55.

25. "Some Evidence: Of the Plots Hatched By The Beijing Expansionists And Hegemonists Against The Kampuchean People," Press Department, Ministry of Foreign Affairs People's Republic of Kampuchea, 1982; Chanda, *Brother Enemy*, 348.

26. Ibid.

27. Becker, *When the War Was Over*, 432–44. Kenton Clymer, "Jimmy Carter, Human Rights, and Cambodia," *Diplomatic History* (April 2003):256–57.

28. Henry Kamm, "Pol Pot Forces Said to Retake Key Port," *The New York Times*, January 17, 1979.

29. They vowed to rebuild "the party as a pure Marxist Leninist one" (Margaret Slocum, *The People's Republic of Kampuchea 1979–89: The Revolution After Pol Pot* [Bangkok: Silkworm Books, 2004], 21). Lee Kuan Yew, *From Third World to First* (New York: HarperCollins, 2000):"He was a totally different character, a tough survivor of the Khmer Rouge, a prime minister appointed by the Vietnamese in the 1980s but agile enough to distance himself from them and be acceptable to the Americans and West Europeans" (327); see also Bekaert, *Cambodian Diary*, 133–35.

30. Howard De Nike, John Quigley, and Kenneth Robinson, eds., *Genocide in Cambodia* (Philadelphia: University of Pennsylvania Press, 2001), 57–58; Kelly McEvers, "The People's Revolutionary Tribunal of 1979," *The Cambodia Daily*, January 8–9, 2000.

31. De Nike, Quigley, and Robinson, eds., *Genocide in Cambodia*, 70.

32. De Nike, Quigley, and Robinson, eds., *Genocide in Cambodia*, 25–26; see also David Chandler, *The Tragedy of Cambodian History* (New Haven: Yale University Press, 1991), 277–78.

33. Ibid. 79.

34. Ibid. 376.

35. Ibid. 26.

36. Ibid. 54.

37. Ibid. 44–45.

38. Ibid. 28–29.

39. Ibid. 507–8.

40. Ibid.

41. Ibid.; "Cambodia Urges Death Penalty At Trial of Ex Leaders in Absentia," *The New York Times*, August 19, 1979.

42. Heynowski & Scheumann Film Studios, *Kampuchea: Death and Rebirth* (Berlin, 1979); Martin, *Cambodia: A Shattered Society*, 183.

43. Gottesman, *Cambodia After the Khmer Rouge*, 43; in the fall of 1980 the new U.S Secretary of State, Edmund Muskie, wanted to abstain from the UN vote for Pol Pot's credentials: "But eventually, under tremendous pressure from China, from American ambassadors in ASEAN capitals, and of course from Brzezinski, Muskie agreed to a U.S. vote in favor of Democratic Kampuchea. The Khmer Rouge retained their seat.... After 1982 Vietnam stopped challenging the Khmer Rouge at the UN, and the number of countries voting for the ASEAN resolution against Vietnam increased from 91 in 1979 to a record 114 in 1985" (382–83, 392); Bernard Nossiter, "Assembly, Rebuffing Soviet, Seats Cambodia Regime of Pol Pot," *The New York Times*, September 22, 1979; Bernard Nossiter, "Victory at U.N. Is Result of Strange Alliance," *The New York Times*, September 23, 1979.

44. Chanda, *Brother Enemy*, 377; MacAlister Brown and Joseph Zasloff, *Cambodia Confounds the Peacemakers 1979–1998* (Ithaca: Cornell University Press, 1998), 13.

45. *Far Eastern Economic Review: Yearbook 1980.*

46. *Documents from the Kampuchea Conference, Stockholm 17–18 November 1979* (Stockholm, 1979).

47. Heynowski & Scheumann Film Studios, *Kampuchea: Death and Rebirth*.

48. Ibid.

49. *Documents from the Kampuchea Conference, Stockholm 17–18 November 1979.*

50. Ibid.

51. Ibid.

52. Ibid.

53. Kenton Clymer, "Jimmy Carter, Human Rights, and Cambodia," *Diplomatic History* (April 2003):272.

54. Norodom Sihanouk, *Prince Sihanouk on Cambodia* (Hamburg: Mittelungen Des Instituts Für Asienkunde Hamburg, Nummer 110, 1980), 81.

4. "The weapon of the mouth"

1. In the spring of 1979, Brzezinski stated: "I encouraged the Thais to help the [Khmer Rouge]. The question was how to help the Cambodian people. Pol Pot was an abomination. We could never support him. But China could" (Kenton Clymer, "Jimmy Carter, Human Rights, and Cambodia," *Diplomatic History* [April 2003]: 273). Nayan Chanda, *Brother Enemy* (New York: Harcourt, Brace, Jovanovich, 1986), 256.

2. John Pilger, "The Long Secret Alliance: Uncle Sam and Pol Pot," *Covert Action Quarterly* (Fall 1997). According to Pilger, "The extent of this support—$85 million from 1980 to 1986—was revealed six years later in correspondence between congressional lawyer Jonathan Winer, then counsel to Sen. John Kerry (D-MA) of the Senate Foreign Relations Committee, and the Vietnam Veterans of America Foundation." Reporter Henry Kamm considered it "Thai blackmail": "either you provide food and we distribute it as we see fit, or we will accept no food aid at all for any Cambodians." The king reported to Leonard Woodcock, U.S. Ambassador to China, that humanitarian aid from UNICEF and the Red Cross "has been in a large part diverted by those 'war lords,' by the 'government,' and by the Cambodian 'resistance,' protected by China and Thailand" (*Cambodia: Report from a Stricken Land* [New York: Arcade Publishing, 1998], 151).

3. William Shawcross, *The Quality of Mercy* (New York: Simon & Schuster, 1984), 355.

4. Jacques Bekaert, *Cambodian Diary: Tales of a Divided Nation 1983–1986* (Bangkok: White Lotus Press, 1997), 17.

5. Bob Woodward, *Veil* (New York: Simon and Schuster, 1987): "There were two other covert support operations that were important, not because of the amount of money, but because of the principle. Casey had still managed to keep them secret. One was the $5 million in the budget for the Cambodian-resistance support operation, and his plan was to add another $12 million at the end of the year, even though this helped the Khmer Rouge indirectly" (425–26); Wilfred Burchett, *The China–Cambodia–Vietnam–Triangle* (Chicago: Vanguard Books, 1981), 112–13.

6. Heynowski & Scheumann Film Studios, *The Jungle War* (Berlin, 1981) and Loch Johnson, *America's Secret Power* (New York: Oxford University Press, 1989), 129. Cline received his Ph.D. from Harvard in 1949 and served as CIA station chief in Taiwan from 1958 to 1962; he was a top CIA analyst during the Cuban Missile Crisis. Charles Ameringer, *U.S. Foreign Intelligence* (Lexington, MA: Lexington Books, 1990), 250; Tim Weiner, "Ray S. Cline," *The New York Times*, March 16, 1996.

7. Evan Gottesman, *Cambodia After the Khmer Rouge* (New Haven: Yale University Press, 2002), 84–85.

8. Heynowski & Scheumann Film Studios, *Kampuchea: Death and Rebirth* (Berlin, 1979).

9. Heynowski & Scheumann Film Studios, *The Jungle War*.

10. "U.N.'s Parley on Cambodia Will Open Tomorrow," *The New York Times*, July 12, 1981; see also Bernard Gwetzman, "U.S. Sees Test of Ties to Moscow In Afghan and Cambodian Issues," *The New York Times*, July 3, 1981.

11. Bernard Ness, "UN's Parley on Cambodia," *The New York Times*, January 12, 1981; "Excerpts from Speech by Haig," *The New York Times*, July 13, 1981; "Mishaps Mar U.N.'s Cambodia Meeting," *The New York Times*, July 14, 1981.

12. Chanda, *Brother Enemy*, 388–89.

13. Heynowski & Scheumann Film Studios, *The Jungle War*.

14. Gottesman, *Cambodia After the Khmer Rouge*, 139.

15. Ibid. 138.

16. MacAlister Brown and Joseph Zasloff, *Cambodia Confounds the Peacemakers 1979–1998* (Ithaca: Cornell University Press, 1998), 19–21; David Hawk, "The Killing of Cambodia," *The New Republic*, November 15, 1982.

17. Chanda, *Brother Enemy*, 377, 382–83. Michael Haas, *Cambodia: Genocide by Proxy* (New York: Praeger, 1991), 312–15.

18. Kenton Clymer, "Jimmy Carter, Human Rights, and Cambodia," *Diplomatic History* (April 2003): 245.

19. Gottesman, *Cambodia After the Khmer Rouge*, 130; Bekaert, *Cambodian Diary*, 65.

20. Ibid. 231; Craig Etcheson, *After the Killing Fields: Lessons from the Cambodian Genocide* (New York: Praeger, forthcoming), 112.

21. Gottesman, *Cambodia After the Khmer Rouge*, 236–37.

22. Ibid. 235.

23. Ibid. 239–40: "The authors of the report arrived at two troubling conclusions: first, that 'respect for legality' had decreased over the past few years; and second, that education had not helped … .That is to say, the abuses are not committed as a result of a lack of understanding. They are committed intentionally for the purpose of winning more absolute power."

24. "Top Khmer Rouge Military Defector Describes a Meeting with Pol Pot," February 23, 1990, DC Cam Archives Document D17440.

25. Ibid.

26. Hun Sen Speech to Phnom Penh aid workers, March 23, 1989, DC Cam Archives Document D17456.

27. James Mayall, ed., *The New Interventionism 1991–1994* (New York: Cambridge University Press, 1996), appendix A, 127.

28. Brown and Zasloff, *Cambodia Confounds the Peacemakers*; Gottesman, *Cambodia After the Khmer Rouge*, 337; Bekaert, *Cambodian Diary*, 58.

29. Robert Kaplan, *The Coming Anarchy: Shattering the Dreams of the Post Cold War* (New York: Random House, 2000), 79–80.

30. Brown and Zasloff, *Cambodia Confounds the Peacemakers*, 84–88; for the text of the Paris Agreement see Mayall, *The New Interventionism 1991–1994*, 133–65.

31. Elizabeth Becker, "Cambodia: Laboratory for UN Dreams and Ambitions," *International Herald Tribune*, October 21, 1991; Andrew Sherry, "Genocide—A Word Not Forgotten in Cambodia" and "Genocide—A Word Forgotten in Cambodia," *AFP* September 17, 1991; see also Tom Fawthorp, "Cambodia: Khmer Rouge Face Permanent Prospect of State of Seige," *Interpress Service*, December 12, 1991; Gregory Stanton, "The Cambodian Genocide and International Law," *Genocide and Democracy in Cambodia* (New Haven: Yale University, Southeast Asian Studies, 1993); David Hawk, "The Killing

of Cambodia," *The New Republic*, November 15, 1982; Christophe Peschoux, "Enquette Sur: Les 'Nouveaux Khmer Rouge,'" DC Cam Archives Document D17437.

32. Serge Thion, *Watching Cambodia: Ten Paths to Enter the Cambodian Tangle* (Bangkok: White Lotus, 1993), 192.

33. Sheri Prasso, "Sihanouk '100 Percent' for Trying Khmer Rouge Leaders," *AFP*, November 16, 1991; "U.S. Senators Want Khmer Rouge Barred from Regaining Power," *Reuters* December 2, 1991.

34. Yasushi Akashi, "UNTAC Views," *Phnom Penh Post*, July 24–August 6, 1992; "NGOs Voice Views on Rehabilitation," *Phnom Penh Post* July 24–August 6, 1992.

35. Mayall, ed., *The New Interventionism 1991–1994*, 52–53; Carol Livingston *The Gecko Tails* (London: Weidenfeld and Nicholson, 1996), 51–52.

36. Ibid. 19–20, 41: "The Cambodian currency, the *riel*, had shot in four years from 87 to 2500 against the dollar. . . . Not everyone joined the UNTAC mission for the good of Cambodia; some needed a 'field' posting to climb the intricate UN salary scale. Others just wanted money, salting away their allowances. More than one paper-pusher from Geneva or New York found themselves in a well-paid, relatively powerful position in Phnom Penh."

37. Kevin Barrington, "Pay Dispute Undermines UNTAC Morale," *Phnom Penh Post*, March 12–25, 1993; see also "An Open Letter to Yasushi Akashi," *Phnom Penh Post*, October 11, 1992; Sara Colm, "U.N. Agrees to Address Sexual Harassment," *Phnom Penh Post*, October 11, 1992; "UNTAC Community Relations Officer," *Phnom Penh Post*, October 23, 1992.

38. Brown and Zasloff, *Cambodia Confounds the Peacemakers*, 281; John Brown, "Interview with Gen. Sanderson," *Phnom Penh Post*, September 24–October 7, 1993. General Sanderson addressed his critics: "There were a lot of suggestions that we should have enforced the relationship. What I am saying to you is if we had done so, we would have lost the whole plot, we would have lost the peace-keeping ethos, the threat that would have emerged from that would have been a threat to all elements of UNTAC, not just the military component."

39. Peter Eng, "KR Spells Out Timeline For Disarmament," *Phnom Penh Post*, July 24–August 6, 1992; Damien Healy, LC, UNTAC HQ, "UNTAC Rebuts Critic," *Phnom Penh Post*, October 23, 1992.

40. Sheri Prasso, "Khmer Rouge Wants a Battlefield in Phnom Penh," *AFP*, September 9, 1992.

41. Peter Eng, "KR Spells Out Timeline For Disarmament," *Phnom Penh Post*, July 24–August 6, 1992.

42. Nate Thayer, "An Interview with Khmer Rouge Leader Khieu Samphan," *Phnom Penh Post*, August 27, 1992.

43. Caroline Gluck, "One Year After the Paris Accords: An Interview with Yasushi Akashi," *Phnom Penh Post*, November 6–12, 1992.

44. "HIV Threatens to Claim UNTAC's Highest Casualties," *Phnom Penh Post*, October 22–November 4, 1993.

45. Steven Edwards, "UN Blamed for Bringing AIDS to Cambodia," *National Post*, August 23, 2000.

46. Kaplan, *The Coming Anarchy*, 96. Mang Channo, "Cambodia's New Challenge: AIDS," *Phnom Penh Post*, January 1–14, 1993; Mang Channo, "Sex Trade Flourishing in Capital," *Phnom Penh Post*, February 12–25, 1993.

47. Moeun Chhean Nariddh, "Deadly Myths Which Help Spread AIDS," *Phnom Penh*

Post, May 6–19, 1994; "HIV Threatens to Claim UNTAC's Highest Casualties," *Phnom Penh Post*, October 22–November 4, 1993; Leo Dobbs, "First Confirmed AIDS Deaths," *Phnom Penh Post*, April 7–20, 1995; Katrina Peach, "Alarm Over New AIDS Figures," *Phnom Penh Post*, December 31, 1993–January 13, 1994; Katya Robinson, "Fight Against Aids Stacked with Problems," *Phnom Penh Post*, December 15–28, 1995.

48. "An Open Letter to Yasushi Akashi," *Phnom Penh Post*, October 11, 1992; Yasushi Akashi's response, *Phnom Penh Post*, November 20–December 3, 1992; Sara Colm, "U.N. Agrees to Address Sexual Harassment issue," *Phnom Penh Post*, October 11, 1992.

49. Ken Stier, "Helicopter Potshots Shoot Down UNTAC Mobility," *Phnom Penh Post*, November 20–December 3, 1992; Nate Thayer, "Khieu Samphan: Gloomy Prospects for Khmer Elections," *Phnom Penh Post*, November 6–19, 1992.

50. William Shawcross, *Cambodia's New Deal* (Washington, DC: Carnegie Endowment, 1994), 14: "Sanderson's then deputy, the French General Michel Loridan, wanted to call the Khmer Rouge's bluff and send U.N. troops into their areas at once. But Sanderson believed that such pressure might at once result in wider warfare"; Kevin Barrington, "Security Concerns Loom Over Polls" *Phnom Penh Post*, May 21–June 3, 1993.

51. Ibid.; Ben Kiernan, "U.N.'s Appeasement Policy Falls Into Hands of Khmer Rouge Strategists," *Phnom Penh Post*, November 20–December 3, 1992.

52. Kevin Barrington, "Bulgarians Executed in Cold Blooded Attack," *Phnom Penh Post*, April 9–22, 1993.

53. Robert H. Reid, "Hun Sen Calls for U.N. to Get Tough with Khmer Rouge," *Phnom Penh Post*, January 15–28, 1993; Nate Thayer, "Sihanouk Poised to Take Control," *Phnom Penh Post*, January 29–February 11, 1993. Ker Munthit, "Hun Sen Accuses KR Leader of Genocide," *Phnom Penh Post*, April 9–22, 1993.

54. Ben Kiernan, "U.N.'s Appeasement Policy Falls Into Hands of Khmer Rouge Strategists," *Phnom Penh Post*, November 20–December 3, 1992. Kevin Barrington, "Boutros-Ghali Says UNTAC Aimed Too High," *Phnom Penh Post*, May 21–June 3, 1993.

55. Nate Thayer, "KR Vows to Foil UNTAC Election; Split Emerges in FUNCINPEC," *Phnom Penh Post*, April 9–22, 1993; Kevin Barrington, "KR Open Bloody Anti-Poll Campaign," *Phnom Penh Post*, May 7–20, 1993; John C. Brown, "Elections: How Free, How Fair?" *Phnom Penh Post*, May 21–June 3, 1993 (excerpt from Khmer-language newspaper, orig. written by Snguen Nemull); Nate Thayer, "UNTAC Fails to Stem Political Violence," *Phnom Penh Post*, February 12–25, 1993.

55. Nate Thayer, "Sihanouk Poised to Take Control," *Phnom Penh Post*, January 29–February 11, 1993.

56. "Voters Mob Polling Stations," *Phnom Penh Post*, June 6–17, 1993; Ker Munthit, "Akashi: Election 'Free and Fair,'" *Phnom Penh Post*, June 6–17, 1993; Nate Thayer, "Samdech Balks at Heading Coalition," *Phnom Penh Post*, June 6–17, 1993; Brown and Zasloff, *Cambodia Confounds the Peacemakers*, 159.

57. Nate Thayer, "Sihanouk Back at the Helm," *Phnom Penh Post*, June 18–July 1, 1993.

58. Richard Hofstadter, *The Idea of a Party System* (Berkeley: University of California Press, 1968), 77; Lee Quan Yew, *From the Third World to the First* (New York: HarperCollins, 2000), 327.

59. Moeun Chhean Nariddh, "Reasons for the Wave of Crime," *Phnom Penh Post*, July 16–29, 1993; Kao Kim Hourn, "Beware the Soft Imperialists," *Phnom Penh Post*, September 10–23, 1995; Moeun Chhean Nariddh, "Rising Theft," *Phnom Penh Post*, October 8–21, 1993; "Act Now or Loose All Credibility," *Phnom Penh Post*, December 17–31, 1993.

60. Chris Burslem, "NGO's Demand Action on Car," *Phnom Penh Post*, September 10–23, 1993; Andrea Hamilton, "UNTAC Hit by Rash of Car Thefts," *Phnom Penh Post*, July 16–29, 1993.

61. Mang Channo, "Assemblyman Holds U.N. Team at Gunpoint," *Phnom Penh Post*, September 10–23, 1993; Chris Burslem, "UNHCR Ultimatum on Theft," *Phnom Penh Post*, September 24–October 7, 1993; Shawcross, *Cambodia's New Deal*, 35.

62. "Red Faces as Last UNTAC Ship Sets Sail," *Phnom Penh Post*, February 11–24, 1994; Chris Burslem, "UNHCR Ultimatum on Theft," *Phnom Penh Post*, September 24–October 7, 1993.

63. Kamm, *Cambodia: Report from a Stricken Land*, 227; Ker Munthit, "Alarm Over AIDS Virus Figures," *Phnom Penh Post* February 25–March 10, 1994.

64. "WHO Chief Takes Tuol Kork Pulse," *Reuters/Phnom Penh Post*, March 11–24, 1994; Ker Munthit, "AIDS Warning Issued," *Phnom Penh Post*, March 25–April 7, 1994; Moeun Chhean Nariddh, "AIDS Threat to 2 Million," *Phnom Penh Post*, October 21–November 3, 1994.

65. Nate Thayer, "KR Vows to Foil UNTAC Election Split Emerges in FUNCINPEC," *Phnom Penh Post*, April 9–22, 1993.

66. Shawcross, *Cambodia's New Deal*, 36.

67. Shawcross, *The Quality of Mercy*, 335–36.

68. Serge Thion, "Meaning of a Museum," *Phnom Penh Post*, August 27–September 9, 1993.

5. "Only the third person knows."

1. "Crimes In Aggression War in Vietnam," Ho Chi Minh City: Printing Factory 7.

2. Ibid.

3. Colonel Mai Lam, November 22, 1994, interview with author, Saigon, Vietnam, tape recording.

4. See "Accounting For Atrocities," Bard College publications 1998 (www.bard.edu).

5. Edward Vulliamy, *Seasons in Hell* (London: Simon and Schuster, 1994), 350–51: "The failure to act decisively, and by sponsoring the carve-up of Bosnia by racial population control through extreme violence, the international community has written a new book of rules for the volatile new Europe: rules under which the motives of those perpetrating the Bosnian carnage can be tolerated and accommodated, and their achievements rewarded and recognised as the basis for new national frontiers"; see also David Rieff, *A Bed for the Night* (New York: Simon and Schuster, 2002), 131–32.

6. Richard Goldstone biography, press release, UN press office; Betsey Pisik, "World Tribunal vs. Sovereignty," *The Washington Times*, October 26, 1998; Jane Perlez, "War Crimes Prosecutor Vents Frustrations," *The New York Times*, May 22, 1996.

7. Author's notes; see also Marlise Simons, "Far from Former Yugoslavia, First War Crimes Trial Opens," *The New York Times*, May 8, 1996.

8. Vulliamy, *Seasons in Hell*, 351: "Not only did the international community decline to defend Bosnia's government, unity and victim population, but it denied that government and population the means of defending itself."

9. Rieff, *A Bed for the Night*: "A 33-year UN veteran, Akashi was an adamant adherent of traditional peacekeeping. Any hint of taking sides or using force against one side was anathema to the bright, but single-minded Japanese diplomat with a dry sense of humor. One aide went so far as to call Akashi a 'peacenik.' He was extremely

uncomfortable with the enormous destructive power he wielded by controlling NATO airstrikes" (131–32). David Rhode, *Endgame* (New York: Farrar, Straus & Giroux, 1997), 365–66.

10. Eric Schmitt, "U.S. Admiral in Bosnia Sees a Crucial Time for NATO," *Time*, December 27, 1995; Jane Perlez, "Officer Says NATO Can Seize Serbs if Ordered To," *The New York Times*, June 21, 1995.

11. "A Toast to UN's Humiliation: Drinks with the Butcher of Bosnia," *The Sunday Times*, July 16, 1995. Rieff, *A Bed for the Night*, (131–32).

12. Heynowski & Scheumann Film Studios, *Pilots in Pajamas* (Berlin, 1967); see also Robinson Risner, *The Passing of the Night: My Seven Years as a Prisoner of the North Vietnamese* (New York: Random House, 1974), 163–64.

13. Gerhard Scheumann, August 22, 1995, interview with author, Berlin, tape recording.

14. Ibid.

15. Jörg Friedrich, August 23, 1995, interview with author, Berlin, tape recording.

16. Heynowski & Scheumann Film Studios, *The Jungle War* (Berlin, 1981).

17. Marie Martin, *Cambodia: A Shattered Society* (Berkeley: University of California Press, 1994), 198–99; a snippet of the Chinese film is featured in Heynowski & Scheumann Film Studios, *The Angkar* (Berlin, 1979).

18. Martin, *Cambodia: A Shattered Society*, 323–25.

19. "A Camp Called Boeung Trabek," *Phnom Penh Post*, January 19–February 1, 2001; Martin, *Cambodia: A Shattered Society*,, 200–1.

20. DC Cam Document D17186.

21. Heynowski & Scheumann Film Studios, *The Angkar*.

22. Ibid. Henry Kamm interviewed Ieng Sary many times over the years, and best describes his changing alibis in *Cambodia: Report from a Stricken Land* (New York: Arcade Publishing, 1998), 137–41. Sary was the only Khmer Rouge leader to admit the existence of S-21 prison. Pol Pot denied it until the end.

23. Seth Mydans, "Official Embrace of Khmer Rouge Leader Roils Cambodia," *The New York Times*, August 16, 1996; for Sary's response, see Seth Mydans, "Khmer Rouge's No. 2 Denounces No. 1," *The New York Times*, August 17, 1996; William Shawcross, "Tragedy in Cambodia," *The New York Review of Books*, November 14, 1996.

24. Jason Barber, "KR Succumbs to Hidden Rivalries," *Phnom Penh Post*, August 23–September 5, 1996.

25. "While Pol Pot Orders Deadly 'Clean-up," *Phnom Penh Post*, January 13–26, 1995.

26. Carol Livingston, *The Gecko Tails* (London: Weidenfeld and Nicholson, 1996), 252.

27. Ros Sokhet, "KR Defections Almost 7,000," *Phnom Penh Post*, January 13–26, 1995; Chea Southeacheath and Chris Decherd, "Mass Rebel Defections Announced by Hun Sen," *The Cambodia Daily*, August 9–11, 1996; Chris Decherd, "Cautious DNUM Transfers Final Troops to Gov't Fold," *The Cambodia Daily*, November 8–10, 1996; Chris Decherd and Touch Rotha, "Ieng Sary's Troops Join Gov't Forces," *The Cambodia Daily*, November 7, 1996.

28. Nate Thayer, "Govts row over defectors," *Phnom Penh Post*, November 4–17, 1994.

29. Ibid.

30. Seth Mydans, "An Amnesty in Cambodia," *The New York Times*, September 18, 1996.

31. "King 'Bowed' Before PMs in Ieng Sary Case," *Cambodia Daily*, October 9, 1996; Laura Ngo, "Prince Urges Int'l Tribunal for Ieng Sary," *Cambodia Daily*, October 9, 1996.

32. Chris Decherd, "Ranariddh Makes Surprise Visit to Pailin," *The Cambodia Daily*, October 15, 1996. Chris Decherd, "KR Radio Lashes Out, Denies Rebel Weakness," *The Cambodia Daily*, October 16, 1996.

33. Seth Mydans, "Official Embrace of Khmer Rouge Leader Roils Cambodia," *The New York Times*, August 16, 1996.

34. "Rebel Dissidents Call for Land Rights and Praise Buddhism," *The Cambodia Daily*, August 19, 1996.

35. "Ieng Sary Lashes Out at 'Dictatorial and Lying' Saloth Sar," *The Cambodia Daily*, August 19, 1996.

36. Ibid.

37. "The Gecko," *Phnom Penh Post,* August 12, 1996.

38. Ieng Sary, "DNUM Presents 'True Facts' About Democratic Kampuchea," *The Cambodia Daily*, September 10, 1996; "KR Radio Says Ieng Sary Involved in Killings," *The Cambodia Daily*, September 13, 1996.

39. Huw Watkins, "King: PMs Jumped the Gun on Sary Amnesty," *Phnom Penh Post*, September 20–October 3, 1996.

40. Seth Mydans, "An Amnesty in Cambodia," *The New York Times*, September 18, 1996.

41. Ibid.

42. Chris Decherd, "The Hard-Liners Give Up; Locations of Others Unclear," *Cambodia Daily*, October 7, 1996.

43. "Hun Sen: Cambodia United 'At Any Price,'" *Phnom Penh Post*, October 4–17, 1996.

44. Ibid.

45. Ibid.

46. Ibid.

47. Laurence Picq, "A Peace in Shame," *Phnom Penh Post*, August 26, 1996.

48. Ibid.

49. Chris Decherd, "Ranariddh Makes Surprise Visit to Pailin," *Cambodia Daily*, October 15, 1996.

6. "I am excellent survivor."

1. "Living with Pol Pot," *Cambodia Times*, February 1996; Seth Mydans, "Cambodian Killers' Careful Records Used Against Them," *The New York Times*, June 7, 1996.

2. Ibid.; David Chandler, *Voices from S-21: Terror and History in Pol Pot's Secret Prison* (Berkeley: University of California Press, 1999), 17.

3. Robin McDowell, "Photographer Recalls Days Behind Lens at Tuol Sleng," *The Cambodia Daily,* February 4, 1997.

4. After reading Doug Niven's and David Chandler's interviews with Nhem En, I was convinced that he was the Tuol Sleng photographer.

5. Carol Livingston, *The Gecko Tails* (London: Weidenfeld and Nicholson, 1996), 66.

6. Sok Sin, September 15, 2000, interview with Lisa Miller, Kompong Speu, Cambodia, videotape.

7. Ibid.

8. Sok Sin, September 15, 2001, interview with author, Phnom Penh, Cambodia.

9. Livingston, *The Gecko Tails*, 13.

10. Lisa Miller, "Pali Sutras for the Soul of 'Survivor' Sok Sin," *Phnom Penh Post*, November 23–December 6, 2001.

11. Author's notes.

12. Sok Sin, September 15, 2000, interview with Lisa Miller.

13. Van Nath, March 11, 1997, interview with author, Phnom Penh, Cambodia, tape recording; for more see Van Nath, *A Cambodian Prison Portrait: One Year in the Khmer Rouge's S21* (Bangkok: White Lotus Press, 1998).

14. Nhem En, March 12, 1997, interview with author, Phnom Penh, Cambodia, tape recording.

15. Him Huy, March 14, 1997, interview with author, Phnom Penh, Cambodia, tape recording; see also Bou Saroeun, "Toul Sleng Torturer: What I've Said Is Enough," *Phnom Penh Post*, January 22–February 4, 1999; Chandler, *Voices from S-21*, 25: "He came to S-21 in early 1977 as a guard, and in 1978 he took charge of documenting prisoners entering the facility and those executed at Cheung Ek, duties previously carried out by Peng. In late 1978 Huy was put in charge of security matters."

7. "Am I a savage person?"

1. Jason Barber and Christine Chaumeau, "Slaughter on Sunday—March 30, 1997," *Phnom Penh Post*, April 4–17, 1997; Christine Chaumeau, "Pain, Horror, and Too Much Blood," *Phnom Penh Post*, April 4–17, 1997; Joshua Phillips and Jason Barber, "Killers on Foot and Moto," *Phnom Penh Post*, April 4–17, 1997; "PM's Soldiers to Be Queried," *Phnom Penh Post*, May 16–29, 1997. "The attackers escaped to the Wat Botum compound, which is the Second Prime Minister's compound and the soldiers prevented people from [chasing] them.' . . . Everyone throughout the country knows who did it" ("FBI Report on Rainsy Rally," *Phnom Penh Post*, October 15–28, 1999).

2. "Grenade Attack on Cambodian Rally Kills 25, 75 Wounded," *The New York Times*, March 31, 1997.

3. Ibid.

4. Ibid.

5. Ibid.

6. "King: 'My duty to ring the alarm bell,'" *Phnom Penh Post*, April 4–17, 1997.

7. "MPs' letter to UN Sec-Gen," *Phnom Penh Post*, April 18–May 1, 1997.

8. Seth Mydans, "Men Once Led By Pol Pot Say They Have Him," *The New York Times*, June 19, 1997; "Son Sen and Yun Yat: Living by the Sword," *Phnom Penh Post*, June 27–July 10, 1997; "KR Radio Turns on Pol Pot," *Phnom Penh Post*, June 27–July 10, 1997; Chea Sotheacheath and Christine Chaumeau, "Hardliners Split as PMs Quarrel," *Phnom Penh Post*, May 3–15, 1997.

9. Bou Saroeun and Peter Sainsbury, "Prince's KR Deal Laced with Treachery," *Phnom Penh Post*, May 22–June 4, 1998.

10. Jason Barber and Christine Chaumeau, "Power Struggle Shatters KR Leadership," *Phnom Penh Post*, June 27–July 10, 1997.

11. "Pol Pot Must Be Tried Properly Says Albright," *Reuters*, July 29, 1997; Elizabeth Becker, "U.S. Spearheading Effort to Bring Pol Pot to Trial," *The New York Times*, June 23, 1997.

12. Seth Mydans, "Chinese Resist War Crimes Trial," *The New York Times*, June 25, 1997.

13. Jason Barber, "Democracy from the Barrel of a Gun," *Phnom Penh Post*, July 12–24, 1997; Robin McDowell, "Coup Carried Out in Cambodia," *AP*, July 7, 1997.

14. "U.S. Department of State: Daily Press Briefing," July 7 and 8, 1997 (www.state.gov/r/pa/prs/dpb/2003/c8043.htm).

15. "Statement of H.E. Samdech Hun Sen Second Prime Minister of the Royal Government," July 7, 1997, press release; "Background on the July 1997 Crisis: Prince Ranariddh's Strategy of Provocation," CPP White Paper 1997.

16. Jason Barber and Claudia Rizzi, "Funcinpec Military Chiefs Hunted Down," *Phnom Penh Post*, July 12–24, 1997; "Amnesty Condemns Cambodia Violence, Intimidation," *Reuters*, July 23, 1998.

17. Ker Munthit, "Cambodia Fighting Escalates," *AP*, July 8, 1997; Jason Barber and Claudia Rizzi, "Funcinpec Military Chiefs Hunted Down," *Phnom Penh Post*, July 12–24, 1997; Jason Barber, "Nat. Police Involvement in Murder Denied," *Phnom Penh Post*, August 29–September 11, 1997.

18. Tyler Marshall, "US Decries Cambodia Takeover," *The Los Angeles Times*, July 9, 1997; *Post* staff and Reuters, "HR Groups Report More Murders," *Phnom Penh Post*, August 15–28, 1997; Katya Robinson, "Cambodian Royalists Cower After Official's Murder," *AP*, July 9, 1997; "Of 4 Men Hunted by Hun Sen, 2 Now Dead," *CNN Online*, July 9, 1997; Ker Munthit, "Cambodia Opponent Killed in Custody," *AP*, July 8, 1997.

19. Bou Saroeun and Peter Sainsbury, "Prince's KR Deal Laced with Treachery," *Phnom Penh Post*, May 22–June 4, 1998.

20. Robin McDowell, "Cambodian Opposition Party Headquarters Looted, Documents Burned," *Boston Globe*, July 11, 1997.

21. Nick Lenaghan, "Report to Gov't as PM Rounds on Rights Staff," *Phnom Penh Post*, August 29–September 11, 1997; Robin McDowell, "Coup Leaders Round Up Hun Sen Forces," July 9, 1997; Elizabeth Moorthy and Chea Sotheacheath, "Another Body Unearthed; More to Come," *Phnom Penh Post*, November 7–20, 1997.

22. "Hun Sen Meets the Press," *Phnom Penh Post*, July 12–24, 1997.

23. Ibid.

24. Nate Thayer, "Brother Enemy No. 1," *Phnom Penh Post*, August 15–28, 1997.

25. Ibid. Ted Koppel, *Nightline*, August 28, 1997; Ker Munthit, "Hun Sen: Pol Pot Trial a 'Farce,'" *AP*, July 31, 1997.

26. Nate Thayer, "Pol Pot: The End," *Far Eastern Economic Review*, August 7, 1997.

27. Nate Thayer, "Brother Enemy No.1," *Phnom Penh Post*, August 15–28, 1997.

28. Henry Kamm, *Cambodia: Report from a Stricken Land* (New York: Arcade Publishing, 1998), 241.

29. Nate Thayer, "Brother Enemy No.1," *Phnom Penh Post*, August 15–28, 1997.

30. Ibid.

31. Huw Watkins and Reuters, "Politics of Trying Pol Pot," *Phnom Penh Post*, October 10–23, 1997.

32. Ibid.

33. Nate Thayer, "'Am I a savage person?'" *Phnom Penh Post*, October 24–November 6, 1997, Nate Thayer, "Pol Pot: Unrepentant," *Far Eastern Economic Review*, October 30, 1997; Nate Thayer, "Fallen Tyrant Defends His Brutal Regime but Now Wants Cambodia Tied to West," *Washington Post*, October 28, 1997.

34. Ibid.

35. Nate Thayer, "The Laughing Butcher That Killed Only 'Yuon,'" *Phnom Penh Post*, October 24–November 6, 1997.

36. Ibid.

37. Ibid.

38. Pierre Sane, "Open Letter to Second Prime Minister Hun Sen from Amnesty International Secretary General Pierre Sane," July 11, 1997.

39. UN Center for Human Rights, "Evidence of Summary Executions, Torture, and Missing Persons Since 2–7 July 1997," August 21, 1997.

40. Jason Barber and Chea Sotheacheath, "Hun Sen Reinstates Ho Sok Suspects," *Phnom Penh Post*, October 10–23, 1997.

41. "Report Revealed as UN Comes Under Fire," *Phnom Penh Post*, June 5–18, 1998.

42. Keith Richburg, "Few at ASEAN See U.S. Concerns as Valid," *The Washington Post*, July 30, 1997; Steven Erlanger, "Asians Are Cool to Albright on Cambodians and Burmese," *The New York Times*, July 28, 1997; "Rights Group Demands ASEAN Act on Members' Records," Reuters, July 24, 1998.

43. "ASEAN Backs Off as Hun Sen Digs In," Reuters and *Phnom Penh Post*, July 25–August 7, 1997; Claudia Rizzi, "Tokyo Bid Prompts Offers but No Talk," *Phnom Penh Post*, November 21–December 4, 1997.

44. "Amnesty Criticizes Cambodian Peace Plan," *Japan Times*, March 4, 1998; *Post* staff and Reuters, "ASEAN Backs Off as Hun Sen Digs In," *Phnom Penh Post*, July 25–August 7, 1997: "Two of Cambodia's biggest aid donors, Japan and France, have refrained from expressing disapproval of Hun Sen."

45. Chea Sotheacheath, "Court Builds Ranariddh Case," *Phnom Penh Post*, September 26–October 9, 1997; Chris Seper, "Cambodian Convicted in Step Toward Election," *The Washington Post*, March 5, 1998; Robin McDowell, "Cambodian Prince Convicted in Plot," *AP*, March 18, 1998; Robin McDowell, "Cambodian Prince Sentenced," *AP*, March 18, 1998; Chhay Sophal, "Cambodia's Ranariddh Sentenced to 30 Years," Reuters, March 18, 1998; Robin McDowell, "Cambodian King Pardons Son," *AP*, March 21, 1998; for more on the Cambodian judiciary, see Basil Fernando and Terrance Wickremasinghe, "Justice in Name Only—No Genuine Courts," *Phnom Penh Post*, November 21–December 4, 1997; Nick Lenaghan and Claudia Rizzi, "Weapons Seizure Ignites Party Sniping," *Phnom Penh Post*, May 30–June 12, 1997; the seventy-eight cases included rocket launchers, rifles, pistols, and ammo.

46. Steven Erlanger, "U.S. Laments Takeover in Cambodia," *The New York Times*, July 9, 1997.

47. Robin McDowell, "Cambodian King Pardons Son," *AP*, March 21, 1998.

48. "U.S. Plays Down Reports of Cambodia Vote Fraud," *Reuters*, July 30, 1998. Seth Mydans, "Was Voting in Cambodia Really Fair? New Doubts," *The New York Times*, August 10, 1998.

49. Seth Mydans, "Thugs Attack Demonstrators In Cambodia; One Shot Dead," *The New York Times*, September 10, 1998.

50. Fareed Zakariah, "The Rise of Illiberal Democracy," *Foreign Affairs* 11/12 (1999).

51. Tina Rosenberg, "Hun Sen Stages an Election," *The New York Times Magazine*, August 30, 1998.

52. "Hun Sen Draws His Line in the Shifting Sands," *Phnom Penh Post*, January 8–21, 1999; Nate Thayer, "Nowhere to Hide," *Phnom Penh Post*, January 8–21, 1999; Nate Thayer, "Dying Breath," *Far Eastern Economic Review*, April 30, 1998.

53. Helen Jarvis, "PM Hun Sen: 'First you need to catch the fish'," *Phnom Penh Post*, February 19–March 4, 1999.

54. Ibid.

55. "Hun Sen Draws His Line in the Shifting Sands," *Phnom Penh Post*, January 8–21, 1999.

56. Ibid.

57. Ibid.

58. "UN Report Says Try Them," *Phnom Penh Post*, March 5–18, 1999.

59. "KR Trial Debate Set for Showdown," *Phnom Penh Post*, March 19–April 1, 1999.

60. For more on Ta Mok, see Jason Barber, "The Life and Crimes of Ta Mok," *Phnom Penh Post*, January 16–29, 1998.

61. Christine Chaumeau and Bruno Carette, "Hun Sen Makes His Case on 'The Trial,'" March 19–April 1, 1999.

62. Ibid.

63. Ibid.

64. "Survey: Prosecute Khmer Rouge," *Phnom Penh Post*, February 5–18, 1999.

65. Nic Dunlop, February 1, 2003, interview with author, Bangkok, Thailand; Nic Dunlop, "The Lost Executioner," *The Independent*, October 3, 1998.

66. Ibid.

67. Ibid.

68. "The Gecko," *Phnom Penh Post*, June 11–24, 1999; Caroline Gluck, "Mass Murderer's Missionary Full of Hope," *Phnom Penh Post*, July 9–22, 1999.

69. Anette Marcher, "Go-It-Alone Tribunal Seeks Foreign Gloss," *Phnom Penh Post*, October 1–14, 1999.

70. "Hun Sen's Speech to the United Nations," *Phnom Penh Post*, October 1–14, 1999.

71. Anette Marcher, "Go-It-Alone Tribunal Seeks Foreign Gloss," *Phnom Penh Post*, October 1–14, 1999.

72. Christine Chaumeau and Samreth Sopha, "'Sorry, very sorry' for So Much Death," *Phnom Penh Post*, January 8–21, 1999; Peter Sainsbury, "Expert: Chea as Culpable as Pol Pot," *Phnom Penh Post*, February 4–17, 2000.

73. Ibid.; Christine Chaumeau and Michael Hayes, "DNUM Nixes KR Trial," *Phnom Penh Post*, February 5–18, 1999.

74. Kenneth Roth, "KR Trial Standards," *Phnom Penh Post*, November 26–December 9, 1999.

75. Ibid.; "Cambodians Talk About the Khmer Rouge Trial," *Phnom Penh Post*, February 4–17, 2000. Anette Marcher, "National KR Tribunal Takes Shape," *Phnom Penh Post*, November 12–25, 1999; Anette Marcher and Yin Soeum, "KR Trial Law Sails Through Council," *Phnom Penh Post*, January 7–20, 2000; Anette Marcher, "Agreement Close on KR Trial," *Phnom Penh Post*, July 17–30, 2000.

8. "She is nice girl, but she is sick."

1. Touch Bunnil, "Beware of NGOs," *Phnom Penh Post*, April 30–May 13, 1999. "Meas Bopha, who runs a guesthouse here, knows what it is like to be victimized. One day she came home and her three children were gone. An acquaintance had simply taken them to sell" (Seth Mydans, "U.S. Interrupts Cambodian Adoptions," *The New York Times*, November 5, 2001).

2. Yin Soeum and Phelim Kyne, "Willing Executioners: Rough Justice in the Communes," *Phnom Penh Post*, January 21–February 3, 2000; "Why Is This Man Dead?" *Phnom Penh Post*, October 29–November 11, 1999; "Swift Trial and a Slow Death in Phnom Penh," *Phnom Penh Post*, December 10–23, 1999; Vong Sokheng and Anette Marcher, "University Mob Beats Thief to Death," *Phnom Penh Post*, July 7–20, 2000; Yin Soeun and Sarah Stephens, "Boy Beheaded for His Blood," *Phnom Penh Post*, December 10–23, 1999; Bou Saroeun, "Militias Bring Spectacle of Lynch Mobs," *Phnom Penh Post*, September 17–30, 1999.

3. "The Pelika Affair: 'We have more,' Say French," *Phnom Penh Post*, October 15–28, 1999: "*L'Express* journalist Alain Louyot said the diary itself had been verified through the hand writing and finger prints"; "Extracts from Piseth Pelika's Diary," *Phnom Penh Post*, October 15–28, 1999; "One Year Later, Pelika's Murderers Still Free," *Phnom Penh Post*, July 7–20, 2000; Anette Marcher, "Bun Rany Fails to Act on Pelika Diary," *Phnom Penh Post*, October 27–November 9, 2000.

4. "No Action on Acid Attack," *Phnom Penh Post*, December 10–23, 1999; Jeff Smith and Kay KimSong, "Healing the Wounds," *The Cambodia Daily*, February 5–6, 2000; "Svay Sitha's Acid-Throwing Wife at Home," *Phnom Penh Post*, June 23–July 6, 2000; Phelim Kyne, "Svay Sitha Picked for Human Rights Forum," *Phnom Penh Post*, August 4–17, 2000.

5. Brian Mockenhaupt and Saing Soenthrith, "Acid Suspect Still at Large," *The Cambodia Daily*, February 18, 2000; Lon Nara and Phelim Kyne, "Tat Samarina's Family in Terror," *Phnom Penh Post*, September 15–28, 2000; Phelim Kyne, "Teen Lover Sues for Acid Attack," May 12–25, *Phnom Penh Post*, 2000; Lon Nara and Phelim Kyne, "Acid Mutilation a Misdemeanor," *Phnom Penh Post*, January 5–18, 2001; Bou Saroeun, "Brave Woman Overcomes Acid Horror," *Phnom Penh Post*, May 12–25, 2000.

6. Beth Moorthy and Pok Sokundara, "AIDS Sufferers Being Urged to Speak Out," *Phnom Penh Post*, November 13–26, 1998; Beth Moorthy and Samreth Sopha, "AIDS Killer Looms Large," *Phnom Penh Post*, April 2–12, 1999.

7. Sarah Stevens, "Cambodia's HIV Toll: 150,000 and Rising," *Phnom Penh Post*, December 25–January 7, 1999; Helen Basili, "Saving Sex Slaves," *Phnom Penh Post*, April 12, 2001.

8. Moeun Chhean Narriddh, "AIDS Epidemic Sees Prenuptial Blood Tests Soar," *Phnom Penh Post*, September 3–16, 1999; "Cambodia Reported Rape Figures Triple," BBC online, April 20, 2000 (www.bbc.co.uk).

9. Donna Hughes, "'Welcome to Rape Camp'—Sexual Exploitation and the Internet in Cambodia," *The Journal of Sexual Aggression* 2000; Anette Marcher, "Slavery and Human Traffic in Cambodia," *Phnom Penh Post*, September 1–14, 2000; Phelim Kyne, "France Seeks Child Porn Suspect's Release," *Phnom Penh Post*, June 8–21, 2001; "Porn Suspect Planned S and M Child Brothel," *Phnom Penh Post*, June 22–July 5, 2001; Phann Ana and David Shaftel, "Court Clears Guynot of Pedophilia Charge," *The Cambodia Daily*, July 27–28, 2002: "The judge said sexually explicit photographs of young boys found in Guynot's possession did not qualify as evidence. Nor did the testimonies of five of his alleged young victims, the judge claimed"; Jason Barber, "Preying on the Vulnerable," *Phnom Penh Post*, June 16–29, 1995.

10. Author's notes.

11. Ham Samrang, "One of Only Two Remaining Tuol Sleng Survivors Dies," *Cambodia Daily*, February 17, 2000; "Tuol Sleng Torture Caused a Lifetime of Pain," *The Cambodia Daily*, February 23, 2000; Brian Mocken Laupt, "Celebrated Sculptor, Im Chan," *Phnom Penh Post*, February 18–March 2, 2000.

12. Craig Smith, "Profiting From His Shots of Pol Pot's Terror," *The Wall Street Journal*, September 16, 1997; Anette Marcher and Mai Rassmussen, "Khmer Rouge Reflect Without Regret," *Phnom Penh Post*, April 14–27, 2000. Nic Dunlop was also critical of En: "When his pictures were exhibited in the Museum of Modern Art in New York accompanied by a book entitled 'The Killing Fields' I wondered whether their meaning had been completely lost, whether what had happened under the Khmer Rouge had been fully understood."

13. Guy Trebay, "Killing Fields of Vision," *The Village Voice*.

14. Nhem En, November 15, 1999, interview with author, Phnom Penh, Cambodia, tape recording.

15. "Cambodians Talk About the Khmer Rouge Trial," *Phnom Penh Post*, February 4–17, 2000. Gina Chon and Thet Sambath, "Former KR Troops Want Trial," *The Cambodia Daily*, November 10, 2000.

16. "A Survivor Who Refuses to Forget," *Phnom Penh Post*, December 5, 1997.

17. Ibid.

18. Youk Chhang, "For the Truth," *Searching for the Truth* 1 (January 2000) and "For Memory and Justice," *Searching for the Truth* 13 (January 2001).In an April 17, 1995, *Wall Street Journal* op-ed entitled, "The Wrong Man to Investigate Cambodia," Stephen Morris, an Australian political scientist at Harvard, blasted the State Department's choice of Kiernan and called on Secretary of State Warren Christopher to "reverse a terrible decision that disgraces American honor and spits upon the graves of more than a million Cambodians." Kiernan responded with an admission that he had been wrong about the extent of Khmer Rouge atrocities and dismissed the charges against him as "only the latest round in a fifteen-year vendetta against a compatriot."

19. Ben Kiernan, "The Cambodian Holocaust," *The Wall Street Journal*, April 28, 1995 and "The Cambodian Holocaust—III," *The Wall Street Journal*, May 30, 1995; "Scholars Speak out on Cambodia Holocaust," *The Wall Street Journal*, July 13, 1995; "Will Yale Deliver," *The Wall Street Journal*, December 19, 1996; Eyal Press, "Unforgiven," *Lingua Franca*, April/May 1997.

20. Youk Chhang, "Accountability," *Searching for the Truth* 3 (March 2000).

21. Kosal Phat, "Mapping the 'Killing Fields' of the Democratic Kampuchea Regime," *Searching for the Truth* 1 (January 2000).

22. Youk Chhang, "For the Truth," *Searching for the Truth* 1 (January 2000).

23. Youk Chhang, "Memory," *Searching for the Truth* 2 (February 2000).

24. Youk Chhang, *Searching for the Truth* 10 (October 2000).

25. Ibid.

26. Robert Birsel, "Khmer Rouge Expert Blasts China Over Trial," Reuters, June 30, 1999.

27. Nhem En, November 10, 2000, interview with author, Phnom Penh, Cambodia, tape recording.

28. Author's notes.

29. Lisa Miller, "Pali Sutras for the Soul of 'Survivor' Sok Sin," *Phnom Penh Post*, November 23–December 6, 2001.

30. Author's notes.

31. John Gallager and Saing Soenthrith, "Not All Were Happy to See the President," *The Cambodia Daily*, November 14, 2000.

32. "Gov't Welcomes Chinese President, Support," *The Cambodia Daily*, November 14, 2000; see also "Hammerberg Claims China Made Moves to Block Trial," *The Cambodia Daily*, November 14, 2000.

33. Author's notes.

34. Nhem En, November 18, 2000, interview with author, Phnom Penh, Cambodia, tape recording.

9. "I am no longer HIV positive."

1. Anette Marcher, "The American Role in Putting Together a KR Trial Deal," *Phnom Penh Post*, April 28–May 11, 2000.

2. Ibid.; Om Yentieng, August 2002, interview with author, Phnom Penh, Cambodia; Vong Sokheng, "KR Draft Law: Slowly She Goes," *Phnom Penh Post*, May 11–24, 2001; Vong Sokheng, "Trial Delay UN's fault—PM," *Phnom Penh Post*, November 23–December 6, 2001.

3. Ibid.

4. Anette Marcher, "Agreement Close on KR Trial," *Phnom Penh Post*, July 7–20, 2000.

5. Anette Marcher, "KR Tribunal Drowning in Smokescreens and Politics," *Phnom Penh Post*, September 15–28, 2000; "Rin Verdict Leads to Khmer Rouge Tribunal Doubts," Phnom Penh Post, July 21–August 3, 2000.

6. Anette Marcher, "Rin Verdict Leads to Khmer Rouge Tribunal Doubts," *Phnom Penh Post*, July 21–August 3, 2000; Anette Marcher, "UN Accepts Flawed Tribunal for Khmer Rouge," *Phnom Penh Post*, October 13–26, 2000; Vong Sokheng, "UN, Ngos Criticise KR Law," *Phnom Penh Post*, February 2–15, 2001; Vong Sokheng, "UN Role in Tribunal Under Fire," *Phnom Penh Post*, July 16–29, 2001.

7. Doug Niven, e-mail to Peter Maguire, April 2001; Anette Marcher, "Law Banning Khmer Rouge Might Be Invalid," *Phnom Penh Post*, August 18–31, 2000.

8. Ibid.

9. Doug Niven, e-mail to Peter Maguire, April 2001.

10. Steven O'Connell and Chea Sotheacheath, "Top Monks Disagree on Role in Fighting AIDS," *Phnom Penh Post*, June 9–22, 2000.

11. Seth Mydans to Peter Maguire, July 13, 2001; Bill Bainbridge, "Chinese Clinic Boasts Free AIDS 'Cure,'" *Phnom Penh Post*, March 5–21, 2001; Chea Sotheacheath, "Illegal Pharmacies Healthier Than Patients," *Phnom Penh Post*, July 9–22, 1999; Bill Bainbridge, "Suppressed Report Shows Failing Health System," *Phnom Penh Post*, February 16–29, 2001; Denise Haywood, "A Cure for 'Everything,'" *Phnom Penh Post*, November 19–December 2, 1993.

12. Lisa Miller to Peter Maguire, October 24, 2001; "AIDS Orphan Figures Soar," *Phnom Penh Post*, February 16–March 1, 2001. By 2005, the study predicted 140,000 Cambodian AIDS orphans.

13. Lisa Miller, "Pali Sutras for the Soul of 'Survivor' Sok Sin," *Phnom Penh Post*, November 23–December 6, 2001.

14. Lisa Miller video footage of the entire event, November 8–10, 2001.

10. "I am not dead. I am alive."

1. Bill Bainbridge and Lon Nara, "'Orphan' Babies Reunited with Their Mothers," *Phnom Penh Post*, December 7–20, 2001; Bill Bainbridge and Lon Nara, "Adoptions 'Like Selling Goods'—FM," *Phnom Penh Post*, December 7–20, 2001; Stephen O'Connell and Bou Saroeun, "Babies Bought for Sale to Foreigners," *Phnom Penh Post*, May 26–June 8, 2000; Vong Sokheng, "Officials Turn a Blind Eye to Child Trafficking," *Phnom Penh Post*, August 4–17, 2000; Stephen O'Connell, Bou Saroeun, and Lon Nara, "Big Bribes Key to US Baby Buying," *Phnom Penh Post*, August 18–31, 2000; Anette Marcher and Bou Saroeun, "Officials Reluctant to Charge Trafficker," *Phnom Penh Post*, August 18–31, 2000; Bill Bainbridge, "Cambodia Suspends All U.S. Adoptions," *Phnom Penh Post*, February 1–14, 2002; Bill Bainbridge and Lon Nara, "Baby Traffic Witness Recants," *Phnom Penh Post*, March 15–28, 2002.

2. Bruno Dagens, "Cent Objets Disparus: Pillage a Angkor" (Paris: Publication du Conseil internationale des musées Réalisée en collaboration avec L'Ecole francaise d'Extrême-Orient, 1993); Stephen O'Connell and Lon Nara, "Virginity Ruling Lets Rapist

Off the Hook," *Phnom Penh Post*, January 5–18, 2001; Rajesh Kumar, "Rape Threat Worsening for Cambodian Women," *Phnom Penh Post*, March 30–April 13, 2001; Bill Bainbridge and Lon Nara, "Pedophile Suspect Free on Bail After Hearing," *Phnom Penh Post*, December 7–20, 2001; Phelim Kyne, "Embassy Accused of Helping Sex Offenders," *Phnom Penh Post*, August 4–17, 2000; Bill Bainbridge, "Billion Dollar Sex Trade," *Phnom Penh Post*, August 31–September 13, 2001.

3. Lor Chandara, "Tuol Sleng Survivor Surfaces in Phnom Penh," *The Cambodia Daily*, January 23, 2003. "I came to visit Tuol Sleng today to show myself to the world that I am still alive," author's notes.

4. Letters to editor, *Searching for the Truth* 4 (February 2001).

5. *Searching for the Truth* 4 (April 2001).

6. Meng Try Ea, January 24, 2003, interview with author, Phnom Penh, Cambodia, tape recording.

7. Meng Try Ea and Sorya Sim, *Victims and Perpetrators? Testimony of Young Khmer Rouge Cadres* (Phnom Penh: Documentation Center of Cambodia, 2001).

8. Khieu Samphan, letter to editor, *Searching for the Truth* 21 (September 2001).

9. Chris Decherd, "Cambodian Newspaper Admits to Printing Rumor That Sparked Anti-Thai Riot," *Associated Press*, February 3, 2003. "The rumor spread on Jan. 25 when the more widely read daily, Koh Santepheap (Island of Peace), published a story based on the Rasmei Angkor article and radio talk shows began taking calls from irate listeners. Prime Minister Hun Sen lent credibility to the rumor on Monday by chastising the actress and urging people to give up foreign products, a reference to Thai consumer goods and television serials that are highly popular in Cambodia." "Rumors Are Staple Fare for Nation's Newspapers," *AFP*, February 3, 2003. Bill Bainbridge, "Blood and Bribes: Inside the Khmer Press," *Phnom Penh Post*, April 27–May 10, 2001: "Truth is often incidental, hearsay is treated as fact."

10. "Tough Talk," *The Cambodia Daily*, January 31, 2003. "Please, TV5, hurry to stop broadcasting the films that have Kop Suvanant Kongying because I am afraid people will go to destroy the television station. . . . The life of Morning Star, or thief star, is not equal to a few bushes of grass near Angkor Wat."

11. "Rumors That Sparked Riots Spread by Media, Politicians," *The Cambodia Daily*, January 31, 2003: "The rapid spread of both rumors was aided by e-mail and mobile phone text messages."

12. "Riots Erupt from Thai Embassy," *Cambodia Daily*, January 30, 2003; Ker Munthit, September 2003, conversation with author, Phnom Penh, Cambodia; "Striking Workers Shot," *Phnom Penh Post*, June 23–July 16, 2000; "Mobs Go Berserk in Anti-Thai Frenzy; Thai Embassy Torched; Businesses Gutted," *Phnom Penh Post*, January 31–February 13, 2003.

13. Wassana Nanuam, "Hun Sen to Blame, Says Report," *Bangkok Post*, February 1, 2003; Ploenpote Atthakor, "Hun Sen Told to Take Partial Responsibility," *Bangkok Post*, February 1, 2003; "Gov't Inaction Broke International Protocol," *The Cambodia Daily*, January 31, 2003; Phann Ana and Kevin Doyle, "Gov't Reels in Aftermath of Riots," *The Cambodia Daily*, January 31, 2003; Robert Carmichael and Michael Coren, "'Deplorable Incident' Ruins Thai-Khmer Relations," *Phnom Penh Post*, January 31–February 13, 2003.

14. "Riots Erupt from Thai Embassy," *The Cambodia Daily*, January 30, 2003.

15. Ibid. 23. For more on the riots and their aftermath, see Ker Munthit, "Thailand Suspends Relations with Cambodia, Evacuates Residents After Anti-Thai Rioting," *Associated Press*, February 3, 2003; Kate Woodsome, "Tour Guides, Hoteliers Shaken,"

The Cambodia Daily, January 31, 2003; Yuwadee Tunyasiri, Supawadee Susanpoolthong, and Achara Ashayagacht, "Minister Seeks Audience with King to Apologize," *Bangkok Post*, February 2, 2003; Songpol Kaopatumtip and Tunya Sukpanich, "Making an Enemy out of Misunderstanding?" *Bangkok Post*, February 2, 2003; "Envoy Denied Royal Audience," *The Nation*, February 1, 2003; "Hun Sen goes hungry," *Bangkok Post*, February 6, 2003; Andrew Perrin and Matt McKinney, "Blast from the Past," *Time Asia*, February 10, 2003. I received an e-mail from a group calling itself "Khmer Intelligence" a week or so after the riots. It claimed that the riots "might have been triggered by a financial dispute between the two largest Thai petroleum companies vying for a multi billion dollar contract with the Cambodian government covering the joint exploration of . . . revenues from promising oil and gas fields in the overlapping zones in the Gulf of Thailand claimed by both countries," February 3, 2003; "Cambodia Apologizes for Anti-Thai Riots as Bangkok Takes Diplomatic Retaliation," *AP*, February 3, 2003; "Hun Sen Blames Extremists for City Riots, Calls for Calm," *The Cambodia Daily*, January 31, 2003: "This event took place by a small group of people who have taken extreme acts and exaggerated the truth that the Cambodian Embassy in Bangkok was destroyed and that some of our officials were killed."

16. Simon Montlake, "Cambodia Keeps Lid on Dark Past," *Christian Science Monitor*, February 12, 2003.

17. Ibid.

18. Ibid.

19. January 30, 2003, interview with author, Phnom Penh, Cambodia, tape recording.

20. Mathew McKinney, "The Art of Survival," *Time*, January 31, 2003.

Conclusion: War Crimes Trials as a Welcome Distraction

1. Seth Mydans, "U.N. Ends Cambodia Talks on Trials for Khmer Rouge," *The New York Times*, February 9, 2002; "Statement from Royal Government of Cambodia in Response to the Announcement of UN Pullout from Negotiations on Khmer Rouge Trial," February 12, 2002; "Cambodia's Quest for Justice," *Asian Wall Street Journal*, February 14, 2002; Puy Kea, "Lead Khmer Rouge Leaders Relieved as U.N. Abandons Trial Plans," *Kyodo New Service*, February 9, 2002; David Brunnstrom, "Door Left Open for U.N. at Khmer Rouge Trial," *Reuters*, February 12, 2002; Human Rights Watch Press Release, "Cambodia: Tribunal Must Meet International Standards," February 12, 2002; Amnesty International Press Release, February 11, 2002; Robert Carmichael, Bill Bainbridge, and Michael Hayes, "KR Trial's Tribulations," *Phnom Penh Post*, February 15–28, 2002; "Annan Says Cambodia Must Comply," *Phnom Penh Post*, March 15–28, 2002; Ker Munthit, "Hun Sen Remains Hopeful About Talks with U.N. on Genocide Tribunal," *AP*, March 12, 2003; "UN Resumes Cambodia Trial Talks," *BBC News*, March 13, 2003; "Deal Reached on the Khmer Rouge Trial," *Reuters*, March 17, 2000; Vong Sokheng, "UN Set for New Mandate on KR Trial," *Phnom Penh Post*, August 30–September 12, 2002; Bill Bainbridge, "UN Votes for KR Talks," December 20–January 2, 2003.

2. Kevin Doyle, "Nuon Chea Interview," *Cambodia Daily*, March 12, 2004.

3. Khieu Samphan, "Appealing to All My Compatriots," *Searching for the Truth* (September 2001); Michael Hayes, "The Khieu Samphan Letter: Smoke and Mirrors," *Phnom Penh Post*, January 2–15, 2004.

4. Rithy Panh, *S21: The Khmer Rouge Killing Machine*, produced by L'Institut National de l'audiovisuel and ARTE; see also Rithy Panh with Christine Chaumeau, *La machine*

khmère rouge (Paris: Flammarion, 2003). Panh spent the Khmer Rouge years working on a compulsory commune and saw "many things not good for a younger guy to see. I lost many people, friends and family." Initially, he wanted to leave Cambodia: "I don't know exactly what I wanted to do but I felt something deep in me, in my heart. If I wanted to survive I had to go away." After reaching the Mairut refugee camp in Thailand, the seventeen-year-old moved to France, where he stayed with relatives and did his best to forget about Cambodia for a few years, "but it is not really a solution. So I came back and taste this story again." Rithy Panh returned to Thailand and worked at the refugee camp at Site 2 from 1988 to 1990. He made his first short film in 1991 and has since directed numerous others examining aspects of the Khmer Rouge regime in close detail.

5. Rithy Panh, September 13, 2003, interview with author, Phnom Penh, Cambodia, tape recording; Cannes Film Festival 2003 program, interview with Rithy Panh.

6. Ibid.

7. Ibid.

8. Ibid.

9. Moeun Chhean Nariddh, letter to *Cambodia Daily*, July 7, 2003.

10. Ker Munthit, "U.N.-Backed Khmer Rouge Trials Attacked," *Associated Press*, June 7, 2003; Dr. Gregory Stanton, "Perfect Is the Enemy of Justice: A Response to AI's Critique of the Draft Agreement Between the U.N. and Cambodia," *Searching for the Truth* (July 2003); Amnesty International, public statement, March 21, 2003; AI Index: ASA 23/003/2003; Amnesty International, public statement April 25, 2003; Human Rights Watch, "Why the U.N. General Assembly Should Require Changes to the Draft Khmer Rouge Agreement," Human Rights Watch Brief Paper, April 30, 2003.

11. David Rieff, *A Bed for the Night* (New York: Simon and Schuster, 2002), 76.

GLOSSARY

AFP Agence France Presse

Sok An senior minister of Cambodia's Council of Ministers; chief war crimes tribunal negotiator on behalf of Hun Sen

Angkar "the organization": Khmer Rouge leadership

Yasushi Akashi Japanese head of UNTAC (1992–93)

Long Boret Prime Minister of Cambodia under Lon Nol

Zbigniew Brzezinski national security advisor to U.S. President Jimmy Carter

Chea Vannath Director, Cambodian Center for Social Development

Youk Chhang Director, DC CAM (1997–present)

Choeung Ek one of the Khmer Rouge "killing fields," on the outskirts of Phnom Penh; where most of the Tuol Sleng prisoners were executed

Ray Cline former CIA Deputy Director; senior foreign policy advisor to President-elect Ronald Reagan

Hans Corell UN Chief for Legal Affairs (1990s–present)

CPK Communist Party of Kampuchea (1979–89)

CPP Cambodian People's Party (1991–present)

DC Cam Documentation Center of Cambodia

Deng Xiaoping Chinese Vice Premier, 1975; Vice Chairman, Communist Party, 1976; Premier, 1978; resigned as Chief of Staff of army and Vice Premier in 1980, to elicit resignations from octogenarian officials, but remains China's paramount leader nonetheless

DK Democratic Kampuchea (1975–82)

Nhem En Tuol Sleng prison photographer

FCC Foreign Correspondents Club Cambodia

FUNCINPEC United National Front for an Independent, Neutral, Peaceful, and Cooperative Cambodia

Geneva Agreement 1954 settlement of the First Indochina War; established Cambodian neutrality after France's withdrawal from Vietnam

Geneva Conventions internationally agreed-upon rules for treatment of prisoners of war

Vo Nguyen Giap Vietnamese general in charge of 1979 Cambodian invasion

Heng Samrin Vietnamese-installed leader of the People's Republic of Kampuchea (1979–82)

Him Huy   Tuol Sleng prison guard

Ieng Sary   first Vice Premier and Foreign Minister of Democratic Kampuchea

Ieng Thirith   Minister of Culture and Social Affairs, Democratic Kampuchea; wife of
Ieng Sary

Ieng Vuth   son of Ieng Sary

Im Chan   Tuol Sleng prison survivor; sculptor

Kang Kech Ieu (Brother Duch)   Tuol Sleng prison commandant

K-5   Vietnamese forced labor program in which impressed Cambodians built border
fortifications and planted land mines

KEG   Kampuchea Emergency Group (United States, Thailand, Malaysia, Singapore);
established 1980 to provide nonmilitary aid to the coalition government of former
Khmer Rouge leaders and King Sihanouk

Khieu Ponnary   wife of Pol Pot

Khieu Samphan   President of Democratic Kampuchea (1976–79)

Lee Kuan Yew   Prime Minister of Singapore (1959–90)

Lon Nol   Cambodian leader (1970–75) installed by the United States; deposed and
went into exile in Honolulu, Hawaii

Long Boret   Prime Minister of Cambodia under Lon Nol

Mai Lam   Vietnamese colonel who transformed Tuol Sleng prison into a museum

Sirik Matak   Cambodian Deputy Prime Minister (1970–75)

Van Nath   Tuol Sleng prison survivor

Norodom Ranariddh   son of King Sihanouk; Cambodian co-prime minister (1993–
1997); head of royalist FUNCINPEC Party

Norodom Sihanouk   appointed King of Cambodia by the French in 1941; abdicated the
throne in 1955 and ran for prime minister; ousted by the National Assembly in 1970;
reinstated as king in 1993

Nuon Chea   Deputy Prime Minister of Democratic Kampuchea after 1976

Rithy Panh   Cambodian filmmaker (b. 1964); directed award-winning film, *S21: The
Khmer Rouge Killing Machine* (2003), featuring many Tuol Sleng prison alumni

Paris Agreement   treaty signed in October 1991 establishing UN peacekeeping force
in Cambodia (UNTAC)

PAVN   People's Army of Vietnam

Ung Pech   Tuol Sleng prison survivor; mechanic during Khmer Rouge regime; later,
first director of Tuol Sleng Museum of Genocide (1979–2000)

PRK   People's Republic of Kampuchea (1979–89)

Pol Pot (Saloth Sar)   "Brother Number One"; Comrade Secretary of Democratic
Kampuchea

Sam Rainsy   founder of Khmer Nation Party (1994), later renamed the Sam Rainsy
Party

General John Sanderson   Australian general; head of UNTAC military division
(1992–93)

Gerhard Scheumann   East German documentary filmmaker

SEATO   Southeast Asian Treaty Organization; 1954 alliance composed of the United
States, France, Great Britain, Australia, New Zealand, Thailand, Pakistan, and the
Philippines

Hun Sen   Khmer Rouge regimental commander; later named Foreign Minister of
People's Republic of Kampuchea (1981); Deputy Prime Minister (1981), Prime
Minister (1985–present)

Son Sann   leader of Khmer People's National Liberation Front (1979–82); leader of Buddhist Liberal Democratic Party (1992–his death in 2000)

Son Sen   Khmer Rouge Minister of Defense

Sopheara Chey   Director of Tuol Sleng Museum

Ta Mok   Khmer Rouge general; in charge of Democratic Kampuchea's Southwest Zone

Tuol Sleng prison   Khmer Rouge interrogation, torture, and execution center (1975–79), also known as S-21; now the Tuol Sleng Museum of Genocide

UNTAC   United Nations Transitional Authority Cambodia (1991–93)

Yun Yat   Khmer Rouge leader, wife of Son Sen

Jiang Zemin   Chinese president; made first diplomatic visit to Cambodia after the fall of the Khmer Rouge, November 2000

BIBLIOGRAPHY

Primary Sources

Documentation Center of Cambodia, Phnom Penh, Cambodia
Documents: D16196–18805

Tuol Sleng Museum of Genocide, Phnom Penh, Cambodia
"Declaration of James William Clark: Agent of the CIA of the USA," May 23, 1978.
"Declaration of Michael Scott Deeds," November 26, 1978.
"Declaration of David L. Scott," December 12, 1978.
"Declaration of Chris DeLance," December 26, 1978.

The Vietnam War Declassification Project, University of Austin, Texas
(www.ford.edu/library/exhibits/vietnam.htm)
"Cabinet Meeting Minutes," April 16, 1975.
"Cabinet Meeting Minutes," January 29, 1975.
Dean, Ambassador John. "Cable on the Cambodia Settlement," February 6, 1975.
Kissinger, Henry A. "Debrief of The Mayaguez Captain and Crew," May 19, 1975.
National Security Council Minutes, April 9, 1975.
Scowcroft, Brent, National Security Adviser. "Life Inside Cambodia." Memorandum for the President, May 10, 1976.
Smyser, W. R., National Security Adviser. "The Situation in Asia," Memorandum for the President, July 15, 1975.

Interviews
Sopheara Chey. April 1, 1994. Interview with author, Phnom Penh, Cambodia. Tape recording.
Karl Deeds. March 31, 1998. Interview with author, Molokai, HI. Tape recording.
Nic Dunlop. February 1, 2003. Interview with author, Bangkok, Thailand.
Nhem En. March 12, 1997; November 15, 1999; November 10 and 18, 2000. Interview with author, Phnom Penh, Cambodia. Tape recording.
Craig Etcheson.August 10, 2002. Interview with author, Phnom Penh, Cambodia. Tape recording.

Jörg Friedrich. August 23, 1995. Interview with author, Berlin. Tape recording.

David Hawk. August 1994. Interview with author, New York City. Tape recording.

Him Huy. March 14, 1997. Interview with author, Phnom Penh, Cambodia. Tape recording.

Chen Kuol. August 7, 2002. Interview with author, Sen Monorum, Mondulkiri, Cambodia. Tape recording.

Mai Lam. November 22, 1994. Interview with author, Ho Chi Minh City, Vietnam. Tape recording.

Kang Li. August 8, 2002. Interview with author, Sen Monorum, Cambodia. Tape recording.

Bou Meng. January 30, 2002. Interview with author, Phnom Penh, Cambodia. Tape recording.

Van Nath. March 11, 1997. Interview with author, Phnom Penh, Cambodia. Tape recording.

Rithy Panh. September 15, 2003. Interview with author, Phnom Penh, Cambodia. Tape recording.

Gerhard Scheumann. August 22, 1995. Interview with author, Berlin. Tape recording.

Sorya Sim. January 2003. Interview with author, Phnom Penh, Cambodia. Tape recording.

Sok Sin. September 15, 2000. Interview with Lisa Miller, Kompong Speu, Cambodia. Videotape.

Sok Sin. September 15, 2001. Interview with author, Phnom Penh, Cambodia.

Meng Tre Ea. August 2002. Interview with author, Phnom Penh, Cambodia. Tape recording.

Om Yentieng. August 2002. Interview with author, Phnom Penh, Cambodia.

Reports

Amnesty International. *Kampuchea Political Imprisonment and Torture*. London: Amnesty International, 1987.

——. *Torture in the Eighties*. London: Amnesty International, 1984.

Central Intelligence Agency. *A Research Paper, Kampuchea: A Demographic Catastrophe*. January 17, 1980.

Human Rights Watch. Press Release. "Cambodia: Tribunal Must Meet International Standards." February 12, 2002.

People's Republic of Kampuchea. Ministry of Foreign Affairs. "Some Evidence: Of the Plots Hatched By The Beijing Expansionists And Hegemonists Against The Kampuchean People." Phnom Penh, 1982.

United Nations Center for Human Rights. "Evidence of Summary Executions, Torture, and Missing Persons Since 2–7 July 1997." August 21, 1997.

U.S. Congress. House of Representatives. *Human Rights in Cambodia: Hearing Before the Subcommittee on International Organizations, of the Committee on International Relations*, House of Representatives, 95th Cong., 1st sess., May 3, 1977.

Films and Television Programs

Heynowski & Scheumann Film Studios. *The Angkar*. Berlin, 1979.

——. *Kampuchea: Death and Rebirth*. Berlin, 1979.

——. *The Jungle War*. Berlin, 1981.

——. *Pilots in Pajamas*. Berlin, 1967.

Koppel, Ted. *Nightline*. American Broadcasting Corporation. August 28, 1997.

Panh, Rithy. *S21: The Khmer Rouge Killing Machine*. By Rithy Panh, produced by L'Institut national de l'audiovisuel and ARTE, 2002.

WGBH Television. *The Vietnam Experience: Cambodia and Laos*. vol. 6. 1996.

Newspapers and Periodicals

Abramson, Rudy. "US Aid Only Hope for Cambodia—Ford." *Los Angeles Times*, March 7, 1975.

——. "Ford Hints at Blame for Cambodia." *Los Angeles Times*, March 9, 1975.

——. "Democrats in House Reject Cambodia Aid." *Los Angeles Times*, March 13, 1975.

Adams, Brad. "Snatching Defeat from the Jaws of Victory." *Phnom Penh Post*, January 22–February 4, 1999.

Agence France Presse Hong Kong. "English-speaking Prisoners Report." January 12, 1980.

——. "Two Escape Lynch Mob After Pinches, Police Say." February 22, 2000.

——. "Rumors Are Staple Fare for Nation's Newspapers." February 3, 2003.

Akashi, Yasushi. "UNTAC Views." *Phnom Penh Post*, July 24–August 6, 1992.

——. "Akashi Responds to Community Concerns." *Phnom Penh Post*, November 20–December 3, 1992.

Ana, Phann and David Shaftel. "Court Clears Guynot of Pedophilia Charge." *The Cambodia Daily*, July 27–28, 2002.

Ana, Phann, David Shaftel, and Kevin Doyle. "Gov't Reels in Aftermath of Riots." *The Cambodia Daily*, January 31, 2003.

Andelmann, David A. "French Express Concern on Embassy in Cambodia." *The New York Times*, April 27, 1975.

——. "Refugees Depict Grim Cambodia Beset by Hunger." *The New York Times*, May 2, 1977.

Anderson, Jack and Les Whitten. "Report Hints Blood Debt Being Paid." *Washington Post*, May 12, 1975.

Bainbridge, Bill. "Suppressed Report Shows Failing Health System." *Phnom Penh Post*, February 16–29, 2001.

——. "Chinese Clinic Boasts Free AIDS 'Cure.'" *Phnom Penh Post*, March 5–21, 2001.

——. "Billion Dollar Sex Trade." *Phnom Penh Post*, August 31–September 13, 2001.

Bainbridge, Bill and Lon Nara. "'Orphan' Babies Reunited with Their Mothers." *Phnom Penh Post*, December 7–20, 2001.

——. "Adoptions 'Like Selling Goods'—FM." *Phnom Penh Post*, December 7–20, 2001.

——. "Pedophile Suspect Free on Bail After Hearing." *Phnom Penh Post*, December 7–20, 2001.

——. "Baby Traffic Witness Recants." *Phnom Penh Post*, March 15–28, 2002.

Bainbridge, Bill and Vong Sokheng. "Take a broader view—PM." *Phnom Penh Post*, June 21–July 4, 2002.

——. "UN Votes for KR Talks." *Phnom Penh Post* , December 20–January 2, 2003.

Barber, Jason. "More Hostages 'Inevitable.'" *Phnom Penh Post*, November 18–December 1, 1994.

Barber, Jason and Christine Chaumeau. "Slaughter on Sunday—March 30, 1997." *Phnom Penh Post*, April 4–17, 1997.

——. "Power Struggle Shatters KR Leadership." *Phnom Penh Post*, June 27–July 10, 1997.

——. "Democracy from the Barrel of a Gun." *Phnom Penh Post*, July 12–24, 1997.

Barber, Jason and Matthew Grainger. "Chhouk Rin—The Turning of a Terrorist." *Phnom Penh Post*, January 13–26, 1995.

——. "Victims Say Shots Fired as They Lay Wounded." *Phnom Penh Post*, September 8–21, 1995.

Barber, Jason and Joshua Phillips. "Killers on Foot and Moto." *Phnom Penh Post*, April 4–17, 1997.

Barber, Jason and Hurley Scroggins. "Panicky Expats Flee in Droves." *Phnom Penh Post*, July 12–24, 1997.

——. "Nat. Police Involvement in Murder Denied." *Phnom Penh Post*, August 29–September 11, 1997.

Barber, Jason and Ros Sokhet. "Train Raid 'Not Planned for Hostages.'" *Phnom Penh Post*, January 13–26, 1995.

Barber, Jason and Chea Sotheacheath. "Hun Sen Reinstates Ho Sok Suspects." *Phnom Penh Post*, October 10–23, 1997.

Barrington, Kevin. "Pay Dispute Undermines UNTAC Morale." *Phnom Penh Post*, March 12–25, 1993.

——. "SOC Likens UNTAC Raid to Pol Pot Rule." *Phnom Penh Post*, March 26–April 8, 1993.

——. "KR Open Bloody Anti-Poll Campaign." *Phnom Penh Post*, May 7–20, 1993.

——. "Security Concerns Loom Over Polls." *Phnom Penh Post*, May 21–June 3, 1993.

——. "Boutros Ghali Says UNTAC Aimed Too High." *Phnom Penh Post*, May 21–June 3, 1993.

Becker, Elizabeth. "Cambodia: Laboratory for UN Dreams and Ambitions." *International Herald Tribune*, October 21, 1991.

——. "U.S. Spearheading Effort to Bring Pol Pot to Trial." *The New York Times*, June 23, 1997.

Binder, David. "New Cambodia Leaders Identified in Radio Broadcast from Vietnam." *The New York Times*, January 9, 1979.

Birsel, Robert. "Cambodia to Vote as Fairness Debate Rages." Reuters, July 25, 1998.

——. "Khmer Rouge Expert Blasts China Over Trial." Reuters, June 30, 1999.

Blumenthal, Ralph. "Russians Seen Unloading Relief Ships in Cambodia." *The New York Times*, January 13, 1980.

Borchgrave, Arnaud de. "Bloodbath in Cambodia." *Newsweek*, May 12, 1975.

Brown, John C. "Elections: How Free, How Fair?" *Phnom Penh Post*, May 21–June 3, 1993 (translation of excerpt from Khmer-language newspaper, orig. written by Snguen Nemull).

——. "The KR, Foreign Aid and the Press." *Phnom Penh Post*, July 30–August 12, 1993.

——. "Interview with Gen. Sanderson." *Phnom Penh Post*, September 24–October 6, 1993.

——. "Rights Groups Mull if They Abet Crime." *Phnom Penh Post*, July 15–28, 1994.

Browne, Malcolm W. "Sihanouk Appeals to UN Council to Get Vietnam out of Cambodia." *The New York Times*, January 12, 1979.

——. "Red Clash on Cambodia: Big Show at UN." *The New York Times*, January 13, 1979.

——. "Third World and West Join to Assail Vietnam in UN." *The New York Times*, January 14, 1979.

Brunnstrom, David. "Door Left Open for U.N. at Khmer Rouge Trial." Reuters, February 12, 2002.

Bunnil, Touch. "Beware of NGOs." *Phnom Penh Post*, April 30–May 13, 1999.

Burslem, Chris. "NGO's Demand Action on Car." *Phnom Penh Post*, September 10–23, 1993.

——. "UNHCR Ultimatum on Theft." *Phnom Penh Post*, September 24–October 7, 1993.

Butterfield, Fox. "Battle on at Phnom Penh's Edge." *The New York Times*, April 16, 1975.

——. "US and China Mark Resumption of Ties in Peking Ceremony." *The New York Times*, January 2, 1979.

——. "Sihanouk in Peking on Way to the UN." *The New York Times*, January 7, 1979.

——. "Cambodia's Regime Reported in Flight." *The New York Times*, January 8, 1979.

——. "Sihanouk Requests Aid of US and UN." *The New York Times*, January 9, 1979.

——. "Defense Secretary Arrives in China for 8-Day Visit." *The New York Times*, January 6, 1980.

Carmichael, Robert, Bill Bainbridge, and Michael Hayes. "KR Trial's Tribulations." *Phnom Penh Post*, February 15–28, 2002.

Carmichael, Robert and Michael Coren. "'Deplorable Incident' Ruins Thai-Khmer Relations." *Phnom Penh Post*, January 31–February 13, 2003.

Channo, Mang. "AIDS: The Next Challenge Facing Cambodia." *Phnom Penh Post*, December 18–31, 1992.

——. "Cambodia's New Challenge: AIDS." *Phnom Penh Post*, January 1–14, 1993.

——. "Sex Trade Flourishing in Capital." *Phnom Penh Post*, February 12–25, 1993.

——. "Assemblyman Holds U.N. Team at Gunpoint." *Phnom Penh Post*, September 10–23, 1993.

Channo, Mang and Gary Way. "Spies in City Aid KR's Train Ambush." *Phnom Penh Post*, August 12–25, 1994.

Chappell, David. "A Letter to the *Cambodia Times*." *Phnom Penh Post*, July 29–August 11, 1994.

Chaumeau, Christine. "Pain, Horror, and Too Much Blood." *Phnom Penh Post*, April 4–17, 1997.

——. "The Boys in Blue Down from Samlot to 'Protect the Country." *Phnom Penh Post*, May 3–15, 1997.

Chaumeau, Christine and Bruno Carette. "Hun Sen Makes His Case on 'the Trial.'" *Phnom Penh Post*, March 19–April 1, 1999.

Chaumeau, Christine and Michael Hayes. "DNUM Nixes KR Trial." *Phnom Penh Post*, February 5–18, 1999.

Chheng, Heng Sok and Gary Way. "Kampot Closed to Hacks, Dips." *Phnom Penh Post*, August 26–September 8, 1994.

Chomsky, Noam and Edward Herman. "Distortions at Fourth Hand." *The Nation*, June 25, 1977.

Chon, Gina and Thet Sambath. "Former KR Troops Want Trial." *The Cambodia Daily*, November 10, 2000.

Colm, Sara. "U.N. Agrees to Address Sexual Harassment." *Phnom Penh Post*, October 11, 1992.

Colm, Sara and Andrew Lam. "Ambassador Tran Huy Chuong of the Socialist Republic of Vietnam." *Phnom Penh Post*, October 23, 1992.

——. "On the Campaign Trail." *Phnom Penh Post*, December 4–17, 1992.

Cranston, Alan. "Arms for Cambodia: The Debate Quickens." *Los Angeles Times*, March 9, 1975.

Daravuth, You. "'Hungry' Guys Will Go to Hell: AIDS." *Phnom Penh Post*, January 1–14, 1993.

Davis, Robin. "AIDS Poses Grave Threat to Cambodian Economy." *Phnom Penh Post*, June 18–July 1, 1993.

——. "Sheer Hypocrisy." *Phnom Penh Post*, July 2–15, 1993.

Decherd, Chris. "Pol Pot Guessing Goes On." *The Cambodia Daily*, June 19, 1996.

——. "PMs Take Unified Stance on Amnesty for Ieng Sary." *The Cambodia Daily*, August 26, 1996.

——. "Ieng Sary: Amnesty Key to Reconciliation." *The Cambodia Daily*, September 10, 1996.

——. "Prince Says Rebel Faction, Gov't in Accord." *The Cambodia Daily*, September 30, 1996.

Decherd, Chris and Ek Madra. "No Word from Thais on KR, Prince Says." *The Cambodia Daily*, October 8, 1996.

——. "Ranariddh Makes Surprise Visit to Pailin." *The Cambodia Daily*, October 15, 1996.

——. "KR Leader Detained in Pailin." *The Cambodia Daily*, October 15, 1996.

——. "KR Radio Lashes Out, Denies Rebel Weakness." *The Cambodia Daily*, October 16, 1996.

——. "Defectors to RCAF Report Hostages Are Still Alive." *The Cambodia Daily*, October 21, 1996.

Decherd, Chris and Touch Rotha. "Ieng Sary's Troops Join Gov't Forces." *The Cambodia Daily*, November 7, 1996.

——. "Mass Defections Directly to Gov't, RCAF Declares." *The Cambodia Daily*, October 9, 1996.

Dobbs, Leo. "First Confirmed AIDS Death." *Phnom Penh Post*, April 7–20, 1995.

Dodd, Mark. "Thai Military Aids KR." *Phnom Penh Post*, January 14–27, 1994.

——. "Former Leader Rejects KR Peace Offer." *Phnom Penh Post*, January 14–27, 1994.

——. "High Life of Hated Ta Mok Is Laid Bare." *Phnom Penh Post*, February 25–March 10, 1994.

Dodd, Mark, Reuters, and Ros Sokhet. "Suspect Held for Foreigners Murder." *Phnom Penh Post*, June 30–July 13, 1995.

Downie, Sue. "Hostage Taking Is Big Money Spinner for KR." *Phnom Penh Post*, August 12–25, 1994.

Dunlop, Nic. "On the Trail of Pol Pot's Executioner." *The Independent*, October 3, 1998.

——. "The Lost Executioner." *The Independent on Sunday*, October 3, 1999.

Edwards, Steven. "UN Blamed for Bringing AIDS to Cambodia." *National Post Online*, August 23, 2000.

Ehrlich, Richard S. "Activist Unearths Further Proof of Pol Pot Genocide." *Washington Times*, July 20, 1998.

Eng, Peter. "American Retrieves Dead Brother's 'Confession.'" *The Associated Press*, February 25, 1989.

——. "KR Spells out Timeline for Disarmament." *Phnom Penh Post*, July 24–August 6, 1992.

Erlanger, Steven. "US Laments Takeover in Cambodia." *The New York Times*, July 9, 1997.

——. "Asians Are Cool to Albright on Cambodians and Burmese." *The New York Times*, July 28, 1997.

——. "Rights Group Demands ASEAN Act on Members' Records." Reuters, July 24, 1998.

Etcheson, Craig. "Pol Pot and the Art of War." *Phnom Penh Post*, August 13–26, 1993.

——. "Genocide: By the Law, Not by Emotion." *Phnom Penh Post*, August 11–24, 1995.

Fawthrop, Tom. "Cambodia: Khmer Rouge Face Prospect of Permanent State of Siege." *Interpress Service*, December 12, 1991.

———. " … But Already KR Feeling the Pinch." *Phnom Penh Post*, December 30–January 12, 1995.

———. "The Khmer Rouge—Unkorked." *Manager* (January 1997).

———. "Wild West Not Yet Won." *Manager* (January 1997).

Fontaine, Chris. "US Senate Resolution Pushes Ieng Sary's Trial." *The Cambodia Daily*, October 2, 1996.

Gallager, John and Saing Soenthrith. "Not All Were Happy to See the President," *The Cambodia Daily*, November 14, 2000.

Gluck, Caroline. "One Year After the Paris Accords: An Interview with Yasushi Akashi." *Phnom Penh Post*, November 6–19, 1992.

———. "Mass Murderer's Missionary Full of Hope." *Phnom Penh Post*, July 9–22, 1999.

Gourevitch, Philip. "Death in the Ruins." *Outside* (September 1995).

Grainger, Matthew. "Govt Nod for Genocide Research." *Phnom Penh Post*, February 24–March 9, 1995.

———. "Hun Sen Steals Show at Corruption Forum." *Phnom Penh Post*, March 10–23, 1995.

———. "Hun Sen: The Power and the Politics." *Phnom Penh Post*, May 19–June 1, 1995.

———. "US Warn Thais About KR Deals." *Phnom Penh Post*, August 25–September 7, 1995.

Gray, Dennis D. "American Goes to Cambodia to Seek Remains of Slain Brother." *The Associated Press*, February 5, 1989.

Gwertzman, Bernard. "US Officials See a Bright Future." *The New York Times*, January 2, 1979.

———. "US Calls for Vietnamese Pullback and Notes Fear of War Widening." *The New York Times*, January 8, 1979.

———. "US to Mute Voice in Cambodia Debate." *The New York Times*, January 10, 1979.

———. "Sihanouk Is Ready for Pol Pot Talks." *The New York Times*, February 26, 1980.

———. "US Sees Test of Ties to Moscow in Afghan and Cambodian Issues." *The New York Times*, July 2, 1981.

Hamilton, Andrea. "Murders of Party Officials Continue." *Phnom Penh Post*, July 2–15, 1993.

———. "UNTAC Hit by Rash of Car Thefts." *Phnom Penh Post*, July 16–29, 1993.

Hawk, David. "The Cambodian Genocide." *Facts on File*, 1988.

Hayes, Michael. "Good Ideas on Human Rights." *Phnom Penh Post*, July 30–August 12, 1993.

———. "Falt Raps Bad Press." *Phnom Penh Post*, October 8–21, 1993.

———. "All Eyes on PMs' Bodyguard Units." *Phnom Penh Post*, May 3–15, 1997.

———. "Scope of Tribunal." *Phnom Penh Post*, October 13–26, 2000.

Heder, Steve. "Pol Pot and Khieu Samphan." Clayton, Australia, *Monash University Centre of Southeast Asian Studies*, Working Paper 70, 1991.

———. "Turning Over a New Page." *Phnom Penh Post*, October 22–November 4, 1993.

———. "A Cure for 'Everything.'" *Phnom Penh Post*, November 19–December 2, 1993.

———. "What Lies Behind KR's Moves." *Phnom Penh Post*, May 20–June 2, 1994.

———. "Shawcross Book Highlights Post-UNTAC Blues." *Phnom Penh Post*, February 24–March 9, 1995.

Hovey, Graham. "U.S. Backs Cambodia at U.N." *The New York Times*, January 4, 1979.

———. "U.S. Is Not Committed on the Cambodia Issue." *The New York Times*, January 5, 1979.

———. "US Reports $58 Million in Aid to the Cambodians." *The New York Times*, January 8, 1980.

Human Rights Quarterly. "International Law and Cambodian Genocide: The Sounds of Silence." 11 (1989).

Infoseek. "Rights Group Demands ASEAN Act on Members' Records." News Article, July 24, 1998.

Japan Times. "Amnesty Criticizes Cambodian Peace Plan." March 4, 1998.

Jarvis, Helen. "PM Hun Sen: 'First You Need to Catch the Fish." *Phnom Penh Post,* February 19–March 4, 1999.

Jeldres, Julio. "Royal Biographer Accuses Hok Lundy." *Phnom Penh Post,* September 12–25, 1997.

Kamm, Henry. "Thais Fear to Return to Border Village Assaulted by the Cambodians." *The New York Times,* January 9, 1978.

——. "Cambodian Assails Vietnam/Embarrassing Thais." *The New York Times,* July 18, 1978.

——. "Vietnam Speeds Cambodia Drive, Pressing Capital." *The New York Times,* January 4, 1979.

——. "Vietnam's Push in Cambodia Has Neighbors Worried." *The New York Times,* January 5, 1979.

——. "'Liberation' Group Says It Has Formed Regime in Cambodia." *The New York Times,* January 9, 1979.

——. "Cambodia, Peking-Bound, Vows War Will Go On." *The New York Times,* January 12, 1979.

——. "Aide Says Pol Pot Regime Is Ready to Join Old Foes Against Vietnam." *The New York Times,* January 21, 1979.

——. "China's Aim in Asia: To 'Contain' Soviet." *The New York Times,* April 20, 1981.

——. "US Condemns Vietnam for Occupation of Cambodia." *The New York Times,* June 21, 1981.

Kaopatumtip, Songpol and Tunya Sukpanich. "Making an Enemy out of Misunderstanding?" *Bangkok Post,* February 2, 2003.

Kiernan, Ben. "U.N.'s Appeasement Policy Falls Into Hands of Khmer Rouge Strategists." *Phnom Penh Post,* Year End 1992.

Kumar, Rajesh. "Rape Threat Worsening for Cambodian Women." *Phnom Penh Post,* March 30–April 13, 2001.

Kyne, Phelim. "Embassy Accused of Helping Sex Offenders." *Phnom Penh Post,* August 4–17, 2000.

——. "Svay Sitha Picked for Human Rights Forum." *Phnom Penh Post,* August 4–17, 2000.

——. "China Enraged by Alleged Links to S-21." *Phnom Penh Post,* November 7, 2000.

Lacouture, Jean. "The Bloodiest Revolution." *The New York Times,* March 31, 1977.

——. "Cambodia: Corrections." *The New York Times,* May 26, 1977.

Lenaghan, Nick. "Report to Gov't as PM Rounds on Rights Staff." *Phnom Penh Post,* August 29–September 11, 1997.

Lenaghan, Nick and Claudia Rizzi. "Weapons Seizure Ignites Party Sniping." *Phnom Penh Post,* May 30–June 12, 1997.

Leslie, Jacques. "Phnom Penh Attack Reaches Stalemate." *Los Angeles Times,* March 13, 1975.

Lewis, Anthony. "In Pursuit of Folly." *The New York Times,* April 21, 1975.

Lewis, Flora. "After Phnom Penh." *The New York Times,* April 18, 1975.

——. "Cambodian Reds, in Paris, Pledge Neutrality Policy." *The New York Times,* April 18, 1975.

Livingston, Carol. "Khmer Rouge Lose Diplomatic Archive." *Phnom Penh Post*, September 24–October 7, 1993.

Locard, Henri. "Les Slogans de l'Angkar." University of Phnom Penh, 1994.

——. "KR Killings More Violent and Systematic?" *Phnom Penh Post*, August 11–24, 1995.

Malcolm, Andrew H. "Chief of Communist Forces in Cambodia Hails Victory." *The New York Times*, April 23, 1975.

Marcher, Anette. "Go-It-Alone Tribunal Seeks Foreign Gloss." *Phnom Penh Post*, October 1–14, 1999.

——. "National KR Tribunal Takes Shape." *Phnom Penh Post*, November 12–25, 1999.

Marcher, Anette and Mai Rassmussen. "Khmer Rouge Reflect Without Regret." *Phnom Penh Post*, April 14–27, 2000.

——. "KR Tribunal Talks Inch Forward." *Phnom Penh Post*, April 14–27, 2000.

——. "Yet Another KR-Trial Proposal." *Phnom Penh Post*, April 14–27, 2000.

Marcher, Anette and Bou Saroeun. "The American Role in Putting Together a KR Trial Deal." *Phnom Penh Post*, April 28–May 11, 2000.

——. "Agreement Close on KR Trial." *Phnom Penh Post*, July 7–20, 2000.

——. "Rin Verdict Leads to Khmer Rouge Tribunal Doubts." *Phnom Penh Post*, July 21–August 3, 2000.

——. "Law Banning Khmer Rouge Might Be Invalid." *Phnom Penh Post*, August 18–31, 2000.

——. "Officials Reluctant to Charge Trafficker." *Phnom Penh Post*, August 18–31, 2000.

——. "KR Tribunal Drowning in Smokescreens and Politics." *Phnom Penh Post*, September 15–28, 2000.

——. "UN Accepts Flawed Tribunal for Khmer Rouge." *Phnom Penh Post*, October 13–26, 2000.

Marcher, Anette and Yin Soeum. "KR Trial Law Sails Through Council." *Phnom Penh Post*, January 7–20, 2000.

——. "Agreement Close on KR Trial." *Phnom Penh Post*, July 17–30, 2000.

——. "Slavery and Human Traffic in Cambodia." *Phnom Penh Post*, September 1–14, 2000.

——. "Bun Rany Fails to Act on Pelika Diary." *Phnom Penh Post*, October 27–November 9, 2000.

Marder, Murray. "Kissinger: No Pangs of Conscience About Vietnam." *The Washington Post*, July 1, 1976.

Marshall, Tyler. "US Decries Cambodia Takeover." *LA Times*, July 9, 1997.

Martin, Marie-A. "L'Industrie Dans Le Kampuchea Democratique." *Etudes Rurales* 89 (91) (January–September 1983).

McDowell, Robin. "Photographer of Death." *The Associated Press*, March 3, 1997.

——. "Coup Carried Out in Cambodia." *The Associated Press*, July 7, 1997.

——. "Cambodian Opposition Party Headquarters Looted, Documents Burned." *The Boston Globe*, July 8, 1997.

——. "Coup Leaders Round up Hun Sen Forces." *The Associated Press*, July 9, 1997.

——. "Cambodian Prince Convicted in Plot." *The Washington Post*, March 18, 1998.

——. "Cambodian Prince Sentenced." *The Washington Post*, March 18, 1998.

——. "Cambodia's Ranariddh Sentenced to 30 Years." Reuters, March 18, 1998.

——. "Cambodian King Pardons Son." *The Associated Press*, March 21, 1998.

McEvers, Kelly. "The People's Revolutionary Tribunal of 1979." *The Cambodia Daily*, January 8–9, 2000.

McFadden, Robert D. "Drawn Slowly Into the Indochina Maelstrom, Cambodia Has Sunk in a Decade of Agony." *The New York Times*, January 8, 1979.

McNulty, Sheila. "U.N. Celebrates Anniversary of Accords It Can't Implement." *Phnom Penh Post*, November 6–19, 1992.

Miller, Lisa. "Pali Sutras for the Soul of 'Survivor' Sok Sin." *Phnom Penh Post*, November 23–December 6, 2001.

Mockenhaupt, Brian and Saing Soenthrith. "Acid Suspect Still at Large." *The Cambodia Daily*, February 18, 2000.

Moorthy, Elizabeth and Chea Sotheacheath. "Another Body Unearthed; More to Come." *Phnom Penh Post*, November 7–20, 1997.

Moorthy, Elizabeth and Pok Sokundara. "AIDS Sufferers Being Urged to Speak Out." *Phnom Penh Post*, November 13–26, 1998.

Moorthy, Elizabeth and Samreth Sopha. "AIDS Killer Looms Large." *Phnom Penh Post*, April 2–12, 1999.

Munthit, Ker. "KR Robs Peace-Keepers." *Phnom Penh Post,* March 12–25, 1993.

——. "UN Marks First Year in Cambodia." *Phnom Penh Post,* March 26–April 8, 1993.

——. "Hun Sen Accuses KR Leader of Genocide." *Phnom Penh Post*, April 9–22, 1993.

——. "Akashi: Election 'Free and Fair.'" *Phnom Penh Post*, June 6–17, 1993.

——. "Will There Be a Role for the KR?" *Phnom Penh Post,* July 16–29, 1993.

——. "Alarm Over AIDS Virus Figures." *Phnom Penh Post*, February 25–March 10, 1994.

——. "AIDS Warning Issued." *Phnom Penh Post*, March 25–April 7, 1994.

——. "Inside Paet's Vine Mountain Hideout." *Phnom Penh Post*, November 4–17, 1994.

——. "PM Laments Hostage Deaths." *Phnom Penh Post*, November 4–17, 1994.

Munthit, Ker and Matthew Grainger. "Hostages: Pawns and Politics." *Phnom Penh Post*, November 4–17, 1994.

——. "King Sihanouk Says Pol Pot Should Go to the Deepest Hell." *Phnom Penh Post*, April 24–May 4, 1995.

——. "Genocide Seminar Calls for 'Commission of Truth.'" *Phnom Penh Post*, August 25–September 7, 1995.

——. "Cambodia Apologizes for Anti-Thai Riots as Bangkok Takes Diplomatic Retaliation." *The Associated Press*, February 3, 2003.

——. "Thailand Suspends Relations with Cambodia, Evacuates Residents After Anti-Thai Rioting." *The Associated Press*, February 3, 2003.

Mydans, Seth. "Official Embrace of Khmer Rouge Leader Roils Cambodia." *The New York Times*, August 16, 1996.

——. "Khmer Rouge's No. 2 Denounces No. 1." *The New York Times*, August 17, 1996.

——. "An Amnesty in Cambodia." *The New York Times*, September 18, 1996.

——. "Men Once Led by Pol Pot Say They Have Him." *The New York Times*, June 19, 1997.

——. "Chinese Resist War Crimes Trial." *The New York Times*, June 25, 1997.

——. "Thugs Attack Demonstrators in Cambodia; One Shot Dead." *The New York Times*, September 10, 1998.

——. "Khmer Rouge in Retirement Needn't Fear a Trial Soon." *The New York Times*, November 29, 2000.

——. "U.S. Interrupts Cambodian Adoptions." *The New York Times*, November 5, 2001.

——. "U.N. Ends Cambodia Talks on Trials for Khmer Rouge." *The New York Times*, February 9, 2002.

Nara, Lon and Phelim Kyne. "Teen Lover Sues for Acid Attack." *Phnom Penh Post*, May 12–25, 2000.

——. "Tat Samarina's Family in Terror." *Phnom Penh Post*, September 15–28, 2000.

——. "Acid Mutilation a Misdemeanor." *Phnom Penh Post*, January 5–18, 2001.

Nariddh, Moeun Chhean. "Reasons for the Wave of Crime." *Phnom Penh Post*, July 16–29, 1993.

——. "Rising Theft." *Phnom Penh Post*, October 8–21, 1993.

——. "Deadly Myths Which Help Spread AIDS." *Phnom Penh Post*, May 6–19, 1994.

——. "AIDS Threat to 2 Million." *Phnom Penh Post*, October 21–November 3, 1994.

——. "Magic Herbs Stay Rooted on Hospital Wards." *Phnom Penh Post*, November 18–December 1, 1994.

——. "They're Serious … Sidesaddle Only Please." *Phnom Penh Post*, December 30, 1994–January 12, 1995.

——. "HIV-Man's Wedding Highlights Lack of Law." *Phnom Penh Post*, March 10–23, 1995.

——. "Experts Angry at AIDS Article." *Phnom Penh Post*, May 19–June 1, 1995.

——. "Magic Art of Bullet-Proofing the Troops." *Phnom Penh Post*, September 8–21, 1995.

——. "AIDS Epidemic Sees Prenuptial Blood Tests Soar." *Phnom Penh Post*, September 3–16, 1999.

Ness, Bernard. "UN's Parley on Cambodia," *The New York Times*, January 12, 1981.

——. "Excerpts from Speech by Haig." *The New York Times*, July 13, 1981.

——. "Mishaps Mar U.N.'s Cambodia Meeting." *The New York Times*, July 14, 1981.

Ngo, Laura. "Prince Urges Int'l Tribunal for Ieng Sary." *The Cambodia Daily*, October 9, 1996.

Nossiter, Bernard D. "Assembly, Rebuffing Soviet, Seats Cambodia Regime of Pol Pot." *The New York Times*, September 22, 1979.

——. "China Victory at UN Is Result of Strange Alliance." *The New York Times*, September 23, 1979.

——. "$200 Million in Cambodia Aid Is Pledged." *The New York Times*, November 6, 1979.

——. "UN's Parley on Cambodia Will Open Tomorrow." *The New York Times*, July 12, 1981.

——. "Hanoi Hints It Might Talk With a UN Panel." *The New York Times*, July 13, 1981.

——. "UN Resolution on Cambodia Keeps Doors Open for Pol Pot." *The New York Times*, July 17, 1981.

Nunan, M. P. "Direct Attack on UNTAC." *Phnom Penh Post*, January 29–February 11, 1993.

O'Connell, Stephen and Bou Saroeun. "Babies Bought for Sale to Foreigners." *Phnom Penh Post*, May 26–June 8, 2000.

O'Connell, Stephen, Bou Saroeun, and Lon Nara. "Big Bribes Key to US Baby Buying." *Phnom Penh Post*, August 18–31, 2000.

O'Connell, Stephen and Lon Nara. "Red Cross Offers Babies for Adoption." *Phnom Penh Post*, September 29–October 12, 2000.

——. "Virginity Ruling Lets Rapist off the Hook." *Phnom Penh Post*, January 5–18, 2001.

Ogden, Jon. "Newsmen Live on the Edge." *Phnom Penh Post*, April 8–21, 1994.

——. "Foreigners Warned to Stay in Towns." *Phnom Penh Post*, April 22–May 5, 1994.

——. "King Washes His Hands of Politics." *Phnom Penh Post*, July 1–14, 1994.

——. "Western Trio Feared Dead After Finds." *Phnom Penh Post*, July 29–August 11, 1994.

——. "Embassies' New Advice." *Phnom Penh Post*, August 26–September 8, 1994.

——. "King's Fax Clarified." *Phnom Penh Post*, August 26–September 8, 1994.

Palan, Anugraha. "Hopes Dashed for Release of Expat Hostages." *Phnom Penh Post*, June 17–30, 1994.

——. "NGO in First Khmer Criticism of UNTAC." *Phnom Penh Post*, September 23–October 6, 1994.

Peach, Katrina. "Alarm Over New AIDS Figures." *Phnom Penh Post*, October 22–November 4, 1993.

Pheap, Aun. "Looking Back at the Fall of Phnom Penh." *Phnom Penh Post*, April 13–26, 2001.

Pilger, John. "The Long Secret Alliance: Uncle Sam and Pol Pot." *Third World Traveler* (Fall 1997).

Postlewaite, Susan. "Troubling Health Stats from UNICEF." *Phnom Penh Post*, August 11–24, 1995.

Pran, Dith. "Khmer Rouge Sabotage the Peace." *Phnom Penh Post*, December 4–17, 1992.

——. "Cambodia Needs Peace." *Phnom Penh Post*, January 1–14, 1993.

——. "An Open Letter to World Leaders." *Phnom Penh Post*, February 12–25, 1993.

Prasso, Sheri. "Sihanouk '100 Percent' for Trying Khmer Rouge Leaders." *Agence France Presse*, November 16, 1991.

——. "Khmer Rouge Wants a Battlefield in Phnom Penh." *Agence France Presse*, September 9, 1992.

Reid, Robert H. "Hun Sen Calls for U.N. to Get Tough with Khmer Rouge." *Phnom Penh Post*, January 15–28, 1993.

——. "Cambodia Premier Seeks Views on Khmer Rouge Trial." Reuters, January 17, 1999.

Rizzi, Claudia. "Ranariddh Says Samphan Welcome." *Phnom Penh Post*, May 30, 1997.

——. "Tokyo Bid Prompts Offers but No Talk." *Phnom Penh Post*, November 25–December 4, 1997.

Robinson, Katya. "Fight Against AIDS Stacked with Problems." *Phnom Penh Post*, December 15–28, 1995.

——. "Cambodian Royalists Cower After Official's Murder." *The Associated Press*, July 9, 1997.

Rosenberg, Tina. "Hun Sen Stages an Election." *New York Times Magazine*, August 30, 1998.

Roth, Kenneth. "KR Trial Standards." *Phnom Penh Post*, November 26–December 9, 1999.

Rotha, Touch and Chris Decherd. "Mass Defections Directly to Gov't, RCAF Declares." *The Cambodia Daily*, October 9, 1996.

Sainsbury, Peter. "Expert: Chea as Culpable as Pol Pot." *Phnom Penh Post*, February 4–17, 2000.

Sainsbury, Peter and Chea Sotheacheath. "Good Intentions Paved Road to Mass Drudgery." *Phnom Penh Post*, April 14–27, 2000.

Samrang, Ham. "One of Only Two Remaining Tuol Sleng Survivors Dies." *Phnom Penh Post*, February 17, 2000.

Saroeun, Bou and Peter Sainsbury. "Prince's KR Deal Laced with Treachery." *Phnom Penh Post*, May 22–June 4, 1998.

——. "Militias Bring Spectacle of Lynch Mobs." *Phnom Penh Post*, September 17–30, 1999.

——. "Brave Woman Overcomes Acid Horror." *Phnom Penh Post*, May 12–25, 2000.

Sary, Ieng. "DNUM Presents 'True Facts' About Democratic Kampuchea." *The Cambodia Daily*, September 10, 1996.

Schanberg, Sidney H. "Reporter's Notebook: Cambodia." *The New York Times*, April 17, 1975.

——. "Truce Was Sought." *The New York Times*, April 17, 1975.

Schork, Kurt. "Torture Allegations in Cambodia." Reuters, August 10, 1997.

Schumacher, Edward. "UN Assembly Bids Vietnamese Forces Evacuate Cambodia." *The New York Times*, November 15, 1979.

Scroggins, Hurley. "Do You Enjoy the Train in Cambodia." *Phnom Penh Post*, January 30–February 12, 1998.

——. "Celebration for Ieng Sary." *Phnom Penh Post*, August 20–September 2, 1999.

Seper, Chris. "Cambodian Convicted in Step Toward Election." *Washington Post*, March 5, 1998.

Shawcross, William. "Cambodia Under Its New Rulers." *The New York Review of Books*, March 4, 1976.

——. "The Third Indochina War." *The New York Review of Books*, April 6, 1978.

——. "Tragedy in Cambodia." *The New York Review of Books*, November 14, 1996.

——. "The Cambodian Tragedy, Cont'd." *The New York Review of Books*, December 19, 1996.

Smith, Craig. "Profiting from His Shots of Pol Pot's Terror." *The Wall Street Journal*, September 16, 1997.

Sokheng, Vong and Anette Marcher. "University Mob Beats Thief to Death." *Phnom Penh Post*, July 7–20, 2000.

——. "Officials Turn a Blind Eye to Child Trafficking." *Phnom Penh Post*, August 4–17, 2000.

——. "UN, NGOs Criticise KR Law." *Phnom Penh Post*, February 2–15, 2001.

——. "UN Role in Tribunal Under Fire." *Phnom Penh Post*, July 16–29, 2001.

Sokhet, Ros. "Hostages Alive but Losing Weight." *Phnom Penh Post*, October 7–20, 1994.

——. "US Visits Prompts KR Push." *Phnom Penh Post*, October 7–20, 1994.

——. "KR Defectors Give No News of Hostages." *Phnom Penh Post,* October 21–November 3, 1994.

——. "KR Defections Almost 7,000." *Phnom Penh Post,* January 13–26, 1995.

——. "KR Defectors Kill on Paet's Order." *Phnom Penh Post*, June 2–15, 1995.

Sophornnara, Sou and Reuters. "Hopes of Captives' Release Decline." *Phnom Penh Post,* August 26–September 8, 1994.

——. "Ban: The View from the Street." *Phnom Penh Post*, September 9–22, 1994.

——. "Kampot KR Break Siege Lines." *Phnom Penh Post,* September 23–October 6, 1994.

Sotheacheath, Chea and Chris Decherd. "Survivor of KR Killings Tells of 'Horrible Ordeal.'" *The Cambodia Daily*, June 27, 1996.

——. "Mass Rebel Defections Announced by Hun Sen." *The Cambodia Daily*, August 9–11, 1996.

——. "Court Builds Ranariddh Case." *Phnom Penh Post*, September 26–October 9, 1997.

Sterba, James P. "Thailand Preparing Camps for Cambodian Soldiers." *The New York Times,* January 12, 1979.

——. "Thais Expecting More Cambodia Refugees." *The New York Times*, January 14, 1979.

——. "Vietnamese Drive Appears to Slow Near the Cambodian-Thai Border." *The New York Times*, January 15, 1979.

——. "China Says the Vietnamese Must be Driven out of Cambodia." *The New York Times*, July 12, 1981.

Stevens, Sarah. "Cambodia's HIV Toll: 150,000 and Rising." *Phnom Penh Post*, December 25–January 7, 1999.

Stier, Ken. "Helicopter Potshots Shoot Down UNTAC Mobility." *Phnom Penh Post,* November 20–December 3, 1992.

Sutter, Robert. "Cambodian Diplomat Is Bitter About 'Way the U.S. Used Us,'" *The New York Times,* April 17, 1975.

Thayer, Nate. "An Interview with Khmer Rouge Leader Khieu Samphan." *Phnom Penh Post,* August 27, 1992.

——. "KR Blueprint for the Future Includes Electoral Strategy." *Phnom Penh Post,* August 27, 1992.

——. "Khieu Samphan: Gloomy Prospects for Khmer Elections." *Phnom Penh Post,* November 6–19, 1992.

——. "Sihanouk Poised to Take Control." *Phnom Penh Post,* January 29–February 11, 1993.

——. "UNTAC Fails to Stem Political Violence." *Phnom Penh Post,* February 12–25, 1993.

——. "Battle Lines Drawn." *Phnom Penh Post,* May 21–June 3, 1993.

——. "Samdech Balks at Heading Coalition." *Phnom Penh Post,* June 6–17, 1993.

——. "Whither the Khmer Rouge?" *Phnom Penh Post,* June 6–17, 1993.

——. "Sihanouk Back at the Helm." *Phnom Penh Post,* June 18–July 1, 1993.

——. "New Govt.: Who's Really in Control?" *Phnom Penh Post,* November 19–December 2, 1993.

——. "King Offers KR Role in Gov't." *Phnom Penh Post,* December 3–16, 1993.

——. "Ieng Sary Dropped from Inner Circle." *Phnom Penh Post,* January 28–February 10, 1994.

——. "Shakeup in KR Hierarchy." *Phnom Penh Post,* January 28–February 10, 1994.

——. "Fury Over Sin Song's Trip to US." *Phnom Penh Post,* February 11–24, 1994.

Thayer, Nate and Ker Munthit. "Govt. Soldiers Take Shaky Hold on Pailin." *Phnom Penh Post,* March 25–April 7, 1994.

——. "Govt's Row Over Defectors." *Phnom Penh Post,* November 4–17, 1994.

——. "Faded Red: The Death Throes of the KR." *Phnom Penh Post,* April 21–May 4, 1995.

——. "Pol Pot: Unrepentant." *Far Eastern Economic Review,* October 30, 1997.

——. "Pol Pot: The End." *Far Eastern Economic Review,* August 7, 1997.

Thion, Serge. "Meaning of a Museum." *Phnom Penh Post,* August 27–September 9, 1993.

Trebay, Guy. "Killing Fields of Vision." *The Village Voice,* June 3, 1997.

Tunyasiri, Yuwadee, Supawadee Susanpoolthong, and Achara Ashayagacht. "Minister Seeks Audience with King to Apologize." *Bangkok Post,* February 2, 2003.

Twining, Charles H., U.S. Ambassador. "US Position." *Phnom Penh Post,* April 7–20, 1995.

Vogle, Paul. "Cambodia Says Five Americans Slain by Khmer Rouge." UPI, October 2, 1982.

——. "UNTAC's Third Choice." *Phnom Penh Post,* March 26–April 8, 1993.

——. "Shallow Sentiments." *Phnom Penh Post,* October 8–21, 1993.

Wannabovorn, Sutin. "Covert Thai Unit 838 Resurfaces." *Phnom Penh Post,* April 8–21, 1994.

Watkins, Huw. "King: PMs Jumped the Gun on Sary Amnesty." *Phnom Penh Post,* September 20–October 3, 1996.

Watkins, Huw and Reuters. "Politics of Trying Pol Pot." *Phnom Penh Post,* October 10–23, 1997.

——. "AIDS Set to 'Destroy' Cambodia—WHO," *Phnom Penh Post,* April 2–12, 1999.

Way, Gary. "Officials Accused of Hostage Scams." *Phnom Penh Post,* August 27–September 8, 1994.

——. "Hostages Plead for End to Bombardment." *Phnom Penh Post*, September 9–22, 1994.

Way, Gary and Mang Channo. "KR Defector Tells of Plan to Isolate Kampot." *Phnom Penh Post*, August 12–25, 1994.

World Headlines. "Amnesty Criticizes Cambodian Peace Plan." March 4, 1998.

Zarembo, Alan. "Judgment Day: In Rwanda, 92,392 Genocide Suspects on Trial." *Harper's* (April 1997).

Secondary Sources

Adams, Sam. *War of Numbers.* South Royalton, VT: Steerforth Press, 1994.

Ameringer, Charles. *U.S. Foreign Intelligence: The Secret Side of American History.* Lexington, MA: Lexington Books, 1990.

——. *Pol Pot, Peasants, and Peace: Continuity and Change in Khmer Rouge Political Thinking 1985–1991.* Ford Foundation, 1991.

Basu, Sanghamitra. *Kampuchea as a Factor in the Sino-Soviet Conflict, 1975–1984.* Ph.D. thesis, Jadavpur University, Calcutta, 1987.

Becker, Elizabeth. *When the War Was Over.* 1986; reprint, New York: Public Affairs, 1998.

Bekaert, Jacques. *Cambodian Diary: Tales of a Divided Nation 1983–1986.* Bangkok: White Lotus Press, 1997.

Bizot, François. *The Gate.* Trans. Euan Cameron. London: The Harvill Press, 2003.

Blum, William. *Rogue State: A Guide to the World's Only Superpower.* Common Courage Press, 2000.

Bowden, Tim. *One Crowded Hour: Neil Davis Combat Cameraman 1934–1985.* N.p., Australia: HarperCollins, 1987.

Brown, Louise. *Sex Slaves: Trafficking of Women in Asia.* London: Virago, 2000.

Brown, MacAlister and Joseph Zasloff. *Cambodia Confounds the Peacemakers 1979–1998.* Ithaca: Cornell University Press, 1998.

Brown, Robert and David Cline. *The New Face of Kampuchea.* Chicago: Liberator Press, 1979.

Burchett, Wilfred. *The China–Cambodia–Vietnam Triangle.* Chicago: Vanguard Books, 1981.

Burr, William. *The Kissinger Transcripts.* New York: The New Press, 1999.

Chanda, Nayan. *Brother Enemy.* New York: Harcourt, Brace, Jovanovich, 1986.

Chandler, David. *The Tragedy of Cambodian History.* New Haven: Yale University Press, 1991.

——. *Brother Number One: A Political Biography of Pol Pot.* Boulder: Westview, 1992.

——. *Voices from S-21: Terror and History in Pol Pot's Secret Prison.* Berkeley: University of California Press, 1999.

Cline, Ray. *The CIA Under Reagan, Bush, and Casey.* Washington, DC: Acropolis Books, 1981.

De Nike, Howard, John Quigley, and Kenneth Robinson, eds. *Genocide in Cambodia.* Philadelphia: University of Pennsylvania Press, 2001

Ellis, Richard. *The Dark Side of the Left.* Lawrence: University of Kansas Press, 1998.

Etcheson, Craig. *The Rise and Demise of Democratic Kampuchea.* Boulder: Westview, 1984.

——. *After the Killing Fields: Lessons from the Cambodian Genocide.* New York: Praeger, forthcoming.

Fleitz, Fredrick, Jr. *Peacekeeping Fiascoes of the 1990s.* Westport, CT: Praeger, 2002.

Gettleman, Marvin, Susan Gettleman, Lawrence Kaplan, and Carol Kaplan, eds. *Conflict in Indo-China*. New York: Random House, 1970.

Gottesman, Evan. *Cambodia After the Khmer Rouge*. New Haven: Yale University Press, 2002.

Haas, Michael. *Cambodia: Genocide by Proxy*. New York: Praeger, 1991.

Hayden, Tom. *Reunion*. New York: Random House, 1988.

Heder, Steve and Judy Ledgerwood, eds. *Propaganda, Politics, and Violence in Cambodia*. Armonk, NY: M. E. Sharpe, 1996.

Herr, Michael. *Dispatches*. 1977; reprint, New York: Vintage, 1991.

Hofstadter, Richard. *The American Political Tradition and the Men Who Made It*. New York: Knopf, 1951.

——. *The Idea of a Party System*. Berkeley: University of California Press, 1969.

Ignatieff, Michael. *Warrior's Honor*. New York: Henry Holt, 1997.

——. *Virtual War*. New York: Henry Holt, 2000.

Jacobs, Ron. *The Way the Wind Blew*. New York: Verso, 1997.

Johnson, Loch. *America's Secret Power*. New York: Oxford University Press, 1989.

Kaplan, Robert. *The Coming Anarchy: Shattering the Dreams of the Post Cold War*. New York: Random House, 2000.

Kamm, Henry. *Cambodia: Report from a Stricken Land*. New York: Arcade Publishing, 1998.

Kiernan, Ben, ed. *Genocide and Democracy in Cambodia*. New York: Yale University Southeast Asian Studies, 1993.

Kiernan, Ben. *How Pol Pot Came to Power: A History of Communism in Kampuchea, 1930–1975*. London: Verso, 1985.

——. *The Pol Pot Regime: Race, Power, and Genocide in Cambodia Under the Khmer Rouge, 1975–79*. New Haven: Yale University Press, 1996.

Kiljunnen, Kimmo. *Kampuchea: Decade of the Genocide*. London: Zed Books, 1984.

Kirchheimer, Otto. *Political Justice: The Use of Legal Procedure for Political Ends*. Princeton: Princeton University Press, 1961.

Kissinger, Henry. *Ending the Vietnam War*. New York: Simon and Schuster, 2003.

Lewis, Anthony, ed., *Written Into History: Pulitzer Prize Reporting of the Twentieth Century from* The New York Times. New York: Times Books, 2001.

Livingston, Carol. *The Gecko Tails*. London: Weidenfeld and Nicholson, 1996.

Locard, Henri. *The Khmer Rouge Gulag*. Paris: Self-published, 1995.

Maguire, Peter. "Nuremberg: A Cold War Conflict of Interest." Ph.D. diss., Columbia University, 1993.

Marchetti, Victor and John Marks. *The CIA and the Cult of Intelligence*. New York: Knopf, 1974.

Martin, Marie. *Cambodia: A Shattered Society*. Berkeley: University of California Press, 1994.

Mayall, James, ed. *The New Interventionism 1991–1994*. New York: Cambridge University Press, 1996.

McCarthy, Mary. *The Seventh Degree*. New York: Harcourt, Brace, Jovanovich, 1967.

Metzl, Jamie Fredric. *Western Responses to Human Rights Abuses in Cambodia, 1975–1980*. New York: St. Martin's Press, 1996.

Miller, James. *Democracy Is in the Streets*. New York: Simon and Schuster, 1987.

Nath, Vann. *A Cambodian Prison Portrait: One Year in the Khmer Rouge's S21*. Bangkok: White Lotus Press, 1998.

Neveu, Roland. *Cambodia: The Years of Turmoil*. Bangkok: Asia Horizons, 2000.

Niven, Doug and Chris Riley, eds. *The Killing Fields*. Santa Fe: Twin Palm Press, 1996.

Osborne, Milton. *Politics and Power in Cambodia*. Australia: Longman, 1973.

Panh, Rithy with Christine Chaumeau. *La machine khmère rouge*. Paris: Flammarion, 2003.

Pelton, Robert and Coskun Aral. *Fielding's Most Dangerous Places*. N.p.: Fielding Worldwide, 1995.

Picq, Laurence. *Au delà du ciel: Cinq ans chez les khmers rouges*. Paris: Barrault, 1984.

Pilger, John. *Heroes*. London: John Cape, 1986.

Ponchaud, François. *Cambodia: Year Zero*. Trans. Nancy Amphoux. New York: Holt, Rinehart, and Winston, 1977.

Poole, Peter. *Cambodia's Quest for Survival*. New York: American-Asian Educational Exchange Inc., 1969.

Porter, Gareth and John Hillebrand. *Cambodia: Starvation and Revolution*. New York: Monthly Review Press, 1977.

Prados, John. *Presidents' Secret Wars: CIA and Pentagon Covert Operations from World War II Through the Persian Gulf*. Chicago: Elephant Paperbacks, 1986.

Pratt, John Clark. *Vietnam Voices*. New York: Viking, 1984.

Ranelagh, John. *The Agency*. London: Weidenfeld and Nicholson, 1986.

Riddle, Tom. *Cambodian Interlude*. Bangkok: White Orchid Press, 1997.

Rieff, David. *A Bed for the Night*. New York: Simon and Schuster, 2002.

Risner, Robinson. *The Passing of the Night: My Seven Years as a Prisoner of the North Vietnamese*. New York: Random House, 1974.

Rivero, Miguel. *Inferno Y Amanecer En Kampuchea*. Cuba: Editorial de Ciencias Sociales, 1979.

Rhode, David. *Endgame*. New York: Farrar, Straus & Giroux, 1997.

Scott, Peter. *Lost Crusade: America's Secret Cambodian Mercenaries*. Annapolis: Naval Institute Press, 1998.

Seabrook, Jeremy. *Travels in the Skin Trade*. London: Pluto Press, 1996.

Shawcross, William. *Sideshow: Kissinger, Nixon, and the Destruction of Cambodia*. New York: Simon and Schuster, 1979.

——. *The Quality of Mercy*. New York: Simon & Schuster, 1984.

——. *Cambodia's New Deal*. Carnegie Endowment, 1994.

Sihanouk, Norodom. *Prisonnier Des Khmer Rouges*. Paris: Hachette, 1986.

——. *Prince Sihanouk on Cambodia*. Hamburg: Mittelungen Des Instituts Für Asienkunde Hamburg, Nummer 110, 1980.

——. *War and Hope: The Case for Cambodia*. London: Sidgwick and Jackson, 1980.

Smist, Frank, Jr. *Congress Oversees the United States Intelligence Community, 1947–1989*. Knoxville: University of Tennessee Press, 1990

Snepp, Frank. *Decent Interval*. Lawrence: University of Kansas Press, 1977.

Solis, Gary. *Son Thang: An American War Crime*. New York: Bantam, 1998.

Sontag, Susan. *Regarding the Pain of Others*. New York: Farrar, Straus & Giroux, 2003.

Sutter, Robert. *The Cambodian Crisis and U.S. Policy Dilemmas*. Boulder: Westview, 1991.

Swain, Jon. *River of Time*. London: Minerva Edition, 1996.

Taylor, Telford. *Nuremburg and Vietnam*. New York: Bantam, 1971.

The Teachings of Buddha. Tokyo: Kosaido Printing Co., Ltd., 1966.

Thion, Serge. *Watching Cambodia: Ten Paths to Enter the Cambodian Tangle*. Bangkok: White Lotus, 1993.

Meng Try Ea and Sorya Sim. *Victims and Perpetrators? Testimony of Young Khmer Rouge Cadres.* Phnom Penh: Documentation Center of Cambodia, 2001.

Vickery, Michael. *Cambodia 1975–1982.* Bangkok: Silkworm Press, 1984.

Vulliamy, Edward. *Seasons in Hell.* London: Simon and Schuster, 1994.

Wettermahn, Ralph. *The Last Battle.* New York: Carroll and Graf, 2001.

Wood, Richard. *Call Sign Rustic: The Secret Air War Over Cambodia 1970–1973.* Washington, DC: Smithsonian Institution Press, 2002.

Woodward, Bob. *Veil.* New York: Simon and Schuster, 1987.

Yew, Lee Kuan. *From the Third World to the First.* New York: HarperCollins, 2000.